MAGGIE GEORGE, published poet : Totterdown, Bristol, during the early p wasn't a misnomer. It reflected the neight the vibrant multi-cultural niche it inhabit

South Bristol was a children's para .... by today's Health & Safety extremes, Maggie ran as wild as the environment invited, pock-marked as it was by bombsites.

Encouraged by hard-working parents, Maggie and her brothers absorbed the foundations of their work ethic. Everyone worked hard, everyone had aspirations for themselves, and for their children.

Maggie was educated at an inner-city Catholic primary school where she thrived. Her academic success meant she continued her education in a prestigious Catholic Girls' school in Bristol. Her unique humour was her saviour...she was no scholar, having barely scraped a pass in the Eleven Plus.

After two years working in the grime of Bristol's then Employment Exchange, her much-loved father suggested the course of her future career. She studied at a Catholic Girls' college, on the outskirts of Newcastle upon Tyne, and became a teacher.

Forty years and three headships later, Maggie enjoys the freedom of writing, travel and, most of all, the constant surprises of her growing family.

Heads
and
Tales

MAGGIE GEORGE

To Claire,
Happy birthday!
Maggie

SilverWood

Published in 2015 by SilverWood Books

SilverWood Books Ltd
30 Queen Charlotte Street, Bristol, BS1 4HJ
www.silverwoodbooks.co.uk

ISBN 978-1-78132-311-3 (paperback)
ISBN 978-1-78132-312-0 (ebook)

British Library Cataloguing in Publication Data
A CIP catalogue record for this book is available from
the British Library

Set in Sabon by SilverWood Books
Printed on responsibly sourced paper

This book is dedicated to my parents

Chapter 1

"If you want to know the time, ask a policeman", that was this morning's song. I woke up and there it was. That's as much as I could recall from the lyrics I'd heard my mother sing during my childhood. I recognised this as a blessing because last week I was stuck with "How much is that doggie in the window?" For three days. It's true what they say, "A dog is not just for Christmas."

The day I wake up with "Like a Virgin" as my ear-worm for the duration, I'll begin to worry, but at least I'll be a decade or two closer to the present. The present, there's a notion. Having lived in the future for most of my career, the present is a luxury I will soon be able to afford, despite the pension crisis. It's a gift I will give myself. All in good time.

With a career bridging two centuries in the la-la land that is education in the UK, I have decided the time is right to leave school, and today is the day to face up. Maybe. Colleagues ask me why. They extol my energy, creativity and *joie de vivre*. Three excellent reasons to quit, I reckon. I am *compos mentis*, I can still summon all three elements at will, besides I don't need their amateur analysis or advice. I already have friends treading the twelve-step journey, on the slippery slope to retirement. In fact, if combined, they'd total several marathons. I wasn't about to join that well-worn trek. For a start, I didn't have any sensible shoes.

However, if I wait another year or two, there's a possibility that the last vestige of all of the above, plus my sense of humour, and almost limitless patience, will have been rung out by the mangle of indecision that is the Department of Education. What to do?

Just how *did* I arrive at today, apart from the inevitable coming of age. The ever-present Father Time, patiently hovering in the wings, licking his thumb, running it along the inside edge of his rusted scythe, reminding me of the probability that my work here is done.

If I steal some moments to think of possible contributors I'd come up with something resembling a list. Okay. Here goes. Tonight's nominees, in no particular order:

1   Change, change, and more change as successive secretaries of state for education lead the raucous parade of protesting ill-thought-out initiatives. Keep those plates spinning and juggling clubs in the air as the political football bounces out of control.

2   The harrowing experience of employment tribunals with their draconian processes.

3   One threatening parent too many suffering the consequences of life in the fast lane, while their children wait for them to join them in play.

4   The suffocating, micro-management of school governors. The few who meander through meetings manipulating and bullying their peers to satisfy some unfulfilled professional life, watching helplessly as it slips over the horizon into oblivion.

5   The dilly-dallying of social services, while families wallow in the fallow territory of unemployment or crime, or worse.

6   Crippling health and safety impositions, stilting opportunities to experience risk or challenges which life inevitably brings us all, leaving children unprepared and vulnerable.

7   The falling roll of talented teachers as the need for rent and food forces them to head for the corporate world, begging bowls outstretched.

Once the dam is breached, I could go on indefinitely. Of this very limited list, any item would stand alone as a reason to hang up my satchel for the last time. *Collectively* one could view it as constructive dismissal. The list will waft into obscurity with time. Curl in on itself, protecting, apologetic, like one of those cellophane fish you place in the palm of your hand, waiting expectantly for it to indicate that you are a passionate lover and a genius to boot. Guaranteed to disappoint.

As with the fish, it's not much use to me because despite every negative event of my career, I still don't truly want to take my kit home for longer than the weekend.

I'm not ready to go, am I? Am I ready to go? Am I actually, *really* ready to go? Is there anything else I'd planned to achieve before temporarily losing my memory stick for the last time? Maybe I should write another list entitled *The pros and cons of the retirement issue.* I'm good at lists. Maybe I'll devise a new therapy, the therapy of the list. I could become the new Oprah, wax lyrical on the holistic properties of the list, sell merchandise, little polka-dot notebooks and matching pencils in soothing shades of aqua. Irresistible. Maybe have T-shirts printed with acronyms like, *Life Is So Tantalising.*

I digress. Retirement, an explanation is due. In fact I owe myself an explanation I guess because here I am poised, albeit tentatively, at the dawning of my new life, as any recovery programme will have me believe, without a strategic plan, risk assessment or even a systematic approach paving the way. I'm teetering on the brink. I'm the reluctant lemming. You know, the one that pauses, the one that risks a backward glance while the others hurl themselves from the cliff, free-falling with glee. I am, in fact, "Lot the lemming". I have metaphorically turned into a pillar of salt, while risking a look into my past. They say time flies when you're enjoying yourself. That may be true, but it didn't slow noticeably during those less enjoyable times either. It can't be relied upon. Time, that is. It skittered along there, the tumbleweed of forty years in schools, blowing in whichever direction the winds of destiny decreed. Sometimes I found myself hankering down against the prevailing hurricanes of discontent, battling against yet another oncoming tide. I squinted up occasionally over the crumbling parapet of the trench in hope of glimpsing reinforcements… back-up…comrades-in-arms…anything but the barrage of explosives trudging their way over prone bodies of exhausted, battle-weary teachers carpeting no man's land. Sometimes, today for instance, I'm blissfully unaware. I have surrounded myself with a marshmallow of nonchalance, hearing only muffled sounds, reclaiming the comfort of my mother's womb.

I was twenty-two when I started teaching. It would be dishonest to say it seems like yesterday. It seems like the forty-odd years it *has* been, it's just that I thought it would feel even longer somehow, to give me time to get used to it. Who was it that said, "Life is something that happens as you while away time with planning?" I think it was John Lennon. Either him or my dad. They shared certain philosophies.

When viewed from the starting block, life stretches out in front of you as you warm-up and prepare to hit the compacted red cinders running. You know what it's like, you gaze into your never-ending future where things progress seamlessly as a sari lifting on a warm breeze, flowing from one phase to another, guided by unfolding maturity, tempered by life's little surprises. It's quite romantic in retrospect, but you don't think of the end of it all do you? After all, you're a novice to the world of work, retirement is for old people. Old people with pensions, and budgies, and Tuesday afternoon at the library after the Tesco trip. Retirement is something your parents mulled over just yesterday – "when the mortgage is paid, when the kids have finished their education, when we come up on the premium bonds." Just thinking of it makes me feel like sliced bread on a hotel toaster, heading for the drop, crisp and dried up.

I want to revisit the innocence, the adrenalin-fuelled outlook of my own starting block before the blast of a gun sent me hurtling toward today.

You can talk until the cows come home before finding the excitement in retirement. Retirement, entry into the beige years. And as for innocence, well, what a willow the wisp concept. Retirement. I can't stomach the word. In fact I can't even bring myself to *utter* the word and, when I hear it in a conversation, I look around with the optimism of a meerkat looking for the person to whom it must be addressed. It's too premature for me. It comes upon me when I least expect it. It's the troll under the bridge and, rather than face up to it, I flee, ducking and flapping like a panicked adolescent.

According to the colossal *Concise Oxford Dictionary* (ninth edition), currently occupying an inordinate amount of space on my desk, the meaning of retirement reads: *Leave office or employment because of age, go away, retreat, compelled to suspend one's innings.* Search as I might, there is no positive definition to be found. The online thesaurus adds "sequestration", and I have to look that up now, as it sounds like something distinctly unpleasant, hinting at some sort of medical procedure involving clipping or cutting with razor-edged secateurs. Ouch!

How did I get here, prematurely occupying this slot in time?

Both my parents are long gone. Children – many years out of the nest – gathering their own twigs and spider silk, house paid for, friends on cruises, granddaughters astounding me every day, young teachers reminding me of me. All circling around in my crazed brain in a monochrome strip of shining memories in the making. I'm tangled in the silicone coils, an abandoned audio tape winding its untrodden path through teasels on the hard shoulder of the A38.

STOP THE WORLD I WANT TO GET OFF!

Chapter 2

I'd like to say that I had always known I was destined to teach but, euphemistically speaking, it was in fact my father who guided me in that direction. In reality I was steered toward the front door, given thirty pounds and sent off to college in the frozen expanse that was, and remains, Newcastle upon Tyne. Having never ventured further north than Gloucester, I had little idea of what to expect. The stationmaster at Temple Meads assured me, "Gloucester, Newcastle, 'tis all the same." Also, I had been a tepid fan of *The Likely Lads* on TV, so I wasn't going completely uninformed.

But I'm jumping the gun. I'm missing my formative years and feel they deserve a skimming over, just a glimpse. After all, we educationalists are forever reiterating the importance of these early years of life, the introduction to the planet we inhabit temporarily. As a "baby boomer", I arrived in a world vibrant with expectation. My parents' generation was demob-happy, and anxious to begin their new lives and loves having conquered the world. However, post-war England was caught on the back foot. Put simply, the country wasn't ready. All that vibrancy and expectation building up a covert head of steam had to be channelled into something, hence us, the baby boomers. With production line efficiency worthy of British Steel we popped into the world one after the other like pods of ripe, round, happy peas. There may have been rationing but somehow the majority of us were bonny babies. Today we would say fat…well no, we wouldn't of course because we'd be sued, but you get the drift. It was as if we were supposed to make up for the deprivation of the war years in weight. And we did. Thick slices of white bread spread with real, yellow butter topped with sugar sprinkles washed down with full-cream pasteurised milk. And we became what we ate – fat! And in my case smothered by layers of family love.

We grew up playing on bomb sites. We didn't know what they were. We just thought we lived in a children's paradise. We climbed, fell, ran pell-mell over hillocks of broken bricks, glass and concrete, fell, made dens amongst the rubble, fell, stayed out all day only returning when our tummies announced the retreat, and our bloodied knees called for attention.

I recall my older brother and I running back home or racing each other on our second-hand bikes, breathless and giggling. Him screaming, "Beat you!" while thrusting out his chest and, breaching the finishing tape which was our back door, he'd burst into the kitchen and flop at mum's slippered feet. Throwing myself down on top of him I'd thump his chest and inhale the sweet outdoor smell of our day. Staggering to our feet we'd grasp extended glasses of orange squash and gulp as if our lives depended on it. Very Enid Blyton.

We had so much to be grateful for and, much like today's children, we took it all for granted. However, unlike today's children our good fortune was rooted in the basics. We had food, a roof over our heads and two parents living together surrounded by an army of relations and drop-in neighbours who hailed a sing-song of "Yoo-hoo, Hilda" on arrival at the back door. I can recall other neighboured cries too. "Rainin'" was one of my favourites because everyone from oldest to youngest in every family in the road leapt to their feet to rush into the garden and retrieve the sun-filled washing before it got drenched. There was sun in those days and its aroma, flapped into drying cotton sheets, beat any fabric freshener boasting fresh air bliss from its lavender label. There's only one authentic fresh air smell and, in the late 40s and 50s, our pants and liberty bodices captured it and swaddled us throughout the day.

"Rag-bone!" was another cry from the streets. How strange. This announced the old man on his cart, creaking, almost toppling, as his horse sidled up to the pavement of number twenty. It was piled high with bags of old clothes, chipped china, and tired shoes worn until the pavement first dusted, then holed our already threadbare school socks. Recycling at its conception. All the children loved to hear Rag-bone because we got to pet the horse. Well, those who could reach high enough got to pet the horse. Not me, I watched and willed myself to grow just so that I could touch the horse's coarse mane which fell matted over its sweaty neck. We rarely had anything to give the rag-and-bone man. Most of our old clothes went to a family in the parish or to Nazareth House where the orphans lived, whoever they were. At that age I had no idea of the refugees that had poured into Bristol as a consequence of the invasion of Poland.

I don't remember feeling deprived of anything. My life couldn't be better. Until 1953 that is. In the year of the coronation, when England was full to bursting with "Hope and Glory", I was to become the most disappointed four-year-old in the country. I feel the need to retell the cause of my deep depression. I believe it might provide further insight into post-traumatic stress disorder in the very young. It is with due diligence that I examine the need to do so, such is the residual pain that remains.

The whole road in which we lived pulled together to prepare a street party in what I guess must've been what they called the "spirit of the blitz" during the war years. All the mums, hair shoved up under turbans, sifted their way through a marathon of baking days. The dads constructed long rectangular tables which, when positioned end to end, reached from our house to the start of the hill a couple of hundred yards away. In years to come we were to roller skate down that hill at breakneck speeds, as proven by Derek Johnson, and fall over in order to stop before hitting the junction risking death by oncoming horse and cart, or possibly even a grey Morris Minor. It was even better during the white winters when all of us children spilled out onto the street like a heap of Russian dolls. All shapes and sizes. Youngest, grasping outstretched gloved hands to keep up with the yelling thrall heading for the hill with home-made toboggans, tin trays transformed into record-breaking luge. My brother and I had a four-man bob sleigh. It was a short wooden ladder we dragged out of the shed, and it flew!

Eventually, Coronation Day arrived. Paper tablecloths fluttered out to claim their space. Enormous metal jugs anchored them, filled to the brim with orange squash or dandelion and burdock. The tables sporting red, white and blue paper plates and dishes. Chairs of every description were lined up like enemy lines opposite each other. Endless plates of jam or spam sandwiches fought for a space in the no man's land between, vying with sausage rolls or pineapple and cheese on sticks made by someone posh from down the road. It was certainly the biggest party I had ever seen and it was all for the new Queen. I helped my dad hang a massive Union flag from one of the front bedroom windows. I knew it was important because as we released it, having wedged one side of it under the window frame, a cheer went up from down below led by Mrs Richards, a lady as loud as she was large, who was my mum's friend. I was so excited I didn't think I could wait much longer, but first of all there was the fancy dress parade. My brother and I always won these wherever they took place because my mum and dad were creative people with standards. My dad was an engineer and coupled with my mum's imagination and practicality they were an unstoppable combination. The previous year at the parish garden party my brother went as W.G. Grace the cricketer, and I went as Little Mo the tennis player. We were three and four-years-old respectively, and had never heard of either of these sports stars. Celebrities didn't get the air-play of today's athletes. However, we knew better than to complain. My brother spent the entire afternoon in cricket gear sporting a thick, black beard, and I put up with the itchy frills of tennis knickers under my Wimbledon-esque white pleated skirt. Naturally we won, we were gorgeous and oblivious to all the fuss. Mum and dad looked fashionably proud, while at the same time feigning surprise. For the coronation fancy dress I was going as a dolly in a box, and my brother, also constrained, was a boxed "Hornby OO" train. Don't ask. Neither made for easy movement but both drew inordinate praise from all and sundry. We won. We were thrilled to bits, not with the winning particularly, we were used to that, we just wanted to get out of the clobber and impeding boxes and on with the party. Keeping still was no easier then than it is now for naturally active young children. We didn't even have attention deficit hyperactivity disorder (ADHD) as an excuse. We were full of life and simply wanted to run and join the adventure!

At last all the tables were laden with months of rationed goodies and everyone sat down after singing "God Save the Queen". I felt it was rude to start without her, the Queen that is. By nine o'clock that night I began to think she was never coming. I looked up and down the street, straining to hear the sound of horses struggling to pull the coronation coach up the hill. I rushed upstairs for a better view leaning out of the bedroom window and inadvertently set the Union flag free. It appeared desperate to leave. It caught a prevailing wind and sallied forth the entire length of the, by now, empty tables only to wrap itself round a wobbly folded wooden chair left out in the echo of a game of musical chairs. On it flew and grabbed the top of a lamp post down the road clinging on determined, I surmised, not to miss the Queen's arrival.

By ten o'clock most of the adults were laughing at nothing, or singing "Roll out the Barrel", followed later by "We'll meet again", with my mum taking the lead with her West End show voice. I couldn't work out why the proceedings were slowing down, although I was almost asleep on my feet. I found my dad helping to dismantle the tables and ran to him yelling, "STOP! She hasn't been yet!" I must've appeared extremely distressed because Mrs Smith from next door picked me up. She rarely even picked up her own distressed children let alone anyone else's, but I'd seen her down more than a few half pint bottles of Baby Blue, and it seemed to bring out the maternal instinct which was usually buttoned up beneath her orange quilted housecoat. Before I had the chance to renew my bellow she'd handed me over to my mum with, "Bless her little cotton socks, time for bed I think." If I'd had the words and the wit I reckon I would've told her where to stick her cotton socks and her beery breath. But I was young, tired, very polite and glad to be handed over. My mum, soaking up the obvious adulation after her Vera Lynn impersonation, snuggled me up close. I could smell her talcum powder, *Je t'aime*, that she kept for special occasions. Between sobs I managed to explain the cause of my upset. She murmured into my drowsy head that the Queen was probably in bed by now after her busy day in London. My incredulity could only be beaten by my exhaustion as I gave in to sleep, a welcome haven after the trauma of the day that would remain forever, the day the Queen *didn't* come to tea.

There were more exciting things afoot for me that year though. I started at school. My big brother, fourteen months older, was already a veteran at it, so after my first day mum let him take me to school on the bus without her. Public transport provided Peter with the opportunity for merciless teasing. Having risen to "big-boy" mode to meet this huge responsibility with all the enthusiasm and reassurance he could muster for our parents, he morphed into Dennis the Menace mode once out of sight and the sport began.

Cautiously building up speed as we reached the bottom of the hill, the transformation would begin. Peter ran, satchel bouncing off his grey-flannelled bottom, through the back lane and across the main road to the bus stop. He left me, confused and crying, with the comforting memory of mum's tea towel waving to us from the front doorstep, and the safety of the other side of the road where the bus picked us up. Five interminable minutes away from home. Each day I summoned up the courage to sprint across the road at a hell of a pace to the comparative safety of Peter and his leering. I should thank him really, these early morning bids for freedom marked the beginning of my sprinting career which, although short-lived, was not without some small success. In later years I enjoyed a modicum of success winning the mother's race when my own children started school, running barefoot as a precursor to Zola Budd in later years. That was a long way off. With the benefit of hindsight I imagine similar scenarios of abandonment played out between siblings all over the country. Today we'd call social services.

After perhaps not the best of beginnings, I grew to love primary school. There were fifty-six children in my class and we sat in a big circle for the register. Thirty minutes later our work began. And I do mean work. We were each given a pencil and told to copy the writing on the blackboard. I already knew how to write and was desperate to show my teacher. My keenness was my downfall, however, as I pressed my pencil too hard and the lead broke. When this happened at home my dad would take a sharp kitchen knife and whittle away at the pencil before handing it back to me, spikey and as good as new. Things were different in school though. I presented my pencil to Miss Kirk. She looked at it, then at me. In between there was an enormous intake of breath and for a moment I was worried she was going to blow me away like the big bad wolf I'd heard of in *Listen with Mother* on the radio. Her eyes dilated and that was the last I saw of her face. Her massive bosom rose and cast a shadow over me as I stood several feet beneath her gaze and her impressive overhang. Then there was a shriek worthy of the banshee which rendered the fifty-five remaining children mute. They looked up without their pencils leaving the paper. It was then that I realised that the object of her disapproval was me. I was completely nonplussed. That is until my pencil was held aloft for the entire class to see. They responded on cue with appropriately shocked gasps, mimicking Miss Kirk. This confused me even more. Had I done something wrong? I hadn't wet my knickers or chewed my cardigan sleeves or hit anyone. What could it possibly be?

I had committed the worst crime. I had broken my pencil lead. The punishment? A sturdy whack across the back of my leg with a wooden ruler. I hadn't experienced corporal punishment before and it terrified me. The adults I knew certainly remonstrated with us at home if we were being too loud, or were late for a meal. But this physicality was new to me and I discovered the first pangs of yearning as I conjured up the safety of my mummy's arms as we sat between the welcoming hearth and the steaming clothes horse on wet days. My home-thoughts were sharply interrupted as expulsion from my own classroom followed. Miss Kirk was a looming monster standing in the classroom doorway. Her right arm outstretched and her massive, chalky hand pointing toward my brother's classroom. As I winced past her, I noticed her face had disappeared and been replaced by a tightly controlled bunch of wrinkles and frowns, underneath which her fleshy lips performed a rolling in-out movement as if she wasn't sure whether to utter another word or whether she had exhausted her safe expletives as she berated me for my heinous crime. The shame of walking into my brother's classroom, when I eventually found it, was trumped only by the ensuing reprimand. It was more grown-up than the first, and involved facing the class of older children, while Sister Mary Assumpta bellowed out my misdemeanour with all the gusto of the Westminster Town Crier. As if that wasn't enough to prompt twelve weeks therapy for accumulating post-traumatic stress disorder, begun with the coronation, I then got a double dose of telling off from mum and dad when Peter regaled them with the shame I'd brought on the family. All this before he'd even dropped his satchel on the kitchen floor that same afternoon. I remember feeling terribly confused. All I had done was try my best with my writing. It was hardly my fault that the bloody pencil wasn't up to it. I decided I wouldn't bother going back to school the following day. I clearly wasn't appreciated. I believe it was then, at that tender age, that I began to realise that life wasn't all smiles. There were actually adults who liked to humiliate and hit children.

Later in that same year I met the boy of my dreams. I didn't recognise this as a landmark in my life at the time, but Frankie was unlike anyone else I had ever met. He was eleven-years-old and so our time together was short. Short but meaningful. I still don't know why Frankie took a shine to me, but we were inseparable at school break times. He always came to find me and hoist me up onto his shoulders. I'd never seen the world from even a decent height before, so perched up on Frankie's shoulders I saw so much that had previously gone unnoticed from my diminutive height. We paraded around the playground, me like the Queen of Sheba, Frankie like Tarzan! Sometimes we'd stand on the school railings facing the tall trees of Victoria Park. If we jumped hard enough on the railings we could make them bounce. It was as if we inhabited a tree house to which no one else was privy. We talked about animals, trees, and how much we loved each other. He took the top off my milk bottle for me so that I wouldn't spray my jumper with globs of cream. He made me a miniature shepherd's crook out of twisted wire, and one day he kissed me. It was a sweet, short, milky kiss. I kept the shepherd's crook after Frankie went to secondary school, and then it went the way of all childhood keepsakes. As, I guess, did Frankie and me.

Chapter 3

My years at primary school weren't all bad. I loved learning and was a good girl. My heartbreak when Frankie left was soon more than made up for when I was chosen to be a flower monitor. Thinking about it now I reckon it still has its therapeutic effect. Maybe Relate could make use of it? "So… Your husband leaves the top off the toothpaste, never empties the dishwasher, falls asleep in front of *Question Time*, leaves the loo seat up, then finally abandons his pants on the bedroom floor before passing out and snoring as his drooling mouth hits the pillow case?

"Yes… Have you considered buying a new vase or two and keeping them filled with flowers in constantly renewed fresh water? I recommend cut-glass vases. That way, if he doesn't mend his ways you have the choice of lobbing the vase at him once the snoring gains momentum, or grinding up the glass and sprinkling it into his final slug of wine during the evening. Can't be detected you see…never fails."

Being flower monitor was my calling. Though I had to work on holding my breath while ditching the slimy stems of dying blooms to stop myself from retching with the stench. Bearing the vases of brazen marigolds into class was akin to a divine ritual as far as I was concerned. I was well on my way to achieving a vision of the Virgin Mary by this stage, so any chance I got to appear other-worldly was met with the enthusiasm of today's *X Factor* wannabes.

We had thought Miss Kirk was strict, but we soon learnt that we'd been lulled into a false sense of security despite her tantrums. The following couple of years introduced us to the firm discipline of the dear nuns. They were known as the Order of the Sisters of

Charity. What a misnomer. God, they had it made didn't they? All the parents held them in dizzyingly high esteem, second only to the parish priest who was second only to the Pope, who everyone knew was second only to God Himself. So the dear sisters could do no wrong. Pinching, slapping, and demoralising, were all deserved according to our parents.

I don't recall ever being dealt corporal punishment at home except once when I had the misfortune to be cowering behind Peter while dad read him the riot act for being rude to mum. Dad pushed Peter with a little more force than anticipated and he fell backward into the hallway taking me with him. We virtually flew up the stairs after that. We'd never even *seen* dad angry let alone felt the force of his frustration before. It was an isolated incident. Peter learnt his lesson and I learnt not to hover behind him if he was on the receiving end of a reprimand.

But it was fine for the nuns to dish out punishment and so we children accepted it as though it were a rite of passage. As much as we hated the nuns, we also loved them. They were so fresh and clean and angelic-looking. Apart from Sister Mary David who had a beard and a wart in the dent directly below her nose. She could be vicious one minute then telling you what an absolute delight you were in the next. I really believe that if one of them had shut us in a cupboard and thrown away the key there would still be parents saying, "You must have deserved it, you little monkey!"

Sister Agnes introduced us to Saint Bernadette and henceforth I waited for my vision. I figured that if a peasant's daughter from France, whose father disposed of dirty bandages from the hospital for a living, was worthy of a celestial visit then so was I. My dad was, after all, a civil servant now, and my mum held down three jobs while I assumed she waited to be discovered and hit the West End. How worthy was *that*? Also in my favour was the fact that Peter and I were dragged to church at every opportunity because dad played the organ and mum was in the choir. In fact I think the choir *was* our family. During 11.00am Mass on Sundays I was in a trance-like state as they sang Latin Communion Motets. Sometimes, as I opened my eyes after such a prolonged absence, I was convinced that I had levitated and would find myself looking down on the congregation as they, in utter admiration, gazed up at my transfiguration. As it was, I'd open my eyes to Peter, his face centimetres from mine, with his eyes crossed and his tongue sticking out. He was jealous of my sanctity I thought. Okay, I may not have actually risen from the pew this time, but there was always Benediction at 4.00pm wasn't there? I was simply being prepared in God's time. I wished he'd hurry up!

By the time I made it to year six in primary school I'd decided apparitions were over-rated. I now prayed *not* to have a vision. You see, I no longer wanted to draw attention to myself. I was ten-years-old, skinny, short and wore national health glasses. Also, I had an over-active imagination which woke me at night in a bedroom as dark as a deserted coal mine, inhabited by morphing shadows of ethereal beings. Apparitions were not for me. Besides, I was in love with my teacher, Mr Coombe, and spent my prayer time asking for him to notice me and make me a monitor.

Mr Coombe resembled Frankie Vaughan, what's more, he could sing. When he opened up our singing lessons with the first few bars of "Shenandoah, I long to see you, away you rolling river", my life was complete. His skills in the classroom were also exemplary. The icing on the cake was his accuracy with the rectangular wooden board rubber. Any hint of bad behaviour was dealt with swiftly and with maximum effect as he took aim and launched the chalky missile. It flew past the innocents. We knew we were safe as long as we didn't move a muscle. Many times it lifted the hair of one of my bunches on its trajectory to the back row and ginger-haired Mitchum. The skill was that it never scored a direct hit. Not the board rubber, not ever. That took skill and my adulation grew in direct proportion to his accuracy. The chalk was another matter. Whenever that was pitched we knew it was with the sole aim of making contact with an unsuspecting ear of the miscreant. Mr Coombe was accurate alright. I believe he died last year. Lovely man.

Being in year six meant you were divided into one of three groups. The Bottom group, as it was called, consisted of those children with special educational needs. As special educational needs were waiting to be discovered, along with ADHD etc. the group was known by parents and children alike as the Bottom group, for children who were "backward".

Not much was expected of you if you were in the Bottom group, so when the other two groups were creamed off the Bottom group got to do colouring in or tidying up. There was a lot to be said for being in the Bottom group. Several of its members have gone on to become terrific entrepreneurs. They saw something that we didn't, even then. To this day I wonder if I missed an opportunity there.

The Middle group was exactly what was written on the tin, children of middling intelligence who may make it through the Eleven Plus if tutored enough.

The Top group was us. I mean me, my brother and six other girls and boys. We were naturally competitive and of above average intelligence, apparently. Basically we were too scared to think outside of the box and could learn anything parrot-fashion, hence we were deemed to have above average intelligence. Simple wasn't it?

We were tutored by the head teacher in his study with the door shut. I had my own theory about this. He smoked a pipe and spent his day in surround-smell. Opening the door risked the possibility of diluting the fugg and shattering the illusion that he was actually in the living room of his sumptuous, smoke-filled Clifton apartment overlooking the Downs in Clifton, not in his shabby study in Bedminster. After handing out our books the head would fascinate us all by lighting up his pipe. It was brown tortoiseshell. He would strike the Bryant and May match and apply it to tobacco in the deep bowl of his pipe while lifting and holding down the box of matches to flatten any escaping tobacco and keep the rest ignited. Throughout the operation the head gradually disappeared behind the growing smoke screen as he sucked, patted, tapped and told us to, "Turn to page, (puff-puff) forty-two, read it through (puff-puff) carefully and complete (puff-puff) the exercise below." Having successfully ignited both his tobacco and our imaginations – it didn't take much in those days because most of us didn't have TV – he'd sit back, stretch, smile benignly and survey each of us one by one.

That about sums up our tutoring. The rest was homework. I think my parents thought I'd learn through osmosis. The head was revered. He'd been to university. The sessions in his office were the ultimate in primary education. The fact that both my brother and I were beneficiaries was a matter for familial pride. I even heard it being discussed after church at Mrs O'Brien's house over Camp coffee and custard creams. It didn't get more news worthy than that.

Osmosis or not, I passed the Eleven Plus and transferred to the girls'

Catholic grammar school. This was a disappointment to me because failing the Eleven Plus would've suited my dress sense so much more. Failure would've resulted in going to the mixed Catholic secondary school and the uniform there was quite remarkable in its time.

Tartan, pleated skirts, white shirts and bootlace ties at the secondary school. Maroon gymslips, coffee-coloured shirts and maroon velour hats at the grammar. No contest. That aside, there were boys at the secondary school, older boys with adorned upper lips and indecisive voices. Bliss.

My parents were pleased of course when I passed the Eleven Plus, but my mum went into a frenzy when she saw the uniform list. It wasn't so much what I had to wear, it was the fact that there was only one supplier and it happened to be one of the most exclusive, upmarket shops in Bristol. You know the sort. Manikins and men wore the same disinterested expression gazing out through immaculate plate glass windows as dreary weather bled dreary people through Saturday's veins and shopping arcades. Normally we stuck to Lewis', British Home Stores, and Marks and Spencer. Mum said you knew where you were with them. What she meant was we could just about afford them.

I didn't much care for shopping, but sometimes mum and I would stop outside Cowardine's coffee shop and we'd inhale the roasting beans as if savouring the elixir of life. I never knew in advance if we were going in or not, but the whole time we wandered from shop to shop my mind would be on the coffee. Standing outside Cowardine's the suspense was almost overwhelming. It was like grabbing my weekly *Boyfriend* comic and turning straight to the centrefold blissfully anticipating George Hamilton the third or, sadly, Cliff. Sometimes we went into Cowardine's. God, how sophisticated (George Hamilton the third). Sometimes we didn't. The sense of disappointment (Cliff Richard) as we turned and headed for the bus station. Outside Cowardine's was where I learnt delayed gratification unlike some of my friends whose learning curve took an impromptu vertical trajectory in the back row of the Rex cinema in Bedminster.

There was an unwritten expectation in the post-war decades that parental tolerance terminated as teenagers flexed their ill-informed, newly-independent muscles to rip the apron strings of obeisance. One look at the role models we had couldn't fail to excite back then in the 60s. The Beatles with their outrageous hair, The Rolling Stones with their disdain for conventionality, Marianne Faithful with her Mars bars (if you weren't there, you'll never know). We couldn't wait to break the mould, don wispy ankle-length dresses and drift off into "Itchycoo Park", fading into the middle distance just as sure as the dot on our black and white, twelve-inch, Ultra TV screen marked the end of the day's transmission.

My teenage years were, relatively speaking, unremarkable. When you're five foot tall and sport bottle-top glasses teenage years can be inhospitable terrain. For my parents it wasn't as fraught as it may have been had I been adorned with breasts and twenty-twenty vision. Thankfully, I was blessed with humour. I wouldn't have made it through to my final year at the grammar school without it. It earned me a following. It was so simple. A couple of jokes, imitations, that sort of thing, and I'd have the class in hysterics. Humour was the reason I was elected form captain year after year. I found I was good at organising people and planning things too and, if I used my sense of fun, there was little I couldn't achieve.

One day, for a laugh, we threw the class swot's maths book out of the window prior to the start of the lesson. She was horrified, while we fell about laughing at her expense. Giggling delinquent girls caught up in the illicit moment. When the first tentative drops of rain began to fall panic seized her, so I opened the window to go get her book lest her simultaneous equations got smudged. We were three floors up. I hitched my gymslip up to my thighs and slung my leg over the sill at the exact same moment the heavens opened. There was a small balcony floored with mosaic tiles enclosed by a rusty wrought iron balustrade to step out onto, and time was of the essence.

Miss Bowls, our maths teacher, was not renowned for her sense of fun and I was already in danger of relegation to the bottom set after yet another year of appalling test results. I stepped out feeling my way with my right foot. I located something non-slip and planted my foot firmly down...on the book. I leapt as if walking on hot coals and grabbed the book while noticing the imprint of my Clark's regulation lace-up on the rain-spattered cover. I turned to climb back into class and caught the puce, stifled expression of my friend Sue as she slowly, but firmly, shut the window while gesticulating that Miss Bowls was in the room! Several expletives came to mind including a couple I'd been saving up for a rainy day. Well BINGO here it was! I silently let rip and finished off with a Hail Mary just to hedge my bets. I *was* three floors up and could actually see the flower bed directly underneath the balcony floor through a chipped tile close to my left foot. I had to get back into class somehow. It didn't take me long to work out that there was only one safe way back in. I may have been a lost cause as far as maths was concerned, but there was nothing wrong with my orienteering skills. I had no option but to go back in the way I'd ventured forth. Shit! I couldn't budge the window. There was one remaining option so I succumbed. I gingerly knocked on the pane twice. Sue opened the window and we stood with our faces inches apart, hers feigning surprise, mine feigning innocence tinged with a smidgeon of menace which left her in no doubt as to her fate at morning break. I squelched up to the podium where Miss Bowls was waiting for the impossible. A plausible explanation.

My glasses steamed up and my Mary Quant hairstyle, now resembling a saturated West Highland terrier, dripped rhythmically into the collar of my sodden blouse and ran down my chest into the elastic waistband of my knickers. Could it get any worse? Of course it could. Miss Bowls pounced. Spittle flew as she remonstrated with me. Her charcoal-grey academic gown flapped like a trapped bat as the class looked on. I zoned out. That aggravated her more than ever, but what exactly did she expect from me? For four years the most she'd ever offered me by way of conversation was, "Whatever's the matter with you, child?" which would usually prompt my imagined response, *Well if you don't know, I sure as hell don't!*

"The pass mark isn't forty per cent and never will be!" she'd screech, her voice prompting goosebumps similar to those I experienced when chalk squealed on the blackboard. I already knew that. What I didn't know was how to keep up with the rest of the class without any help. I was swept along on the tidal wave of a syllabus which meant little to me. I truly did not care one iota how long it took three men to dig a hole on the last Tuesday of the month when gallons of water soaked through it at an indeterminable speed rendering the hole unworkable for twelve and a half days of said month. I can't say it's had a profound effect on my life either. Finally, the tyranny stuttered to a halt as the puddle of rainwater around my feet sought refuge in the welcome cracks of the waxed wooden floorboards.

I envied that puddle finding sanctuary in the PE kits abandoned in the changing rooms below.

Miss Bowls swept out of Form 4A as a round of applause from thirty-nine hysterical classmates resounded. I took my bow, and felt the power of performance. Fast forward to the end of my fifth year when the fun seemed to have dissipated, and there was an edginess in the beeswax air of the endless corridors and disappearing flights of stairs which still haunt my dreams. This was the defining year as far as school went. "One's future was within one's grasp." I already had "one's future" planned having met the man of my dreams, Sid. He was a rocker who worked as a cinema projectionist. I told my friends he was in the film industry. Every Tuesday he picked me up from school on his motorbike. I persuaded him to ride up to the end of the school drive in his creased black leathers, then I'd wait until those I wished to impress were ambling their way out of school at the end of the day. I'd casually drop into step with them, and wait to see their surprise as Sid grunted his salutation while chewing mightily on black bubblegum and revving the engine. Too sexy!

Tuesdays were cookery days so travel by motorbike wasn't ideal. I became quite adept over the weeks though. I'd hitch up my gymslip, stuff my velour hat under my bottom where I knew it would remain for the duration of the journey through town, grab Sid's leathers with my left hand and steady my cauliflower cheese, or whatever, with my right. We'd sweep away from school to a fanfare of backfiring exhaust and a deep growl from the meticulous silver engine. I felt so cool. Cornering wasn't easy. One week I arrived home with a rice pudding in my lap. I think that may have been the week that I decided Sid wasn't the man of my dreams after all.

At the all girls Catholic grammar school I attended, careers guidance was a dismal affair. It was assumed that one would either marry money, become a secretary (which would subsequently lead to marrying money), or enter a convent, in which case one would have no need to worry about money. After my disastrous results at GCE O level, my parents went to their second parents' evening of my secondary school career. My parents didn't believe in interfering. I couldn't have cared less. In the five years to date I had got away with murder and, on the whole, had a blast. This parents' evening was different though. I felt the tension mounting in the musty air as

I pushed my rose-tinted specs to the top of my head and rubbed my eyes in an attempt to appear half awake. Looking back, I am swathed in nostalgia as endless corridors close around me once more, and I see myself practising invisibility as a gossip of sixth formers jollies on past me not even noticing my forlorn, dropped coat as it laps itself playfully about their ankles before being kicked into touch under year eight's shoe rack. God how I wanted some of that sophistication.

But this was parents' evening and my fate was about to be decided for me. My dad threw his weight behind the towering, studded oak front door of the school entrance and stepped back to allow mum in first. She in turn ushered me in. A *pas de trois*. I noticed her wary expression as dad ran his finger along the underside of his collar and coughed. The echo didn't help. For once, I was the more confident one of the three of us. We joined the queue outside Sister Dominic's study where we telepathically agreed a vow of silence. Other parents sounded so *posh*. Even Sue's parents who were local bakers. Even her mother, who was from Wales, sounded like Princess Margaret for God's sake. She had nothing on us, I remember thinking, they didn't even own their own house. I think I was a bit of a snob. An aspiring one maybe. Sister Dominic, "Dom", wore a sylph-like mask which belied her steely temperament. If looks were an indicator you daren't face-up to Sister Dom for fear she would keel over. Her threadbare, black habit hung on her as it had since she whispered her vows a millennium ago. The truth was she could have survived Guantanamo Bay without so much as a hair out of wimple.

Leaving a pile of shredded tissues at my feet, I followed my parents into her study. It smelt dry and tired. It smelt like Sister Dom. The sad net curtains offered no relief as they hung, exhausted, longing for a better offer. She kept us waiting. I knew this tactic from old. Dom liked to unsettle her victims in the same manner that ants do by anaesthetising their prey pre-devouring. I could wait as long as she liked, I was counting the change in my Robert Hirst secret purse attached to the inside pocket of my Burberry. Just about enough for a packet of No 6 ciggies on Saturday. Yes!

Papers were shuffled, my dad looked up, he could out-psych her any day. Sister Dom shook her head, bit her lip and launched into the good news/bad news. Apparently, due to my abysmal results, I would not be able to stay on at school to study English literature before

28

being discovered by Lawrence Olivier and leaving to take the West End by storm. Shame, that was my only career plan.

The good news followed. I could continue into the sixth form provided I studied Doctrine, aka religious education. Doctrine, the word fell between us where we stared at it. It lay there like yesterday's fallen plums, bruised and embarrassed beneath the tree. Discussion wasn't invited and my parents accepted Dom's decree. It was as if we had been pardoned some unspeakable crime and absolution had set us on the path to redemption. We felt obliged to thank her, copiously, before taking our leave, almost backing out of the door and doffing our forelocks in deference.

Within the hour I was seated between my parents on the number twenty-two bus back to the sprawling outskirts of the city. "Doctrine?" my dad chuckled as he lit up his second ciggie of the journey. And again, "Doctrine?" fifteen minutes later as he cleared the condensation and smoke from the top deck window with the back of his hand and shook his head at his reflection.

Mum sat with her gloved hands crossed in her lap. She wouldn't be seen dead outside the house without appropriate gloves and hat in those days. I tried to gauge her feelings and concluded that her upwardly tilted head, elevating her above the smoking classes, could only indicate that she was beyond disappointment. I sat on the crack between their two seats, physically uncomfortable, and emotionally in the desert-whirl of nowhere sensing an oncoming sandstorm from which there was a distinct lack of shelter. I knew mum wouldn't demean herself by expressing her opinion on the top deck of a number twenty-two bus, so I willed the journey to stretch into a fantasy filled with dragons, evil stepmothers and avenging knights as it took the corner at Bedminster Down far too fast. We reached the mid-point of our journey and I attempted to conjure up the world of CS Lewis in an attempt to save me from the retribution I had coming. Where was the damned wardrobe when one needed it? It was virtually impossible for my mum to demonstrate anything other than perpetual optimism in public. As a much younger child I used to wonder if there was a saint of perpetual optimism. It sounds feasible doesn't it? As long as my mum lived the outside world saw a perfectly groomed, perfectly harmonious family. Today was no exception. A neighbour boarded the bus, sat down in front of us and turned to my dad for a light.

He worked for the cigarette factory WD and HO Wills and was always generous with his allocation of ciggies. He proffered the pack to my mother. She declined gracefully, although she was a smoker. Smoking on the bus was one of those unwritten rules of etiquette as far as she was concerned. Like eating in the street, one didn't do it. Dad lit up, his third of the journey. Mum smiled and managed a perfectly civil conversation which continued as we alighted the bus until the neighbour turned, slipped the latch of his garden gate and walked up the path to the green front door with its minuscule oval window of dimpled glass. I counted the steps before she spoke. There were twelve. Then a distant rumbling mutter escalated as we walked up the path to our own front door. It reached its hiatus as mum tugged at each individual finger of her dainty beige, nylon gloves and shoved them mercilessly into the pocket of her gabardine mac. Dad disappeared upstairs seeking refuge in the bathroom. I removed my battered velour school hat and stood holding it as if it were some cherished object, smoothing and turning it between forefingers and thumbs with an overanxious Laurel and Hardy mannerism. There were no answers to the questions which were bouncing like hail around a rockery. "How have you managed to waste all these years? Do you realise how much that uniform has cost your father and me? How could you be so bright at primary school and so SLOW now?" Then the *pièce de résistance* which I knew heralded the end of the conversation, "What will I say to everyone?"

An hour or so later my dad had managed to resolve the situation. He had a gift for finding the opportunity hidden behind the twisted mesh of any obstacle. I was to join the civil service, go to college one day a week to boost my meagre qualifications, then proceed to teacher training college. Resolution. My protests fell on deaf ears. Even when I insisted that I couldn't stand children my father was adamant: "You'll be a great teacher. You're bright when you want to be, artistic and a good laugh." Strange… These were not the qualities I recognised in any of my current teachers, but I trusted my dad and I needed to leave home.

Chapter 4

Eighteen months in the civil service was enough for me to realise that there must be more to life despite the opportunities I'd managed to wring out of it to date. Four good things actually. I earned a salary, and it was a veritable fortune in those days. Seven pounds per week, a vast improvement on the nineteen shillings I was paid for peeling onions in a greasy spoon café in town every Saturday. Secondly, I got out of the office once a week to attend further education college. Thirdly, my tutor was a young Hugh Grant. He was my ideal teacher. He was mysterious, shabby and remote, but still held a look of promise. It was as if he hadn't given up on his dreams and this was simply a humdrum episode in the novel of his life which paid his rent. The fourth piece of good fortune was Rod. He was the man occupying the space in my head for the remaining four days of the week. The man of my dreams.

He worked in the offices below mine. He was a mod. He was a trainee architect with a scooter on which hung more mirrors than those boasted by Gaudi. He also drove a mini and wore a parka. Our song was, "When a man loves a woman". I discovered, three months into our relationship that when a man loves a woman his devotion may be sorely tested if the woman in question is transferred to the centre of Bristol, as I was. Young love...transient.

I was transferred to the claims section of the Ministry of Labour aka Department for Employment in the centre of Bristol. It was an experience I shall never forget. On the one hand I learnt how to deal with the GP (the general public). From the great unwashed i.e. those "awful young layabouts" who today would be travelling the world and skyping their parents from Bali before moving on to Taiwan and Goa on what is commonly called a gap year, to those for whom life had dealt a lousy hand. All humanity was there. And a large percentage took one look at the diminutive teenager behind the counter, while metaphorically rubbing their hands together in anticipation and whispering, "Game on". Part of my job was to interview new claimants. You know the sort of thing, name, address, family members, last job etc. Perfectly straightforward. So it's with a smile now that I remember my gullibility when I swallowed, hook, line and sinker, the information volunteered to me by Mr S.

After twenty minutes struggling with his unfamiliar Asian accent I realised that we were not on the same page so to speak. Mr S was claiming benefits for his family. Absolutely right. However, his family was not living in the UK. His family was "at home over the other side", the "other side" being Pakistan. I felt so sorry for him when the supervisor came up to my station and, realising my dilemma, was able to explain the situation to Mr S whose face fell. I forced a smile as feeble as the last rays of Tuesday afternoon's sun which barely limped through the grilled windows of that forlorn place. His shoulders sagged and, as he turned to leave, he gave me a wonderful smile which I returned sympathetically. My supervisor, Mr Andrews, took me to one side. Due to his advanced years – he was at least forty – he knew a scam when he saw one. It seems that Mr S was one of the regulars at the labour exchange. I didn't really care. At the tender age of sixteen you don't do you? I just wanted to give him all the benefits he was clearly *not* entitled to just so that his wives and family could scrape together a meal. I wasn't bothered if they lived in Pakistan, Singapore or Barton Hill. Mr Andrews was bothered though.

After six months on Fresh Claims, my interview skills honed to perfection so I thought, I was promoted to the pay section. This meant getting to work incredibly early almost at "sparrow's fart" as I moaned to my friend Sue. Arriving at the red-brick building, so much a part of Bristol's architecture, I was ushered into a secure room. No windows, artificial light worthy of Dickensian Britain, and tea in which you could stand your standard issue pencil. You didn't though. It was the only one you got and, at the risk of repeating myself, I was still suffering from post-traumatic stress disorder after the Miss Kirk episode.

And there we sat. Three pay clerks faced with heaps of filthy lucre. And it really was filthy. Thousands of pounds in fivers, threadbare pound notes with the Queen's head fading into the back pockets of the nation, and then stacks of silver and copper all waiting to be counted, bagged and carried to the pay stations in the main area. After half an hour my hands were layered with the detritus of a million pockets and sweaty palms, sneezes and chesty coughs bequeathed to the cash. Thank God I didn't think with a clinician's mindset in those days. Then came the dramatic bit which I loved. The security guys arrived complete with coshes, helmets and industrial steel-capped boots to escort us and carry the money to where the hall had fogged with cigarette smoke and mugged-up with alcohol as the first claimants of the long day gathered to collect their unemployment benefit. The walk from the vault through the Fresh Claims Department and the length of the counter, from behind which we perched on chairs so high I almost needed a leg-up, was like the opening of a Broadway burlesque. Cheers and wolf whistles pierced the erstwhile impenetrable atmosphere as we took our places. Graham, one of the other pay clerks, blushed, fluttered his eyelashes and bit his lip. Graham was gay. He didn't think anyone knew. Bless his heart. *Everyone* knew. And if there was any room for doubt it was dispelled forever as he promenaded his swaying booty along to his high chair, arranged his immaculate shirt cuffs, and licked his forefinger to flick open the first claimant's dossier.

The laborious task of counting each claimant's money, recording it, getting said claimant to sign, or mark with an X that they'd received it, and then handing it over began. I eventually relaxed enough to enjoy the camaraderie of the first twenty or so claimants. The flirting was outrageous but I took it with all the superior charm of a posing heron on a grassy bank, safe behind the pane of glass separating me from the GP. All of this was, of course, in the 1960s. Sexual harassment, along with the aforementioned ADHD, hadn't been invented yet. It was good fun. No one was groomed, no one was hurt, or felt in the least bit threatened.

That is until Mr Evans approached. Mr Evans was an alcoholic, a genial alcoholic in my experience to date. He brought an air of the Caribbean in from the insidious, damp reality that was Bristol in winter. He wasn't from exotic climes but he had aspirations.

Regardless of the temperature Mr Evans wore a short-sleeved shirt lurid with printed palm trees, surfers and macaws. What an optimist! He was a total sensory experience. He was always heard first. He sang Irish rebel songs and was often joined in the chorus by several other claimants. I must admit I sometimes hummed along too and allowed myself to feel part of something bigger than the political demography of the labour exchange. Then there was the smell of warm summer nights in sleepy bars and sun-kissed shores, his preferred poison being Bacardi. As he came into sight, his florid face, the beacon at the head of the squadron beamed. His eyes like pissholes in the snow, disappearing as time marched headlong into the day, betraying his carefree demeanour. No Bacardi today. White spirit substitute was his default when there was a cash flow problem. I wondered if he would combust if his lighter caught a whiff of his vaporous breath.

He stood peering across at me as I tried to locate his dossier from the hopeful pile on the counter between us. I opened it and read the word Nil at the bottom of the column titled Total. I checked and double-checked but whichever way I looked at it the word Nil would not compromise. I looked into Mr Evans's red eyes as he called out to acquaintances in the hall, "God love 'er, she's just a babber this 'un."

I ventured, in my clipped Sylvia Peters accent, "I'm afraid there is nothing for you this week, Mr Evans." I felt sick. Not in anticipation of his response, but because I sounded like a holiday rep. saying, "Welcome to Tagisi" as if it were the ultimate in luxury travel and not a Thompson two-star destination complete with burger bar and Mickey Club for the kiddies. Mr Evans smiled. Well, he didn't actually *smile,* at least not an amicable "don't-you-worry-my–dear" smile. It was more of a quizzical "run-that-by-me-again" smile. Actually, there was no mistaking. It was a more of a sneer. So I did as I was requested and ran it by him again. By now I thought I'd make a really convincing holiday rep. My smile was setting, but it hadn't yet reached my eyes. I was fooling nobody. Mr Evans' affable body language changed. His face suffused to purple from his open-necked shirt, past his sprouting nostrils right up to his unruly eyebrows. He pulled his right hand through his greasy, thinning hair and looked around at his audience, as if he'd been given respite enough to phone a friend for an opinion on what action to take next. They knew something was about to kick off. I caught the eye of a young man leaning against the wall lighting up the stub of an earlier cigarette retrieved from behind his left ear. He looked at me with something verging on pity I think. Yes, pity, tinged with an inkling of a warning stare which held my glance for longer than was socially acceptable.

Mr Evans took a deep breath and boomed out, "Give me my *fucking* money!"

Oh God, I thought, wincing with the impact. The F word! I knew I was in trouble now. I lifted the dossier in front of me as if hoping to find his money cowering underneath. I didn't. I cleared my throat and in my enviable received standard pronunciation said, "I'm afraid there's nothing for you this week, Mr Evans." The charm offensive didn't stand a chance. Mr Evans reached inside the baggy pocket of his creased, stained trousers, and pulled out a gun. They say time stands still in this type of situation. It's true. It lifts up and suspends itself like a centre court tennis ball lobbed by Virginia Wade before crashing down to alert you to the fact that some action is expected of you. I knew *something* was expected. I just didn't know *what!* Every trembling muscle of my seven stone, sixteen-year-old body knew that. Every trembling muscle of my seven stone, sixteen-year-old body also knew that if I tried to climb down from my lofty perch my legs would fail me miserably and I'd end up exposing more than my youthful inexperience from an undignified angle on the mottled flooring. He mouthed the words again, this time waving the gun in front of the window of my booth. Keeping my eyes firmly fixed on the gun, I gripped the sides of my seat and slipped off letting Mr Evans know that I would ask my supervisor if he could come and help, and assuring him that I'd be right back. I walked the length of the interminable counter in front of hundreds of claimants, some of whom had seen the scenario unfold. Cat-calls, whistles and whoops preceded me once more, and this time I didn't like it. For a split second I wished I was in school, in a maths lesson even. Anywhere but here. It couldn't get more serious unless I lost control of my bladder. I didn't. Oh, thank you, God!

Mr Andrews calmly pressed the hidden panic button which was connected to the police station adjacent to the Ministry of Labour, and within a few minutes Mr Evans was being escorted out of the building clutching his methylated spirits and shouting over his shoulder that he would be back. I didn't doubt it.

In minutes I was reinstalled on my perch, much against my will. Today, of course, in a similar situation I would be offered counselling and a couple of weeks off, but back then such treatment was called, "Get a grip". Mr Andrews reassured me that it was like getting back on a horse once you'd fallen off. If you didn't do it immediately you probably wouldn't pluck up the courage again. Wrong analogy for me. I was pretty fearless in those days, but horses I didn't trust, and they knew it, taking delight in throwing their heads forward and down on the only two occasions I'd ever ridden, pitching me onto the sand at Brean Down on a lacklustre Bank Holiday Monday three years ago.

However, I did as I was told. This time a rousing chorus of cheers erupted accompanied by a round of enthusiastic applause as I began to count out the next claimant's money with the string of sausages that had once been my nimble fingers.

It may have been at that moment that I decided to work even harder for my upcoming exams. I had to get out.

I began to think that maybe college wasn't such a daunting option after all. Perhaps I was more intellectual than I gave myself credit for. After all, only one small barrier stood between me and the world of academia. Passing some exams. Unfortunately, to date, I was showing little aptitude. However, the competitive side of my personality kicked in. I *would* go to college simply to prove my secondary school teachers wrong. And now I had the added incentive of wishing to live beyond my seventeenth year. I still didn't like children, but I could *learn* to like them couldn't I? After all, there was a time when I couldn't stomach celery, but with the enhanced sophistication of a sixteen-year-old I was quite partial to it now.

I worked relatively hard at day release and managed to date two police cadets in the time I was there. I never quite made it with Hugh Grant, although I suspect he might have fancied me a bit by then. I was going through my Yoko Ono phase and, with a touch of eyeliner sweeping upward at the edges, I believed I had a touch of the Orient about me which he would find overwhelmingly attractive. The power of a strong imagination eh? I'd never know for sure because I'd not been wearing my glasses on college days and was virtually blind as a consequence. Blind, but mysterious.

The summer before my nineteenth birthday was momentous. I lived with the kind of abandon which is the norm today, perhaps even tame by comparison. I was leaving for college soon. My results had been sufficient to jettison my career. Just. "Purple Haze" was my favourite song. Jimi Hendrix was God. He really was. I worshipped him and was word perfect with all his songs although I never sang them out loud, certainly not in company, just in the bath. I even provided my own electric guitar accompaniment. Not so much air guitar as water guitar as I thrummed the rhythm out on the long-handled back scrubber my mother bought from the Ideal Home exhibition in the Victoria Rooms, along with a doughnut maker.

I stayed out late. I came home in the early hours of the morning in an open-top sports car belonging to the boyfriend of a fellow civil servant, and rode the inevitable storms of protest from my parents with the nonchalance of an albatross borne on the ocean thermals. I was eighteen and flying! Euphoria has a shelf life too though, and, in September, I boarded the train for Newcastle upon Tyne to begin three years in a girls Catholic college. Oh God, is this karma? My older cousin Annie, who I worshipped because she had been a Tower Ballroom dancer in Blackpool, had studied at the very college I was bound for having decided she had a teaching vocation four years previously. I had initially attempted to follow in her dainty footsteps by applying for an audition with the Bristol Old Vic Theatre School. Imagine my amazement when I was summoned to audition! Before casually mentioning this to my parents I'd read the prospectus. I thought I'd impress them with my background knowledge. You know, show them I'd been serious enough to do some research. It was then that I pulled out of the audition. There were fees to be paid. Large fees which I knew were beyond the already stretched budget at home. My acting career was over. Annie, however, fell on her feet. Not literally of course. As a dancer she had met and dated Adam Faith. Then she met Lonnie Donegan who swept her off her blistered feet to the echoes of "Hang down your head Tom Dooley". But the glamour and promise of glittered mirror balls isn't everything it would seem and she had just completed her qualification at St Mary's, Fenham, Newcastle upon Tyne. Unknown to me she had called my dad to let him know they still had places left if I was interested. Or, should I say, if *he* were interested. I guess my application was successful due in part to Annie's impeccable college career. I also guess that the dear sisters had no idea of Annie's dalliance with the bad boys of rock and roll prior to becoming a teacher. As the train pulled out of Temple Meads Station, my tin trunk (dad's from the war) settled into the luggage carriage. Inside…all my worldly goods. Everything from my cousin's hand-me-down pyjamas to my thigh-high purple patent leather boots with platforms Elton John would envy. Was it really that long ago and that serendipitous? I suppose yes is the answer to both of those questions. Life wasn't as complex then. There wasn't the lure of *X Factor*, or the celebrity status of sports personalities photographed advertising underwear stuffed with socks. Choices were still limited despite the best efforts of everyone after the war. And most choices were made by our parents too. Remarkable how we acquiesced. My journey up north was interminable. I felt like an evacuee. Not that I knew what that felt like of course, but I was alone, away from my family for the first time ever, heading for a city my mother read about in every one of her treasured library books written by Catherine Cookson. All I needed was a luggage label tied through the button hole of my grey duffle coat and the picture would be complete.

The countryside didn't flash by as in *The Railway Children*. The backdrop varied according to the time of day and condition of the weather. So far it had rained non-stop. Wall to wall greyness compromised the view. Occasionally steam billowed horizontally past, obscuring what I was able to see of the alien landscape. Sheep, sodden and static, appeared and were gone. A game of I Spy would've been out of the question.

Six hours into the journey rolling hills were replaced by factory chimneys and belching funnels. This must be the north I thought. The remnants of a poem flitted briefly through my mind. Something about "dirty rotten steamer with its smoke-stacked" something or other, the memory dims, I only learnt it for the GCE after all. *Dante's Inferno* presented itself and as we rattled and chuffed along a kind of decoy night fell. Abandon hope all ye who enter here, I thought as malevolent orange clouds fused with black billows to form a puffed up soufflé over the spewing factory funnels. God, where are all the happy poems when you need them? An hour later daylight reappeared much to my surprise! We were definitely through the industrial north. Skies cleared just enough to see housing estates budding like back to back rows of latent strawberries recognising summer. This was virgin territory to me and I realised I already missed living close to undeveloped fields where sheep actually moved from time to time.

After my packed breakfast and lunch had been reduced to the remains of a curly edged sandwich and the crumbs of a Jammie Dodger biscuit, I ventured into the toilet for the third time. I couldn't hang on any longer. My first trip had resulted in mopping the floor with a bundle of Jeyes toilet roll as the train lurched from side to side in an enthusiastic rhumba, and I hovered above the pan. The next visit was slightly more successful as we had pulled into a station and I broke the rules by *not* "refraining from urination while the train is in the station". This time a passenger with the girth of Hattie Jacques almost smothered me in her attempt to squish her way out of the over-frequented cubicle. After our do-se-do I almost fell into the cubicle only to find that I could barely manage a trickle. The confined space and second-hand air proved too much for me.

The eight-hour journey ended with a spectacular crossing over the River Tyne, and for the first time I felt a stir of excitement in the pit of my stomach. As I stepped off the train at Central Station in Newcastle, I realised that I was totally alone in the throng of rush hour hoards. Everyone had a purpose. They knew where they were going. I was the last swallow catching up with the flock, and flying forth in search of summer. A porter swung my battered tin trunk out of the carriage onto a trolley and made for the exit with me following like orphan Annie. Newcastle smelt cold. People with pinched faces pushed by. Breath hung in the smutty air and my nose ran copiously.

Dumped in the lay-by, my tin trunk and I waited for a taxi. I stared down at the trunk and noticed the remnant stains of brown glue and a scuffed old label with half of my dad's name penned on it. I wondered what its last journey had entailed at the end of the second world war. Whatever it was, it was likely to have been more exotic than Newcastle upon Tyne late in the afternoon of an early autumn Monday. It was almost dark before I got to the front of the queue. A burly cabbie rolled out of the driver's seat, lifted the trunk as if it were a feather-filled pillow, and launched it at the open boot. In one swift movement he was back in the taxi. Then came the revelation.

English is not spoken this far north. The cabbie turned to me and spoke. I had no idea what he said, but guessed it was a question as he stared at me expectantly. I foraged around in my pocket with the ripped lining for the address of the college. I pulled out the creased piece of Blue Vellum headed notepaper and along with it a mucky five pound note and a dead match. A lump came to my throat. The last time I'd seen the letter I was at home with mum and dad, "oooohing" and "aaaaaahing" as they read the offer from St Mary's College. Home seemed like a warm millennium away. I longed for the smell of washing drying in front of the coal fire and the sound of dad whistling his bike along the path and shutting it up for the night in the garden shed.

I read the address and we swung away from the station before I pushed the letter back from whence it came, hanging on to the fiver in the hope that it would cover the taxi fare. No point in dwelling on thoughts of home. Independence, freedom, responsibility were all waiting at the end of this long journey. It was nine hours thirty-five minutes door to door. I've since flown to San Francisco in less time and arrived to more clement weather and English-speaking cabbies.

As the taxi pulled away I stood on the drive of St Mary's and wondered when the welcome committee would appear. I'd still be standing there now if realism hadn't hit in the form of a north-easterly gale howling up from nowhere, and flinging leaves spitefully, at my tin trunk and biting at my bare legs. My mum's parting words came back to haunt me, "You'll catch your death wearing that mini-skirt up north." Having been born in Sunderland her advice was sound. Sound, but ignored.

I followed a group of girls lugging their trunks up the curved, gravel drive. I made a point of not catching them up but lingered a few metres behind, close enough to grasp snippets of their conversation. It turned out they had arrived from Belfast. I had absolutely no idea why anyone would want to leave the country of their birth to go to college, and knew less than zilch about the "troubles" in Northern Ireland which had prompted their flight.

Reminiscing now, I'm ashamed of my ignorance and lack of understanding. In later years, while in the throes of labour with my third baby, I read a novel about the Black and Tans as I paced up and down the maternity unit of our local hospital waiting for the action to crank up a productive notch. It compounded the fact that my knowledge of the history of Ireland had indeed been shameful. I could've been a far more compassionate and informed listener while at college. Instead I assumed most of their stories had been wildly exaggerated. Surely no one believed the tales of regular searches made by the Brits on unsuspecting young children and their mothers, or the surprise calls in the middle of the night when fathers and brothers disappeared. It made my exploits in the labour exchange tame by comparison. Anyhow, we pitched up on the same corridor in the halls of residence and soon became firm friends, united by our sense of mischief and need to survive. My room was directly opposite the lift which meant that my first six months in the halls of residence had the constant accompaniment of heavy iron concertina gates yielding to allow rowdy students to alight, and slamming of the same on the return trip. What a nightmare! Even worse was the unwanted responsibility forced upon me for shutting the lift gates and doors should anyone mistakenly leave them open. Why? Because left open an irritating buzzer was activated to ping continuously until some eejit got up and closed them. The eejit was the hapless student in Room 262, always a fresher, this year, 1967, me.

Respite came in the shape of Clare Mooney in Room 235. After six months in Newcastle, she decided to return to Belfast and take her chances with the IRA and the British army which she deemed a safer option than teaching. I took the opportunity to move into her vacated room leaving the ominous Room 262 to the new girl who was transferring from Durham. I'd done my time.

First things first. Huddles of freshers grouped in the lounge all fervently discussing which courses they had chosen, and why. How come they all seemed to know what their main subject was to be? Due to a lack of career guidance combined with my own apathy I had no idea that going to college meant studying the subjects of your *choice* in addition to the prescribed curriculum. Oh God! Faced with choice, I was stumped. I mean, I hadn't even heard of some of the subjects. Dance for instance. Imagine…dance was a subject! And humanities. What on earth was that?

Feeling slightly under-confident I chose English literature and music. I could think of nothing safer. It wasn't as simple as that though. I made the mistake of thinking English literature posed the least threat. After all, I'd just passed my A level. It has to be said that the emphasis is on the word *just* in that last sentence. How wrong can one be? After two weeks at St Mary's spent in a stifling study lined with books written by authors with unpronounceable names, I threw in the towel and changed to drama where a little knowledge could be disguised during heart-rending improvisations, quotes from *An Actor Prepares*, and name-dropping Brecht during break. After all, I had been invited to the Bristol Old Vic…oh, we've done that already.

To gain access to the music course there were auditions. Music was a popular choice for students hoping to become primary school teachers. If you had a music qualification it stood you in good stead in the jobs market when competing against men, 'specially men with maths or PE qualifications. The queue for auditions babbled down the main staircase on the music block and kept time through the passage of practice rooms. As the queue shortened strains of a familiar melody escaped from the audition room. It was "Early One Morning, just as the sun was rising". Apparently, we were to sing a song of our choice before a panel of tutors. I couldn't imagine anything less likely to impress the panel, than "Early One Morning", and I felt increasing pity for the tutors after the umpteenth rendition. I started to wrack my brain for a good song from my large selection. "Hey Joe" by Jimi Hendrix came to mind followed by "Strawberry Fields" courtesy of The Beatles. I ran them both in my mind before deciding that neither was appropriate in a Catholic college, and anyway, I didn't think playing air guitar would be an accurate indicator of my musical prowess. By now I was next in the queue. I strode through the open door. There they were. The panel. A fatuous-looking elderly gentleman asked me what my chosen song was, and, while silently struggling with "Only the Lonely" by Roy Orbison, I cleared my throat, took a deep breath and out came "Early one morning". I'd hardly got past hearing a maiden singing in the valley below when I was stopped and waved to the other side of the room where I picked up my timetable. I was *in*!

Chapter 5

The North-East of England was as alien to me as Kathmandu. At least in the latter they speak English. I was adjusting to the Northern Irish accent surrounding me on corridor three due to the influx of girls from over the water. After my first holiday back in Bristol my mother asked why I was speaking like an Irish navvy. I blamed my musical ear. While in college we had to wear academic gowns as seen on graduation days. This wasn't as onerous as we first imagined and presented us with an opportunity to bolster our meagre diet and keep us relatively warm when crossing the quadrangle which hummed twenty-four hours a day for three quarters of the year with a north-easterly wind which did not take prisoners. Necessity is the mother of invention they say, and we soon put our gowns to use.

All first year students lived in halls and we shared everything. We would've starved together had someone not had the idea of sewing large pockets on the inside of our gowns, possibly the first Bags for Life. From the refectory we stowed away bread, fruit, pies and the more adventurous students balanced milk jugs in these voluminous pockets. Getting back to our rooms we sorted out the booty like Fagin's ragged scavengers. Consequently, no one became more emaciated than was fashionable in the 60s. Regular food parcels for the girls from Northern Ireland were a great source of nutrition too, and had the double advantage of introducing us to foreign food. Apart from Vesta packet curry I'd had little experience of foreign cuisine so relished the offer of soda bread or potato bread shipped from Belfast and Armagh.

Curfews were imposed the like of which I hadn't experienced

since my early teenage years. My *very* early teenage years. This was quite permissible for girls who'd come to college straight from school, but for a bunch of us over nineteen-year-olds it was simply a challenge to be overcome. I discovered I'd inherited my father's penchant for finding the opportunity behind every obstacle, and it wasn't long before I uncovered areas of the college grounds which were accessible without having to dodge Alf the gatekeeper at the main entrance.

I got to know a girl, Noreen, whose room overlooked the side street just along from the gatehouse, and had the added advantage of being on the first floor. This was invaluable. I'd let her know if I was going to be late back after a date and, for a couple of ciggies or some coffee, she'd open her window for me to climb in. She thought she was getting Nescafe. She wasn't. Well, she got a Nescafe jar alright, but I filled it with what can only be described as goat droppings posing as coffee from the local open all hours. She was happy. I was happy.

Alf was prone to dozing after 10.00pm when he assumed all his girls were safely tucked into bed. He was partial to Newcastle Brown Ale so there was no danger of waking him once he'd sunk a couple of bottles and dropped off. All I had to do was scale the wall, which was just level with the top of my head, sling my handbag in through the open window of Noreen's room and heave myself up. The degree of difficulty increased, however, when under the influence of alcohol. Somehow, limbs did their own thing with amazing flexibility if haphazard accuracy at such times.

On one such night in the middle of winter, with more snow on the ground than the rest of England had seen for centuries, I staggered back to halls with a friend, Oonagh, who was also planning to get back into college through the alternative route. We slid and skittered along the drive like a couple of kids shushing each other exaggeratedly as we approached the gatehouse. Having taught her the rudimentary process of getting oneself, one's self-respect and one's handbag through the window without detection, she decided I should go first to demonstrate. My first attempt at getting my bag through the window was an abysmal failure and resulted in a shower of chewing gum, ciggies, lighter, Rendezvous lipstick, brush, tissues and two pound ten shillings in loose change raining down on the pair of us. We collapsed into a snowdrift behind the college wall. We

44

composed ourselves and took in the beauty of our surroundings, then we lit up and waxed lyrical about the joys of the frozen north-east after midnight in December.

Meanwhile Noreen appeared at her window in her pjs and academic gown. She poked her head out of the window sporting my sponge rollers, also part of the deal, and hissed at the pair of us, "Jesus, are you coming in or building an igloo?" in her harsh Northern Irish twang. It was enough to start us off again and it was a good fifteen minutes before the pair of us swung our sodden feet onto the bedside rug of Noreen's cosy room. She wasn't amused. It was way beyond the acceptable time for good Catholic girls to be coming home she remonstrated. I mimicked her nasal accent as we crept back to our own rooms along the deserted corridor and collapsed onto unmade beds. Oh yes Tracey Emin, we know where you're coming from.

Those three years in Newcastle upon Tyne were confirmation to me that all those Catherine Cookson novels my mum had read, plus a previous addiction I'd had for autobiographies of holy Irish people were true. The college was run by the dear nuns as we called them with our tongues sidling into our cheeks. They expected immediate compliance, and they invariably got it. Some of it makes sense now with the benefit of hindsight. For instance, there were strict rules about personal appearance in the classrooms where we observed teachers and helped with small groups. St Mary's was a sprawling campus which incorporated education facilities from pre-school through primary, secondary and college. As future educators it was essential that we set an example they said. Everything from the writing on our hand-painted posters, which had to be italic with each letter measured to within a millimetre to ensure precision, to our hair, clothes and make-up. Mini-skirts were not tolerated as our knickers may be glimpsed by impressionable children. Skirt lengths were henceforward below the knee. Hair was to be off our shoulders or tied back for purposes of hygiene. My attempts at emulating Yoko Ono evaporated overnight. Dusty Springfield make-up was a no-no, nail varnish was out of the question, and earrings were anathema. Human Rights hadn't been invented then. We simply did as we were told. Fail to comply and the consequences were spelt out in impeccable italics: *permanent exclusion*.

As term three approached prep for our teaching placements

began. We were finally going to leave the security of St Mary's and travel to distant places with exotic names like Ashington and Newbiggin-by-the-Sea to teach in *real* schools. Planning was a lengthy business but we frequently left schemes of work and lesson plans to the last minute as we ransacked each other's wardrobes for anything resembling suitable schoolwear, and experimented with our newly discovered and soon to be abandoned minimalist foundation *crème*.

We devised all kinds of scams to get round the issue of lesson planning. Remember this was pre-ICT, so we copied from one another in longhand. We adopted a systematic approach before even hearing of the management guru Coverdale. In order to maximise potential and minimise writer's cramp and exhaustion, as night after night we sat burning the midnight oil, there had to be a system. We played to our strengths. I planned English, drama and music, Noreen planned geography and history, Frances planned dance, and so on. Eventually the whole corridor was involved in the master plan. What we hadn't banked on, however, was the acuity of the nuns. They'd seen it all before. The result was pandemonium as we were all dismissed from our pre-placement appointments with tutors with more than a flea in our ears to rewrite every single plan and present each one at the end of the week for approval. We learnt that the midnight oil had barely been scorched. Now the incineration was about to occur. The corridor wreaked of cigarettes, everyone smoked, as we churned out pages and pages of planning, all handwritten, without a single spelling mistake. No one wanted to risk a second dismissal, especially not the week before our placements began.

I remember queues of students anxiously waiting outside study doors, unvarnished nails bitten to the quick, hair scraped back into an elastic band, spotless academic dress. We resembled an agitated line of self-recriminating, repressed schoolgirls. Nothing got past the nuns though. All attempts to divert attention were sussed and dealt with before the study doors were quietly closed. All that mattered were the plans. Attention to detail came close to being anal. More than a dozen of us were sent back to amend the already amended plans due to some error or other. But by the end of the weekend we were, miraculously, ready. Exhausted, but ready.

As the first week of placement dawned most girls were sporting short hair, or had pulled back their manes into neat buns resembling

46

the *corps de ballet*. By the end of the week all of us had followed suit. The motivation? Nits.

Depleted of long, straight hair, faces emerged which had until now been half hidden by curtains of swinging tresses. We got to see complete faces of friends for the first time! Weekends took on a whole new structure as we sat on the floor in the common room, one behind the other in a line, grooming. Lifting and separating each lock of hair, checking for nits, screaming and leaping up if we found any, destroying any chance of anonymity. It was great "crack" as the Belfast girls said, unless you were the poor unfortunate with "visitors". We became neurotic. If someone was caught so much as taking a sideways glance at a friend it prompted the retort, "What? What are you staring at?" as the friend was grabbing handfuls of her own hair and inspecting it with the ferocity of some homeless feral creature in fear of discovering NITS! The nuns told us our bodies were temples of the Holy Spirit, but we were more worried about our crowning glory – our hair.

The language barrier was an issue during my first teaching practice near the centre of Newcastle. The children gawped at me when I spoke and I stared at them when they answered trying to lip-read. But it wasn't just the accents hindering communication, we used different words for heaven's sake.

One day I told them we were going into the hall for a dance lesson. So far so good. Then I asked them to put on their daps. I heard a child snort. His friend whacked him and he squealed like a cat with its tail caught in a door. That was it. The signal. The whole class lost control as infectious laughter spread with the rapidity of chicken pox, and girls blushed away their giggles as best they could. The problem? Daps. There is no such word in Geordie. The translation is pumps. Now *that*, in my opinion, is worth laughing about! We called a truce, and were all bi-lingual by the end of the placement.

My gift for colloquialisms improved each day and I was now almost fluent in the local dialect. We regaled each other with tales of misinterpretations leading to all kinds of unforeseen incidents in class. We were all suffering from fatigue exacerbated by lack of healthy diet. Too much smoking and shrieking with laughter until the wee small hours. My disinterest in children was slowly but surely becoming a thing of the past. Looking back I put my indifference down to immaturity, and a spell of working in a nursery in Bedminster where I learnt that the emerging vocabulary of three-year-olds included the knowledge and correct usage of the F word. Changing nappies wasn't my forte either. I guess at the age of sixteen I was as selfish as the next teenager. There was no room in my egocentric world for anyone else in life apart from the current man of my dreams. That was then, now was a very different scenario. It was with some surprise that I found I wasn't looking forward to the end of my first placement. My class of ten-year-olds had won my heart and I had become quite possessive, preferring to have them to myself rather than sharing them with their class teacher on the days she observed. She was aware of the development of our relationship and was secure enough to leave me with the children in the classroom most of the time while she caught up with her lesson notes and planning for the next term. On my final day in school we presented a dance performance to the rest of the school. I remember every step of the dance to this day. The chosen music was "Ground Control To Major Tom" by David Bowie. Our performance was a kind of dance/drama and involved lots of slow-motion-no-gravity movements. The children hung on Bowie's every warbled word and their serious expressions left no one in any doubt that they were all taking the performance incredibly seriously. The applause at the end was deafening. I cried. The children beamed and presented me with a beautiful bouquet. I found myself smiling through the tears of sheer joy and saying, "Thank you, Pet," to the upturned face of the most challenging boy in the class as he proffered the rather heavy bouquet. A riot of colourful flowers. My initiation was complete.

Chapter 6

Naturally, I met the man of my dreams in Newcastle upon Tyne. He was a one-man band in his spare time, and a student by day. He stood on the corner by Fenwick's department store and busked there at weekends. His name was George. He was never short of money, so there was always ample supply of menthol ciggies and Newcastle Brown.

He came to the college folk club which I was roped into organising as I was already singing with a group of local lads in pubs along the coast, and as such had some sort of minor celebrity status in college. I cringe now as I see myself crossing the college quad with my guitar flung across my back heading for music lessons. What a poser. The truth was I had only mastered three chords which enabled me to accompany a variety of children's favourite songs such as "Momma's taking us to the zoo tomorrow", and "Froggie went a-courting". That was a well-kept secret. But, as I feigned the height of disinterest dreaming my way across the quad, I was Joan Baez. Oh yes. A further rise in status came when George asked me out. He was by far the most gorgeous man at our college folk club. This being the only time in the month when the campus was inundated with men from the university and other local colleges of education. Preparation for the prospect of a night of flirting in the innocuous dark offered by the college lounge, while listening to Gateshead's idea of Bob Dylan giving "How many roads..." an airing, reached epic proportion by Saturday afternoon.

Needless to say, interest in folk music was not a necessary prerequisite for membership to the club. I put the revival of the folk music industry in the late 60s down to girls colleges all over the UK. Folk club was the only event where the presence of men was permissible. The prolonged frenzy of activity constituting getting ready for the folk club began days beforehand. The entire three floors of halls reeked of perm solutions and bubble baths. Clothes were exchanged, new make-up tried out, long before the doors opened. No alcohol was permitted, but where there's a will there's a way, and copious amounts of Newcastle Brown Ale arrived in guitar cases throughout the evening, or were smuggled down in academic gowns from rooms above.

The night George sang, "The first time ever I saw your face" he stared directly at me. At least I thought he did, but I couldn't be sure because I wasn't wearing my glasses. Anyway, it was either me or the third year student standing close by. She had enormous "attributes" which strained at the threadbare front of her pink, fluffy, skinny-rib jumper. I chose to believe it was me George was serenading. Against the odds it turns out it was. We had six idyllic months together and then he told me he had to go away as he had a project which needed his undivided attention. I swooned, and assumed it was the possibility of a recording contract which he talked about incessantly. We spent that last night planning our future. Dreams of touring with The Beatles or Peter, Paul and Mary as his support acts were surely going to become reality. Four kids, two Labradors and a jeep were thrown in for good measure. The suburban dream. He assured me of his love, kissed my ears (he was obsessed by them) promised he'd be in touch, and disappeared in his green, three-wheeled car. That in itself should've been a clue.

Weeks of heartache followed, then I heard from a reliable source that the project needing his undivided attention was in fact called Cathy, a twenty-three-year-old shop assistant, the mother of their two-year-old daughter, Sonia. I wondered whether he had ever sung her, "The first time ever I saw your face", and vowed that the next time ever I saw *his* face I'd rearrange it for him.

Shunned, I turned my thoughts to the political arena. It was a mistake. I knew diddly-squat about student politics but played the silent recluse listening, smoking, nodding in agreement and turning up for demonstrations. Politics didn't come into it, but Gemma and I had our sights set on intelligent men having both become disillusioned by good-looking folk singers with come to bed eyes, and there was always a party at the end of the long, foot-weary day of protesting.

I didn't burn my bra indicating solidarity with Women's Lib because I needed all the help I could get in that department, but I joined in demonstrations now and then if there was nothing more exciting on offer, or if the group I sang with didn't have a gig, or if Jeff, the current man of my dreams, wasn't coming up for the weekend, or if I didn't hitch down south to Leeds to see him. I don't suppose you'd call it commitment exactly, but I swelled the ranks now and then.

We'd all meet in the centre of town wearing home-made maxi dresses, paisley headbands and daisies between our flip-flopped toes. I remember one evening after a long day of singing "We shall overcome" and chanting "What do we want? When do we want it"? I turned to the boy sporting a baby beard, sharing my Newcastle Brown and asked, "What *do* we want exactly?" He looked at me with disdain, reclaimed his beer, gave me a snappy response and disappeared. I can't remember exactly what he told me, but I think it had to do with student grants. It was the taking part that counted, and by now my sojourn with intelligent men was losing its gravitas. It turned out they were not the geniuses their doleful brown eyes would have us believe. Who could one trust?

As we marched on so did time, and suddenly finals were upon us and everything became serious for a month or two as the midnight oil was replenished, and all candles well and truly burnt at both ends as we crammed like furtive squirrels storing nourishment for harder times to come. Futures were discussed. It began to dawn on us that pretty soon we would all go our separate ways. A regular diaspora of forever-friends. I guess deep down we were ready for the upheaval. Somehow our time was over. Transition of the most formidable was on the distant horizon, and we watched it edging forward at an alarming speed. The words "upwardly mobile" were yet to enter the English language during those halcyon years in Newcastle. However, the time was fast approaching for women to join the ranks of the male masses pouring out of college and universities. The seeds had been sewn, and we were ripe to compete in the world of work. Perhaps some of those marches with their fearsome chants hit home. Thousands of graduates came successfully through the milk rounds with more female graduates than ever making the grade and competing for careers, no longer content to play understudy to their male counterparts. So, three years as "Nanuk of the North" and I was ready for warmer climes. London or Birmingham? Heads or tails, or a simple twist of fate? Jeff and I were ready to spend more time together. Our relationship deserved more care and attention than the frantic weekends we grasped throughout each term. I found myself wondering if Jeff was *the one*. He was incredibly good-looking with the longest eyelashes any of my friends had ever seen. No, he didn't use mascara. In addition to his looks Jeff was kind, clever, athletic, thoughtful, and I loved him and his family. I began to reflect on the prospect of us as parents. Our children would be stunning, if they had his looks, and between us we had enough idealism to raise the perfect family.

Jeff had been offered a graduate apprenticeship with British Leyland in Longbridge, Birmingham, the previous year, but I still hankered after a career in theatreland, London. So I headed south-east and stayed with Jeff's best friend, Ben, for a week. I had dreams of walking through Covent Garden in my grey duffle coat with the furry trimmed hood, a kind of waif-like, lonely figure which would be of immediate interest to a passing theatrical agent looking for a Rita Tushingham replacement. I'd given up on Yoko Ono. I must've been there on a bank holiday. I wasn't discovered. I wondered about gatecrashing through the stage door of the Apollo and telling the resident director just how fortunate it was that I'd finished my drama training, happened to be passing and noticed he needed a talented leading role. "Look no further," I'd say as I launched into my rendition of "I met a boy named Frank Mills" from *Hair*. The contract would be pressed into my hot little hands before I got to the end of the song.

What a dreamer.

There was a time when I had harboured feelings for Ben. In fact he was almost the man of my dreams once except that he lived with Jeff and they had become good friends. Ben also had an entourage. Not any entourage. He had an entourage headed up by a Julie Christie lookalike. She just happened to be unbearably intellectual too and, worse still, her waist-length hair was naturally straight. How lucky can some girls get? I had even resorted to ironing my hair to achieve the same effect. All I accomplished was a burnt eyebrow. Ben never seemed to see me.

One week in London was enough to know that Jeff was, after

all, the man of my dreams, but with Ben still very much in the higher echelons of the first division. After a week in London with two job interviews and offers of teaching posts, I was grimy enough to know I didn't want to live my life below ground, mole-like, scraping my way up to daylight every morning and evening and breathing historical blackness into my lungs for the remainder of my days. I was young and impressionable and believed that there wasn't a friendly, well-disposed person living in London. On my first day there I'd emerged from Bank Tube Station and approached a newspaper seller. I asked him directions for somewhere I thought to be close by. Flicking his cigarette to the corner of his mouth and squinting, he looked down at me before spewing, "'Ow should I fuckin' know? MORNING STANAR," all in one continuous sentence. No, the streets of London were definitely not paved with gold and I was not staying.

At Paddington Station, after scraping my hair into bunches and donning my grey, faithful duffle, I managed to persuade the ticket office that I was a half-price passenger of fourteen. I was in fact twenty-one. I bought a one-way ticket heading north to Birmingham where I was to interview for a teaching post in a newly opened Catholic primary school nestled in the shadowy suburbs of the city. Jeff and I would be together for more than a hurried weekend at the end of the A4.

The interview was a breeze but it seemed I still couldn't prise myself away from the dear sisters. The head teacher was Sister Mary Edward. Her bullying techniques, implemented to humiliate even the most hard-nosed child, had been honed to near perfection on the staff. She kept us in no doubt as to who ran the place, and nobody had the courage to challenge her. In those days the sisters still clung to their black habits and flamboyant headdresses. Hers framed her face with what can best be described as a white, starched porch so that her profile could not be seen from the side. Daunting.

She kept the stock cupboard locked to avoid pilfering by the teachers. Try as I did to find something worth pilfering in the stock cupboard, unless one had a penchant for rubber bands or steel paper clips (varying sizes), nothing caught my eye. Weeks into my first term it was with fear and trembling that I approached her for the key to the cupboard to get some adhesive. I didn't think that was unreasonable. After all, I was employed as the art teacher for the school. Glue was pretty important. I didn't realise that glue was also desperately expensive. What followed confirmed for me that the nuns must've undergone some kind of rigorous training on interview techniques with MI5 prior to taking the veil. Short of turning the bare, single hanging light bulb in my face, or rationing the staffroom biscuits she tried everything to break me. Why did I need the glue? Which children would have use of it? Was there no alternative? I suggested mixing flour and water. Her eyes widened, her crêpe paper neck began to blotch like a four-year-old's poster paint fingerprint picture, garish red. "Where do you imagine you will purloin the flour, dear child?" I looked around for the "dear child" and realised that it was me. Oh God, was there no end? I leant against the cold, magnolia wall for support. Time was of the essence. It was ten minutes to the end of the break. My class would be lining up soon and pouring back into class, flushed and sweating from playground excesses. Worse still, I needed to go to the toilet. The only two loos for staff were constantly occupied during the fifteen minute morning break earlier today which meant I'd had to hold on for a further two hours until the lunch break. Now, in fact. I snapped out of my self-pitying interlude and heard her voice babbling on. For a moment I'd thought I'd fallen asleep in front of the TV and surfaced, confused. "When did you last have glue? When did you last see your father?" No, she didn't ask that. She didn't need to because she listened in to phone calls from my dad, on the odd occasion that he decided to call from work in Bristol. I got the glue. She got the hump.

She brought out the best and the worst in me. Because of her, or even in spite of her, I determined to be the most creative teacher in school. Not difficult. Most of the staff had transferred from the old building where they'd merged with the peeling wallpaper and brown, curling, sticky tape in a mutual comfort zone. The brand new school building did nothing to revitalise their vocation. It was as if they had a signed DNR agreement i.e. not to resuscitate in the event of death, or transfer to a state-of-the-art new school. The year six teacher was Irish, ageing and frustrated. He never married and in those days, as a good Irish Catholic middle-aged man, one didn't have partners. I wonder now whether he was gay, but I think he was just a sad, under-confident old dolt. He verbally beat the children into passing the Eleven Plus. I wasn't allowed into his classroom for fear I might introduce PAINT!

He kept spare pants in his cupboard as it was a common occurrence for terrified children to lose control of their bladders in the weeks leading up to exams in year six. I hope to God he retired before SATs arrived. I picture him now soiling his own pants in a residential care home on the west coast of Ireland. I wish him well nonetheless.

He often sat opposite me over a meal at lunchtime and spat his conversation at me until I could no longer contain my revulsion and asked to be excused. Recalling this today I can picture him with crystal clarity, and the chicken and vegetable bake congealing in front of my eyes. I imagine there are scores of past pupils who, unfortunately, have that same perfect recall, while blanching at the memory of wearing school pants home. It wasn't all bad though. I learnt so much about socio-demographic influences while teaching in supposedly middle-class Birmingham. My first encounter with a "trophy child" was in Birmingham. His name was Dominic. He was delightful. He was bright, articulate, took holidays during term time and regaled his classmates with stories of hiking to the top of volcanos and swimming with dolphins (obviously not on the same trip). Back then this was tantamount to saying your dad was an astronaut. Most holidays were taken during the Factory Fortnight when Brummies took over Weston-super-Mare for fourteen days. Fourteen days of fish and chips and the ramma-langa-ding-dong of the Winter Gardens entertainment, while Somerset grockles shimmied back under the Cotswold stones from whence they had emerged, resurfacing only when the all-clear sounded.

From the outside looking in being a trophy child seems to be something to which we would all aspire given half a chance. The family appears to have it all. Money, big house, two vehicles – one resembling a car, the other reminiscent of a child's transformer truck – several holidays per year and, eventually, a second home abroad. Take a deep breath! Gorgeous-looking dad, designer-clad mum, grandparents living miles away, and no, absolutely no sleepovers at home!

Dominic had no friends. He was loved, maybe even adored by his parents, looked up to by his peers, and excelled academically, but at playtime he was the last one leaving the classroom to make the most of pelting about like a mad thing with two hundred other little mad things on the same mission outside. He would often linger and try to engage me in conversation. Most of the time he was successful and break times came and went without having the chance to grab a coffee and, yes you guessed it, chase to the toilet. After a while I noticed the pattern and began to observe Dominic in different situations in an attempt to figure out why he was alone. Sometimes he accepted an offer from another child to play, but it rarely lasted longer than ten minutes or so. He was simply too sophisticated for his peers. Not for him the rough and tumble of playground politics, chasing the girls and diving at their skirts for a glimpse of school knickers amidst a flurry of laughter and mock admonitions. He watched, taking himself off behind a goal-mouth, seemingly making mental notes of play in progress as though charting the behavioural habits of a newly discovered rain forest species like a Richard Dimbleby wannabe. He wasn't unhappy. This is what he knew. This was how he coped when faced with a whoosh of ten-year-old hurly-burly boys.

One parents' evening Dominic's parents arrived straight from work for their 7.00pm appointment. They were early, I was running late due to an angry parent giving me his opinion on bullying in the school. Needless to say he finished with a threatening flourish as he reminded me, with jutting forefinger aimed at the bridge of my new red specs, that I was "just out of school knickers" and "knew nuffink". I felt uneasy about the knickers reference, and he left me in no doubt as to whose genes his son had inherited. Relief of sorts came in the form of Mr and Mrs Watson, Dominic's parents. They swept into the classroom. He looked every inch the self-confident young executive alpha male. His suit, although not Savile Row, was pretty sharp and certainly not off the peg. Mrs Watson's perfume announced her arrival with all the subtlety of a trumpet voluntary released into the vaulted ceilings of a cathedral as she slid onto the rather low junior chair. She crossed her legs, rearranged her rather striking mini-skirt and looked across at me as though about to interview me for a position in her firm.

The next ten minutes were a comparative breeze when compared with the previous thirty minutes with the bully boy and his son. As a clue that our session was about to end, and the official bit was over, I asked how they'd enjoyed their recent holiday with Dominic. There was a pause as they exchanged glances, and it seemed to me that they were momentarily struggling to register who Dominic was.

Then Mrs Watson gushed, "It was perfect. On day one we signed him up to the Mickey Club and he spent the *whole week* out of our hair, didn't he, darling?" Mr Watson patted his wife's knee. What a patronising gesture I thought.

"Yes, sweetie." He turned his attention to me. "So…nice to meet you, Miss…" I let it hang there just long enough for him to feel the first stirrings of discomfort.

"Yes…you too," I said, as if it were actually the last thing I meant. I didn't bother to remind him of my name. I figured if he couldn't be arsed to spend time with his only child on a family holiday he didn't deserve to be reminded of my name.

I remember catching the bus home to my cosy bedsit that night. I'd never thought of it as cosy before but, as I opened the front door and bent to sift my mail from that of the guys who lived upstairs, I spotted my dad's familiar handwriting on a thick brown envelope (a perk of the civil service) and felt all the warmth of my childhood wrap itself around me. We didn't have the money to holiday abroad. We didn't know of the existence of the Mickey Club. In fact we'd never flown anywhere as a family. But our parents' love was tangible even when angry words stung and justification for some denied request was rammed home to the sullen teenagers we sometimes were. We never doubted their love. We knew who we were. We learnt how to communicate with our peers. We learnt how to choose friends. We learnt that being well off was probably a bonus for some families, but that was all it ever was. A bonus. Not a replacement, or a stop-gap, or a substitute for love. We were rich indeed.

As I sat nursing my hot chocolate I thought of Dominic snuggled in his maximum tog duvet – physically comfortable, but emotionally empty, and cold.

Chapter 7

At the other end of the scale, and in a younger age group than Dominic, was Brigid. Her family was large, boisterous and poor. She was eight-years-old when we met, and she remains the giver of the most precious gift I have ever received from a pupil.

Unlike Dominic, Brigid was not a loner. Despite the prevalent smell of poverty, which she wore like an identity tag, there was always a little group of girls around her. They swapped beads, well, the others swapped, Brigid watched and found joy in their negotiations. She had no beads of her own. They compared pencil cases and traded free creatures given with breakfast cereals. Brigid watched. The only thing she owned was her filthy uniform, battered-too-big shoes and a huge smile freely given to all and sundry.

Being Brigid's teacher was an enlightening experience for me and, after a while, I was able to control the wrinkling of my nose as I approached her desk. The wrinkling was totally involuntary I hasten to add, it was purely a reflex triggered in response to the smell. It was unmistakeable. Unwashed hair, neglected teeth, mucky uniform and bed-wetting, nature's bouquet of the impoverished family. I wanted to take her home for a decent meal, a bath and a change of clothes. Bless her, she wet the bed and it didn't help that she wore the same underclothes day in, day out.

I remember thinking that she was old before her time probably because she was the carer of her younger siblings for much of her free time. She wore an air of forced maturity. Christmas was coming and we were casting for the class production. I decided that Brigid was to be the Virgin Mary. As each part was allocated the whole class sat totally silent waiting to hear if they had been chosen for any of the lead roles. As I called Brigid's name and the part she was to play there was a collective gasp from the other girls, and the boys turned to take a look at her like she'd just fallen in the last shower. Brigid herself looked confused but pleased. Apparently she'd been the donkey last year, and the year before.

The following morning dawned and Brigid arrived four and a half minutes late as she did every single day. She handed me a piece of cardboard. On the one side was the tail end of the words porridge oats, and the muscular left leg of a large man wearing something tartan. It was a note from home. This was a first. It read, *Dear missus, our Brigid can't be Mary, we've nothing blue for her to wear.* Brigid looked up at me and I saw something move in her hair...it was a head louse. Those of you who know anything about these wee visitors will know they hang out in peer groups, large numbers, they do not usually appear alone. Without turning a hair, literally, I told Brigid not to worry. I had a blue nylon sheet at home and knew I could make something convincing from it, something worthy of a young girl from Nazareth, albeit with a lively dose of nits. She turned, scratched her head and hopped back to her seat without a care. The head lice would have to wait.

The night of the nativity came and Sister Mary Edward introduced the evening, welcoming parents and grandparents, amongst them Brigid's parents and nine siblings. I couldn't tell you how the play went. My eyes were on Brigid's family. There wasn't a hint of a shuffle even from the youngest, eighteen-month-old Donal. Her parents sat holding hands and their eyes never left their Brigid who was clad in an old discoloured white nightie belonging to her ten-year-old sister, Niamh, and a blue nylon bed sheet veil. She was a most reverend, respectful and loving Mary, and a natural mother. She held the audience with her smile and the baby Jesus, a black male dolly from the "Home Corner", with expertise.

The last day of term came with the first snow of the winter. I took my class out onto the playground to tilt our heads way back and catch snowflakes on our tongues. Magic! To this day, I've never met a child who wasn't thrilled into a giggling heap when catching snowflakes this way.

Sister Mary Edward was away taking Irish coffee with our parish priest, so I intended to break as many rules as possible starting with the snowflakes. YES! Once the children got the hang of it I closed my mouth and watched them. For a few minutes we were inside one of those glass paperweights that you shake up to make a snowstorm. No one to interfere. No one to wag a disapproving finger at us. No one to stop us being the children we were. Yes, I include myself there. What a privilege to be able to slip so easily, without fear of falling, back to the unappreciated world of childhood I'd been so desperate to leave. After a while we'd had our fill of snowflakes and skidded across the playground back in to the warmth of our festooned, Christmassy classroom. The day passed as end of term days still do. Children played games, tidied up and gathered their Christmas goodies as they left for home. Windows steamed up and we became calm in our own world of holiday anticipation as a winter wonderland was gently forming on the playground where parents gathered. Many of the children had brought gifts for me too. In fact I had more boxes of Newberry Fruits than I care to recall, and they were so sweet that the mere thought of them sets my teeth on edge even today! Still, they came in handy as gifts for various family members I had missed from my Christmas list. My mum was impressed by my thoughtfulness.

Brigid hung back from the procession of thank yous and Christmas wishes. I was glad because I'd noticed her socks were soaking wet as a result of playing in the snow wearing the worn-out shoes with the flapping soles, and I had a spare pair of wellies in the cupboard which I wanted to give her.

As I turned to fetch them, she whispered quietly, "This is for you, Miss." She held out what looked like a ball of newspaper. I took it. It was heavy and the paper slipped to the ground. In my hands was a rusty tin of skinless tomatoes. "Happy Christmas, Miss," she said, looking up at me with such a sense of pride, anticipating my response. I reached for her hands which were smudged with newspaper print, and she launched herself at me. We hugged. A big, squeezing-type hug, the type of hug forbidden in twenty-first century schools. As I grinned and wiped tears away from us both I thanked her with all my heart for the tomatoes not caring about the other, as yet, unseen gift of the head lice variety I had most certainly received too!

That was over thirty years ago and I wonder what happened to Dominic and Brigid. As an Indian friend of mine once said, "Maggie, we plant the seeds of the trees under whose shade we will never sit." I hope Dominic and Brigid both grew tall and strong and beautiful.

Months later I woke one morning and wheezed, "I can't breathe," at Jeff, my gorgeous husband as he now was. Two years out of college and into the reality of working for someone for whom I had little if any respect, I felt in danger of suffocation. I had to have a change of school. Either that or have a baby. Personally, I yearned for a baby. The auld biological clock ran fast in those days, and the first baby was almost always anticipated within a year or so of marriage. And what was to stop us? We had a house, a car, and Jeff's job was secure. On top of that the girl I shared a lift with every morning was about to have her first baby and I was insanely, unashamedly jealous. Jeff was more down to earth. I think he knew a baby wasn't the solution to my cabin fever and he was right of course. Damn!

I decided to bite the bullet, quit whingeing and knuckle down. How commendable. Then something happened which made me realise that Sister Mary Edward and I were simply not compatible. She told me I was to sing Gounod's "Ave Maria" at the next parents' soiree – evening to you and me. Now, she could've *asked* me and I've no doubt that would've appealed to my ego. I might even have done it. But no, she *told* me. It was the last straw. Not that I couldn't sing it, of course I could. I was Catholic, knew Latin inside out, and had learnt to play Gounod's "Ave Maria" on the piano at the age of nine. Singing it before an audience of four hundred parents held no fear for me. After all, I had sung in most of the working men's clubs along the north-east coast for two years. Admittedly not Gounod's "Ave Maria", there wasn't much call for that.

Anyone surviving those audiences could survive anything. No, that wasn't the issue. The issue was that here I was approaching my mid-twenties and *still* allowing myself to be ordered to do something by *yet another nun*. Enough! The only way was out and, on this auspicious Tuesday, I was going to take action. I determined to beat everyone else to the staffroom at lunch break. Today was the day we received the bulletin which detailed all the teaching vacancies in schools throughout the county. If there was one in there that caught my eye I'd give it a go. There were two. One was closer to the centre of town which would mean travelling by bus during the rush hour, both ways. Still, I thought, it's an opportunity. I sent for the application forms.

Then another vacancy leapt up at me from the same page. Now this one would really be the challenge I sought. It was a Middle school, closer to home and I would be teaching the top class, twelve/thirteen-year-olds, in a team-teaching set-up. Oh yes! So I sent for the application forms and mentally set aside Saturday afternoon's rugby match to complete them both. It would mean not watching Jeff who was captain of the club, but at least I would be in the relative peace and quiet of the musty clubhouse, and could glance up intermittently to catch enough of the action to have a credible post-match conversation. Usually I watched from the sucking mud of the touchline, but my grasp of the game still left much to be desired.

As the blast of the final whistle pierced the wind and hail on a dismally cold Saturday afternoon I was nearing completion of both application forms. Pretty soon the sweating stampede of thirty, hulky, boy-men panted their way through to the awaiting bath, resembling the annual bull chase in Pamplona. They piled in and began the lusty bellowing of risqué songs which were all part of the Saturday ritual. "Swing low, sweet chariot…" By the time I was called into the dining area of the clubhouse to help dish up the hallowed pie, beans and builders' tea, the applications were done and dusted. I'd pop them in the post before getting home to cook a liver and bacon supper. Another Saturday ritual. Pie and beans? That was a mere snack providing an opportunity to re-run the whole game, the glory, the near misses, the decisions of the partially sighted ref, the foul play of the opposing team and last, but not least, who was the redhead on the touchline?

Oh, how we indulged our men, revering the Saturday afternoon worship. We stood in all wind and weather, shouting encouragement, screaming at the opposition if they menaced our men. Ears froze, hair frizzed, hands purpled and noses ran as we steadfastly watched and feigned knowledge, while sneaking a peak at our watches in the hope that it was all over bar the shouting.

A couple of years later I was standing on the touchline with our two-year-old daughter pulling her wooden, quacking duck through the muck, while breastfeeding our recently born son under my woollen poncho. That's dedication. Multi-tasking was initiated up and down the country on rugger field touchlines such as this.

For now though I was excited about taking control of my career again. I was two years into teaching when I realised that children had captured my heart and soul. My dad was right. Three weeks later the letters I'd waited for plopped onto the doormat, one day after another. I was invited to interview first at the inner-city school. I re-read the advert and a chill made the hairs on the back of my neck prickle. In my frantic skimming of the job description I had somehow missed the following sentence. *The successful candidate will lead and manage science throughout the school.* Science? Me? Why on earth did I apply? Why in heaven's name did they invite me to interview when there was clearly no sign of a science subject in the meagre list of my O Level and A level passes? In fact I'm fairly sure that if it was possible to detect science aptitude through DNA testing there would be no evidence with which to suggest the presence of any such aptitude in my screening!

What should I do? The options presented themselves. I could call off the interview risking a smearing of my character by messing about during the appointment process, OR I could use the interview situation as a dummy-run for the middle school interview which was on the following day. It was a no-brainer.

I found myself, after a fifty-five minute bus journey followed by a fifteen minute walk through an estate cursed with 50s architecture, at the school. By the time I got there I was hot, bothered and cross with myself. However, it's not in my nature to go at things half-cock as they say, so I did my best to smooth out the creases in my smart new suit and strode toward the school entrance. Ten minutes later, after scouring the boundary of the school grounds and finally dragging along on the heels of year nine stragglers, I found the one gate that was still open at 9.00am. I made it just in time to see the candidate before me being led, like a clone to the slaughter, into the study. Now *there* was a scientist if ever there was one. Long mousy hair, long mousy skirt, flat shoes, duffle bag, camel coat slung half-heartedly over her free arm. Her other arm clutched an enormous file entitled, *Experiments with Junior Three.* I hoped it wasn't a literal translation. Suddenly I felt agitated. What was I doing here? What if they liked me? What if they offered me the job? EEK! I could blag with the best of them, and had a tendency to get carried away during interviews. For some reason it never failed, I had been offered every job for which I had been interviewed to date! It *had* to fail this time.

I didn't want the job. I couldn't do it. Previously, the only good ideas I'd had in the science department were pinched from *Blue Peter*. They were all literally "one I made earlier". Still, my pride had me rehearsing coherent answers to, as yet, unheard scientific questions so as not to "show yourself up". Oh God, I could hear my mum's voice from Bristol!

I smiled, a diluted effort, at the guy opposite also waiting for his big chance. He nodded perfunctorily, and adjusted his large Buddy Holly specs. The door of the study opened and the candidate with the suspect file came out, red-faced, wispy hair escaping from half-hearted elastic bands, camel coat hanging on her every word while trailing one of its arms seductively along the grey-tiled floor. She smiled, a real chummy, good luck smile and I felt bad for my unchristian thoughts.

Half an hour later, my knowledge of primary science exhausted, I returned to the plastic seats outside the study where the other candidates were waiting for the verdict. I did the only thing I could under the circumstances. I prayed. Oh how I prayed. Dear God, PLEASE don't let them offer me this job! Well, they say be careful what you pray for but, when the chair of the appointments committee approached and asked fluffy-haired Miss Clark back into the study, it took all my reserve not to leap up and shriek "Eureka"! Oh, thank you, God.

Being invited back in to the study meant you had the job. The two of us on the subs bench looked sheepishly at each other, said our goodbyes, and left. I was ecstatic and spent the return journey reading up my prep notes for the following day's interview. This time I read the advertisement and felt this job had my name on it. Art, French, English...okay my French wasn't anything to write home about, but my accent was *pas mal*.

Chapter 8

I started at Dovecote Middle School the following September. I was to be part of a team of four teachers working with the twelve – thirteen-year-olds. We rotated the subjects we taught and it couldn't have been better for me because the two guys who taught maths and science didn't specialise in art or French so, with a bit of rearranging of the timetable, I taught English, art and French the entire time... NO MATHS!

I was in heaven. The head teacher, Mr Salter, was everything I thought a successful head teacher could be. He was encouraging, noticed everything and frequently commented on the artwork the children were producing. He was quick to praise if something warranted praise, and he dealt with under-performance with a firm but fair countenance, in fact, in the manner most of us who've experienced poor performance would *love* to employ today. But all that was before employees' rights became *de rigueur*. In addition, Mr Salter was human. He laughed a lot and wasn't beyond shedding a quiet tear of pride when a less able child flourished, which many did at Dovecote. He was larger than life in stature and personality. Children and teachers were respected by him and, in return, we worked hard to do our best for him. The school was happy, industrious and very large! With Mr Salter I learnt the importance of empathy, compassion, diligence, fun and sheer hard work. In fact everything which had made him and eventually all of us professionals in an improving school in a relatively challenging area of Birmingham. Can you imagine going to the pub on Friday lunchtimes and actually having an alcoholic beverage to accompany your double egg and chip butty, then returning to face art with forty boisterous children eager to attack a bowl of *papier mâché* and create? Well, that was the Friday routine at Dovecote. Some would say they would *only* attempt *papier mâché* after sinking an alcoholic beverage of some kind on a Friday afternoon. I relished it though. I viewed *papier mâché* as frog spawn with a creative purpose, and the children loved that I openly delighted in it, watching with bated breath as I immersed my hands in it and squelched the living daylights out of it. Very therapeutic. Their guffaws were music to my ears, and they were quick to follow my lead plunging their own hands into the jellied bowls in a kind of squidge-fest. There was a sense of camaraderie. We were in this together, up to our slime spattered elbows!

My art room was a dream. It stank of oil, white spirit, scorching polystyrene, wrought iron, enamelling, glue, glue and more glue, and PAINT! As with employees' rights there was a reasonableness about life, a common sense approach as far as health and safety was concerned. Teachers were trusted. There's a notion! As a result we didn't shy away from the more outlandish activities and the children surely reaped the benefits of each exploration. They became co-creators, designing and producing original works of art far surpassing the heaps of elephant poo we are led to believe is worthy of exhibition in the Tate Modern. We cut models out of chunks of polystyrene using an electrically heated wire, and used welding tools to create wrought iron candelabra. We heated enamelling kilns at off the scale temperatures to create jewellery, and operated jigsaws to bring to life interesting sculptures in balsa wood. In four years I didn't lose one child, and received no complaints from parents. I just had to read that over once more and let it sink in through the mire and heaving swamp of eighteen years of bizarre governmental fussiness, and the over-protective parents spawned from the nanny state.

None of us could foresee the rise of the blame culture which would become the reason for so many creative people losing the will to continue in education. During my upcoming years as a head teacher I became the equivalent of a sin-eater as all and sundry railed, blamed and threatened. I digested tasteless, petty grievances delivered as verbal staccato, and allegations of such magnitude which, if accompanied by an evidence base, would've seen me carted off to the gallows. They still permeate my late-night disturbances.

Hey-ho. No wonder I adored Dovecote Middle School. While teaching the oldest children I accompanied them to camp in Wales during the spring term. I had no idea what to expect, but every time camp came up in conversation in the fogged-up staffroom there was hilarity, and lots of "d'you remember when…" and raucous rendering of the camp song which began, "Dolfriog Hall is in north Wales, that is where we go at every Easter time…" and was followed by other such incomprehensible fits and starts stuttered between gulps of coffee and much inhalation of Embassy Filter Tips. Most of the staff had been to camp in previous years. This year I was the newbie.

Mr Salter always went to camp. This time was no exception and I took comfort in knowing that his ever-present fatherly figure would ensure everything went according to plan. There was no way he could climb any mountains or ford any streams due to his physicality, but he knew every inch of the valleys and always journeyed to where the activity played out for the day with his car stacked with goodies. First aid kits, blankets, flasks of hot tea, Kendal Mint Cake and chocolate to soothe a tired child or flagging adult appeared from the boot of his muddied Escort like rabbits from a conjuror's hat. The children loved to reach the end of a circular walk or descend a mountain and catch sight of his car in the distance. They loved him and he greeted all and sundry with arms open wide and his familiar smile, while he congratulated each child as though they had just returned from the summit of Everest. Which of course, in their imagination, they had.

After showers and dinner there was always a sing-song or competition involving plenty of teamwork and too much fun. As I watched the children and teachers playing together like one enormous family, I felt again that we were completely isolated from the real world in our own cocoon. I wanted us all to stay there forever and protect the children from growing up too soon.

Once the children were safely in bed enjoying midnight feasts (at 9.00pm) we took a look at the rota for night duty. Night duty at the local pub that is. Every night two of us were allowed, rather encouraged, to partake of the local beer in the nearest village. We'd roll home after a lock-in just in time to grab a couple of hours sleep before setting off like sheepish Sherpas for the next day's gruelling activity. Mr Salter positively thrived on watching each hungover teacher braving the early morning mists and demonstrating, with forced vim and vigour, the scaling of a gate which pitched one upside down for a second before landing with cartoon-like rolling eyes safely on the other side. Even now I can remember my brain hitting the side of my already thumping head after one such demo. Still, there were sparkling, crystal clear, gushing streams to race alongside under cover of thick, leafy tunnels. "Let's go!" Thirty-eight years on I have instant recall of how that week changed me forever. It was as if I had returned home somehow. My home which, put simply, was childhood with a new adventure every day. I saw nature through the eyes of the child I had been such a short time ago, and the transition was seamless. We were the lost boys and girls, and all we had to do was romp our way through the countryside squealing as we splashed through ice-cold brooks giggling in surprise at a scurrying newt silenced at the glimpse of sun on dew.

The week ended as gloriously as it had started. After hours spent coaxing and chivvying the children to the summit of one of Snowdon's foothills we opened our lunch packs to find Creme Easter eggs amongst the cheese and tomato sandwiches. Mr Salter was indeed with us in spirit. Naturally enough my biological clock received a hammering during that memorable week at camp, and I returned home to find that Jeff also had thoughts of starting our own family, while I had been away rehearsing with a family of forty almost teenagers in the wilds of north Wales. Why wait? The time was right, the baby boomers were about to enter parenthood.

Leaving Dovecote Middle School was never going to be easy. There's something so special about the bond between the children in their final year of the primary phase of their education and their teachers. For obvious reasons this isn't replicated in any other year group. I always felt the challenge of continuing to prepare the children for their secondary phase while offering them a balance of exploration and fun into the bargain. Naturally, in the days before SATs this was an exciting challenge which I absolutely *loved*. During the final few months, aside from camp, we gave the children a taster of secondary school life with ever-increasing responsibilities which the majority lapped up. It was a kind of weaning process designed to make the transfer to secondary school less of a shock. It also served to help us teachers detach from our emotions as we waved off another shoal of little fish as they plunged into the much bigger pool.

My class had the added responsibility of looking after me too as I was by now blossoming in my first pregnancy. They were in awe of the changes taking place in my diminutive body, and sex education that year was arguably the most productive, for want of a better word, in my limited experience to date. I was determined to show that pregnancy was not an illness and continued to take netball practice and participate in the rounders tournament of teachers v pupils. One day Mr Salter caught me standing on a table stretching up to pin some artwork on a display board. I was reprimanded severely, but as he continued on his way he turned, smiled and winked. He'd fulfilled his professional duty, but knew me well enough to know that pregnancy wasn't going to stop me showing off my children's work in a fabulous display.

A group of girls from class organised a leaving party and baby shower for me. I was completely overwhelmed at their generosity and by the love they showed for me, Jeff and our unknown wee one. We invited them to our home after our little girl was born and they spent an afternoon positively drooling over her. I found myself hoping that they had listened well to the sex education tutorials at Dovecote and wouldn't be too eager to have babies of their own. The girls continued to visit for a couple of months and then became embroiled in the demands of secondary education, boys, athletics, boys, musical tuition, boys etc. by which time contact dwindled to the occasional letter. I missed them, of course I did, but being a new mum is a full-time adventure and I was hooked. I never quite mastered a routine with Rebecca our first-born. There were women who sallied out of their front doors pushing immaculately dressed babies in carriage-like prams appearing calm and unruffled at the same time each day. They puzzled me. Rebecca and I had our own flexibility largely governed by her penchant for sleep. So, while others joined the promenade into town at 2.00pm sharp, Rebecca and I were often fast asleep in the back garden catching a few rays. The harmful rays of the sun hadn't been discovered at that time, and this is something for which I am very grateful. We soaked it up. I continued to read avidly at that time too with music as our constant companion throughout the day just as I had while carrying Rebecca.

Housework suffered, much as it does today, but obviously for different reasons. Life was too short. Rebecca was so much more fascinating and such an amenable baby. We were even able to maintain a healthy social life carting Rebecca around in her carry-cot to the various events at the rugby club. She slept through the pounding of disco music while snugly wrapped in a cellular blanket in her carry-cot surrounded by boots, shirts and buckets in the club's kit cupboard. I wonder sometimes that we never found ourselves halfway home before realising that we'd left her at the club. It seemed such a shame to disturb her! Today we'd probably be facing a grilling by social services.

I remember a neighbour who had her second baby at the same time as Rebecca entered the world. I often met her coming out of her house. I began to think she waited until she saw me before appearing and regaling me in a Brummie accent as undulating as the Lickie Hills with, "I've got me meat in." One could be forgiven, due to the number of occasions she uttered it, for thinking this was some kind of colloquial salutation, but actually it wasn't. She just enjoyed telling me as if to reinforce the fact that she was Little Miss Organised to my Little Miss Whatever's in the Fridge is Tonight's Meal. Her timing was uncanny and tempted me to play along. One day, as I stepped outside the front door, she stepped outside *her* front door. She threw down the gauntlet. I set out to pass her house on the usual route to town then turned back as if I'd forgotten something crucial like my purse for instance. It worked. By the time I re-emerged she was gone. I smiled and quashed the urge to celebrate in classic goal-scoring mode by lifting up my shirt and flashing my enlarged boobs! I set off with a terrific sense of one-up-mum-ship. How quickly we sink to these levels! With a self-congratulatory smirk I rounded the corner only to see her a few paces ahead. "I saw you going back for something but thought I'd wait for you anyway. I'm in no hurry, 'I've got me meat in'." AAAAAAAAAAAAAAAAHHHHHHHHHHHHHH!

Chapter 9

The last real summer I recall in England was in 1976. While the country heaved saturated sighs and moaned its weary way through each scorching day, Rebecca and I sat in a home-made paddling pool in the back garden and waited for the new baby. We must've poured gallons of water sitting there surrounded by plastic containers, ducks, funnels and measuring jugs, while playing shops or schools or swimming baths. It didn't matter what the game was, we did exactly the same activities for each. It was too hot to think of anything else to do and my creativity was stifled in the unrelenting sun. Rebecca was content to play anything that involved pouring water over mummy.

Jeff and I decided we didn't want too much of a gap between Rebecca and our next baby and it wasn't long after making that decision that I became pregnant again. Had we known we were in for a record-breaking summer in terms of temperature and hours of sunlight that year we may not have been so hasty. I vowed not to give birth until it rained. It would be asking too much. So we sat perfectly happily, with wrinkling fingers and toes, keeping cool in Jeff's prototype of a paddling pool. It was all I could manage to heave myself out at the end of the day and prepare some salad. Cooking was out of the question unless Jeff did it. Rebecca was in seventh heaven. She had been a water baby from day one and loved nothing more than to throw herself headlong into the pool like a young penguin, slide along the polythene bottom, only to emerge opposite me, a shining, brown, well-covered little body with rapidly bleaching hair. What a beauty.

One day after a night threatening rain of biblical proportions (I lived in hope), John decided to arrive. During the final stage of labour in my bright delivery room with the midwife and Jeff, I heard the first few drops of the long-awaited rain falling onto the window ledge through the open window. Okay, action stations! It was cool enough to give birth so, with just the midwife and a very excited Jeff, John made his gentle entrance into the world. Having been banished from the delivery room when Rebecca, a breech baby, was delivered under the direction of the resident consultant and his team, this was a totally new experience for Jeff and he wasn't going to miss a second. To this day if given the chance he will retell the event. It usually begins with a graphic representation of my birthing bits as he uses his two hands to form a large circle and begins, "his head was right there… black hair and everything, then he disappeared again…" by which time every woman in the room winces in recognition, squeezing a collective pelvic floor, while every man pushes plates of half-eaten food away, while finding an excuse to leave the room. At the same time there's a chorus of "SHAME" from any member of the family who happens to be present, and embarrassed, yet again.

Time was something other people seemed to regulate their lives with. My life was regulated by the children and Jeff's dinner. The notion of getting me meat in before going out in the afternoon was a fantasy I'd long ago given up. With another baby in the house it wasn't even worth attempting to establish a routine as far as I was concerned.

As John grew I began to miss school. Not too much, but my mind was beginning to suffer. I knew we'd reached some sort of crisis the day I turned the one downstairs room we had, apart from the kitchen, into a replica classroom. I heaved furniture around and set up a construction corner, a book corner and a home corner with all the paraphernalia therein. Just outside the back door we had a sandpit and so I created water play with various bowls and watering cans. All done in the time that Rebecca and John were having their morning nap. Happy days.

I made a cup of coffee and gave myself a pat on the back. Multi-tasking again! It was perfect. All that I needed was for the children to wake up and be overwhelmed by their learning environment. Bang on cue, just as my bottom eased into my favourite cream leather chair with my well-earned coffee and Rich Tea biscuit, snuffling began upstairs followed by Rebecca plonking down the stairs with the cat over her shoulder.

I popped up to get John, eager to see the reaction to their very own Early Learning Centre. After five minutes my home-classroom was rearranged. Everything was scattered, books ploughed through by an enthusiastically crawling John, while Rebecca attempted to climb into the bowl of water outside, while clutching the terrified cat, and pouring the watering can over her head. Oh God, how am I ever going to manage a whole class again?

Meanwhile, Jeff was working nights. Even after the purchase of blackout curtains and a fan in constant use, whirring to block out all other sounds, it was hardly ideal. Sleep seemed to be a long forgotten luxury. I took the children out as much as I could, often walking over to my sister-in-law's beautiful schoolhouse in the country for the day. She had two children of her own just a couple of months younger than Rebecca and John. There we had the freedom of the rambling house and the quiet countryside to enjoy. Bliss. Mary was a teacher too, and we watched the progress of our children with a little more knowledge than is possibly helpful. Visits to the clinic were a source of amusement for other mums. Sharing the same surname we were called Mrs Urban and Mrs Rural. Amazing what people find amusing after giving birth isn't it? After clinic we would sometimes go shopping in town comparing prices from one supermarket to the other before deciding where to spend our family allowance. We could've managed a job-share as a cross between Nigella Lawson and Gok Wan if only we'd realised it then. I could even tell you the price of bread and where to get the best fruit. One morning after clinic Mary and I decided to do some research in town. I started at one end taking in Key Market and other such smaller outlets, Mary completed the pincer movement from Tesco and the opposite end of the high street. Our task was to compare prices of standard groceries in order to shop more efficiently. As I write I find myself shaking my head in disbelief! These days it would take weapons of mass destruction or threat of starvation to get either of us into any supermarket let alone compare prices of such staples as wine and chocolate. But life was less complex then although we hardly had time to appreciate it. Jeff's star was in the ascent at work and he continued as captain of the first team at the rugby club. We were both enjoying his success professionally and socially. As wife of the captain of the rugby club first team... I'm tempted to put that to the music of the "Ladies of the harem of the court of King Caraticus", it occasionally fell to me to launder the team shirts. Fifteen giant white shirts bearing red and black stripes across the chest. One week, when this particular task fell to me, I loaded up the machine after relieving it of the last nappy wash of the day. This was in the days of terry nappies, disposables had just come on the UK market but I was fiercely eco-aware, and broke, so we didn't have them. In went the shirts, up to bed went the children, out came me meat, on went the veg. All completed to the strains of "'Cos I'm a woman, W-O-M-A-N".

I just had time to get the shirts on the line for some fresh air before Jeff came home from work. Boy, would he be impressed. He was more than impressed, he was speechless. I had forgotten to reset the temperature dial on the washing machine and had washed the shirts on maximum heat. The result? A blush of baby-pink rugby shirts blowing in the breeze ready for tomorrow's match.

And the first fifteen wore them with pride! We had no spares so it was pink or nothing. I will never forget the moment I heard the scrunching of studs on the concrete pathway leading from the changing room to the pitch like a legion of Roman soldiers. Roman soldiers... in pink! What happened next has gone down in history. As our hulky macho men trotted onto the pitch a cannon of wolf whistles pierced the chilly air followed by unrepeatable cat-calls from the opposing team and their spectators. I slunk away into the clubhouse with the children, smothering giggles. I didn't take a backward glance, I didn't need to, I could feel the recriminatory looks without turning round. Thankfully they all took it with good humour and, at the end of a tough match which we won, some of the lads minced off the pitch hamming up the shirts. I remember that it was shortly after this that a new washing rota was drawn up. My name was mysteriously omitted.

During this time I had made more friends with children of their own and, during one of those interminable coffee mornings when you sit and compare your children's antics with all the others exploring the room at breakneck speed, someone mentioned the National Housewives Register. I'd never heard of it. Was it some kind of census or cult? What was I missing? I'll explain for the uninitiated. It was a national group set up for housewives who wanted to make more of their leisure time. To date my leisure time alluded me, but I was keen to resuscitate my vegetating brain.

The whole idea fascinated me. The only housewife I knew with leisure time was the one down the road with her meat in and she'd never told me she was on a register anywhere, and believe me she would have. Apparently, groups of housewives all over the country were meeting to have meaningful conversations verging on debate, and even to learn something that wasn't necessarily to do with teething, nappy rash or worms. I was interested and before I knew it found myself agreeing to go to a group one evening provided it wasn't on a rugby training night. Luckily it was on a Wednesday. Count me in.

What do National Housewives wear to an evening meeting? Denim dungarees would hardly cut it. I dug out a floral skirt and white blouse in an attempt to look the part whatever that was. I was aiming to achieve a cross between Margo and Barbara of the TV sitcom *The Good Life*.

The group was always held in someone's home and this evening it was in a huge, mock Tudor house on one of the new estates. Approaching it I began to have reservations. What if they were all very clever housewives? What on earth would I have in common with them if they were all wadded and owned horses? My imagination ran away with me as I conjured up the Jilly Cooper Polo set, or even the Bromsgrove glitterati. I almost did a U-turn. Instead I gave myself a good talking to, parked the car and walked up the mammoth well-gravelled drive to arrive at the same time as a girl I knew from ante-natal classes. She was wearing jeans and an ordinary-looking T-shirt which I recognised from one of the cheaper high street shops I frequented next to Oxfam. Oh God, am I going to be overdressed? She reassured me and we went in together. After the register, yes there was one, the newbies were introduced. There were two of us. Then came the subject for discussion. "The effect of the three-day week". Well I knew all about *that* thank you very much. After all, Jeff was a foreman at Leyland. Before I opened my mouth I took in the rest of the group. Their husbands were probably company directors or something political. I didn't want to upset anyone. I kept shtumm. Lack of confidence again. I enjoyed the heated discussion though and felt reassured that my mind wasn't morphing into chewing gum quite yet. It was still actually functioning at quite an impressive level. Maybe I was one of the lively-minded housewives in their strapline after all!

At the end of the evening, proposals for the next session came up. By far the most popular was "The life and works of John Updike". I remember thinking, *I hope it's not next week, I'll need a month to get through enough reading to make any kind of contribution.* I'd done Thomas Hardy and DH Lawrence at A level. I'd never heard of John Updike. I'd never heard of American literature. It was a bit like American humour wasn't it? Hardly worth a mention. It probably wasn't considered worthy by the dear nuns. Maybe it was *risqué?* Things were looking up. To my relief the group met monthly. A couple of meetings later, to Jeff's amazement and mine, I offered to host a session at our house. I decided to present an evening on Cezanne. Looking back I can hardly believe I actually volunteered. I think I was fortified after the session on John Updike in which I offered my opinion, twice, and wasn't scorned. My offer to host was made in the heat of the moment. Someone mentioned artists and wouldn't it be interesting to have an evening featuring the life of one of the impressionists, and before I gave it any thought I volunteered. My offer was immediately taken up and someone asked, "Which one?"

"Which one what?" I replied.

"Impressionist, which one?"

"Cezanne," I said confidently, no doubt giving everyone the impression that I knew all there was to know about impressionism. I knew Cezanne was one because I had a postcard of one of his paintings sent from France by an old school friend who was now living there. It was pinned on the corkboard next to other important things like a recipe for Salad Niçoise and the dates we were going to the caravan in Devon. Driving home the words, "you can fool some of the people some of the time..." echoed in my mind. What did I know of Cezanne? Absolutely nothing except that he was an impressionist painter. Well, that's a start isn't it? In fact I enjoyed my research. I felt a sense of purpose over and above the norm. What did I care that me meat wasn't in, I was the National Housewives Register's expert on Cezanne. I had tasted absinth. I almost wished her down the road to appear just so I could astound her with my intellect.

The actual evening was a great success albeit only four lively-minded housewives turned up instead of the usual nine or ten. Their loss. I set up visuals. Posters of Cezanne's more popular works, an art easel, painting smock I had recently made for my father-in-law, and a palette. I thought it all gave off an air of the absinth-tainted Paris art scene. It certainly had more ambience than the previous evening sessions, although John Updike gave us a good excuse to eat hot dogs and corn cakes. I didn't bake anything, but I did offer wine and cheese. The teacher in me was still very much alive – in a parallel universe – but still as close and neatly fitting as a second skin.

Two years went by and our two adorable children had sparked off a baby boom at the rugby club and with their cousins close by they had plenty of playmates. Jeff continued to do well at work and I was so proud of him. I had passed my driving test at the second attempt and had my own Allegro Estate which I managed to prang all in the same month, but all was well with our world.

We'd always said we would settle either in the south-west or north-east and our destiny was taken in hand when Jeff was offered a job in Bristol. Another round of fond farewells ensued. Leaving Mary would be the hardest thing for me, but I felt sure that we would end up living close to each other again very soon. It was my way of persuading myself that I could cope without her.

The rugby club had been the hub of our social life for many years and it was where we had met most of our friends. Jeff's involvement had a massive impact not only as captain of the first fifteen, but also as the founder of the mini rugby sessions for aspiring rugby players which were hugely popular with the children. There were long sessions of alcohol-infused goodbyes and promises to keep in touch. Promises which faded with the passing years and growing families. This really was goodbye to my ex-pupils at Dovecote Middle School who continued to visit and had become more like extra family to me. Again, promises were made and subsequently broken. Visits became fewer and farther between. We hardly kept in touch even with our closest friends once we'd moved. Families took over and weekends were precious.

The moving day arrived with all the pre-imagined chaos and some. The removal men were great, but I felt like a spectator at a pantomime as I watched cupboards, beds, cots and fluffy creatures all bundled into the enormous van transporting us to the south-west. It was surreal. I kept watch like a nosey neighbour as our hand-me-down furniture settled in the back of the van.

Toward midday, at my wits end, I went to collect the children from a friend who lived close by. I swore that if "I've got me meat in" put in an appearance I'd have her bubble wrapped, gaffer taped and deposited on her front garden. The removal men suggested that I might want to take some things in the car with us. I couldn't imagine what could possibly be that important apart from Rebecca and John until they suggested the kettle and the potty. Such wisdom eh? Thank God for removal men with forethought. I was excited about our new beginning, but so sad about leaving Mary and her husband Paul and their two lovely children, the Rural family. It was hard to imagine not having them within walking distance. Apart from Mary and I seeing each other during the week we established a routine of meeting up on a Sunday afternoon with the children. Jeff and Paul analysed Saturday's match while Mary and I dawdled behind with the children. The walk was invariably in the glorious woods around their picture book home and always ended with tea in front of the Aga. Joanna Trollop wasn't making it up after all. Mary had a bone china tea set and it came out every Sunday, very prim and exceedingly "country", after the walk, and it became a kind of standing joke between us all. As we were about to leave Bromsgrove, Paul and Mary presented us with a pretty floral tea set of our own. It was an emotional moment with giggles and wiping away of tears as intermittent as the roses round the rim of the tea cups. I still have the tea set.

It was then that the thought came to me that our life would be very different down south, and maybe moving back to our roots was a trifle premature. Too late for retrospect. Jeff's new role was beckoning and I convinced myself that I was looking forward to new horizons albeit on familiar turf.

As we pulled away in our Allegro Estate, with Jeff following in the company Rover, everyone came out to wave us goodbye. I put on a show of joviality like Bromsgrove was death row and I'd just been granted a last-minute reprieve. In fact I felt as if the early years of our marriage were left behind in our tiny townhouse and the lump in my throat took up residence as we approached the motorway and images of Bromsgrove lost interest in us. Doubt crept in as spraying trucks bossed us out of the centre lane to cower near the hard shoulder. With notices pasted and clinging onto the filthy rear doors demanding *how is my driving? Call 01834... Your comments are appreciated.* I could hardly resist gesticulating as the muck from their too-close wheels splattered the windscreen causing a temporary wipe-out. My comments certainly wouldn't have been appreciated, or probably even read.

I couldn't visualise our new house. I'd only seen it once and that was when Jeff decided it was *the one*. I couldn't argue with his rationale. The house had aluminium window frames and would never need maintenance. To Jeff this was Nirvana. The deal was done.

So, armed with potty and kettle we braced ourselves for the next transition. Ten minutes into the journey Rebecca piped up, "Are we nearly there yet?" and I shed silent tears. Moving on the 23rd December is not a sensible idea. We were relatively well prepared for the weather although heather-grey, laden clouds looked ominous. Our convoy pulled up outside the empty house. It was cold and verging on bleak. I had a pre-cooked evening meal all ready to go. Bedding was handy and followed the beds up the stairs into the allocated bedrooms. The children's favourite cuddlies had travelled with them and were raced around the new house with an energy I envied. First things first. Let's put the kettle on. It was then that we realised we were being welcomed to the south-west with a power cut. Things could've turned nasty if it hadn't been for a neighbour arriving at the front door with a tray of teas, coffees and biscuits. My heart sank. I braced myself for, "I thought you'd appreciate some refreshment" and "I've got me meat in so it's no bother for me...". What I got was the exact opposite. The kindest smile and a welcome as warm as the mug I clasped to my chest for comfort. I decided I liked being back in the south-west.

Next on our list of priorities was a Christmas tree and so it was that three hours later, in the almost dusk of fairy tales, that we were all cosied up in front of a beautifully-dressed tree, without lights, basking in the romance of flickering candlelight. Lengthening shadows crept across the tea chests distorting the profile of haphazardly placed furniture, and as the children fell asleep the snow thickened laying a coverlet over the front lawn. What a wonderful sight they would behold in the morning, surely more than enough to dispel any little fears they may be harbouring. We mounted the stairs slowly, not yet knowing which tell-tale creaks might wake a dozing child. We needn't have worried even though the aching stairs would've done any fairground haunted house proud. Rebecca and John were in that unreachable zone that is infant sleep. Just as we checked on them for the last time we noticed Wraxall Church a mile away leaning on the side of the hill. Its bell tower was, by now, lit for Christmas. After the tucking in Jeff and I stood gazing out of the window (aluminium-framed), at the church and the swirling snow. It felt like we were in the middle of a Disney winter wonderland. We were filled with the deep peace that comes with snow.

The traditional saying goes, "New house, new baby", and who were we to mess with the tradition? Just over one year in our new home, with Rebecca and John both at the local nursery, and a new social circle which didn't involve the National Housewives Register, number three babe decided it was an opportune time to arrive. I remember the exact time my waters broke because I was making spag bol for Jeff and I. The children were in bed and as I stood sipping a pre-dinner sherry (which didn't affect unborn babies in those days) and stirring the sauce, it happened, my waters broke. I carried on stirring for a moment thinking that moving was probably not a good idea. Better to keep the bodily fluids to one area and the bolognaise sauce from burning in another!

We called my brother who was living in Bristol at the time and he arrived to baby-sit while Jeff and I left for the hospital shortly before midnight. After a long day spent reading a very large history of Ireland and the Black and Tans, and pacing the corridors of Southmead Hospital in Bristol, things were still not moving. This one was taking its time. As unpredictable as the English rain. Stop, start, stop, start. It was thought that an enema would help. I'd kept quiet about this, but was soon rumbled by the more experienced midwife beginning her shift at 5.00pm. She rolled up her sleeves, donned her latex gloves and disappeared between my knees with her evil tubing. Ten minutes later, the indignity over with, I simply had to wait for nature to take its assisted course. I chose to wait in close proximity to the bathroom having been caught off guard when John was on his way. I didn't have to wait long and just about made it to the toilet before the world dropped out of my bottom. Panting and sweating like the Labour party candidate for Brighton (this was 1979 general election time), I spotted the name Cascade emblazoned on the porcelain toilet bowl. Despite my discomfort I found it funny. In fact I found it hilarious and couldn't reach over to retrieve my pants for at least another five minutes when my heaving guffaws finally took a breather and I was able to hoik up my knickers. The midwife said it was the first time she'd seen that reaction to an enema in the thirty years she had been in business! Needless to say that was enough to start me off again with the laughter followed swiftly by another cascade. Ooops!

Three hours or so later I had nothing to laugh about. It seemed an eternity since my labour had started and now, at the time when all my energy was necessary, my body gave up. I'd had enough and simply could not rally at that time of night. To make matters worse the general election was on the TV round the clock, and feverish discussions from the various TV sets that had been set to BBC 1 for the night accompanied the protests and blue language of some of the more vociferous mums-to-be.

An epidural followed. For someone such as myself who relishes control this was a strange situation. Each time the midwife said "Push," I had to ask her, "Where?" After an epidural you have to draw on your imagination and rely on past memory to direct your efforts to the appropriate part of your anatomy. After several non-productive pushes the contraction we'd all been waiting for reached a crescendo and Claire was born. She resembled an Eskimo with the blackest hair and fairest skin I had ever seen.

Just at the same moment history was being made as Margaret Thatcher was elected as first woman prime minister of the country. Staff were amazed that we didn't decide on Margaret for a name! Oh Please!

Chapter 10

The decision to be a stay-at-home mum hadn't been difficult for us. It was so different in those days. Property was cheap, so was the cost of living. Add to that a plethora of female authors waxing lyrical on childbirth and the growing National Childbirth Association waving the banners for breastfeeding and there wasn't really any decision to be made. It was around this time when I discovered that my mind really *was* turning into a cauliflower. I was no longer a member of the National Housewives Register, and the only outside pursuit I had the energy for was amateur drama in which I enjoyed some success. However, I found myself wondering whether I would be capable of returning to teaching, or whether in fact my brain had calcified. I decided to take up my parents' offer of childcare for Claire and I registered as a supply teacher. My first couple of days were in local schools where the children were well behaved and just like little sponges soaking up all the ideas offered for investigation.

As my confidence increased I ventured further afield into south Bristol. My dad called the area, "Apache territory" because the inhabitants knew their own and didn't appreciate outsiders muscling in. I had no intention to muscle anywhere. I was going to teach. I'd proved to myself that I still had the magical gene which dedicated teachers possess, and now I was magnanimously sharing it elsewhere.

I was soon put in my place by some of the most streetwise children I had met since Newcastle upon Tyne!

One school I particularly loved was on the outskirts of Bristol, and it was tough. Really tough. The head teacher possessed the essential qualification for leadership, a sense of humour. Each morning he would appear in the staffroom and put the kettle on. As each teacher arrived he made them their usual. He knew who took sugar, who preferred coffee to tea, who liked to start the day with a digestive biscuit and silence, and which mug belonged to the more fastidious (read fussy). As a supply teacher, entering a staffroom is a precarious business. There may be all kinds of unwritten protocols and this particular school was no exception. First of all it's important to ascertain if anyone has a favourite chair. This is done by moving from chair to chair with your bottom hovering slightly above the seat at the point just before gravity takes over, while scanning the room for any body language hinting that the chair belongs to someone. This is hilarious to watch, but not in the least bit funny if you are the hovering one! On more than one occasion the bell for the end of break sounded before my bottom had touched down.

So, Mr Casey, the head, removed the obstacle of "Who's been using MY mug and left it on the drainer?" simply by having drinks at the ready. As if that weren't enough, he was funny. I was in love immediately and wanted to work forever in his school. Nothing sordid, you understand, I had just met the leader of my dreams as opposed to the man of my dreams. As time for the early morning bell approached, Mr Casey began to relate a funny story which rendered us all helpless with laughter as we picked up our bulging bags of resources for the day and struggled off to bring the children inside.

I was in a classroom upstairs, and as the neighbouring teacher and I patrolled the stairway as shoals of children swirled along the corridor narrowly missing us he said, "Don't take any flack mind… any monkey business. I'm just across the corridor…no worries." I had never sought to be bailed out by any other teacher and I wasn't about to begin today, so I smiled sweetly and thanked him, at the same time saying it wouldn't be necessary. He smiled and simultaneously yelled at a group of sparring boys stumbling up the stairs. "Up on the LEFT, boys… The LEFT… Down on the RIGHT! How many more times?" They whooped and carried on. Don't take any flack mind, I thought.

After introducing myself to the year five class I gave them a rundown of the day. As I finished a rather large boy stood up, grabbed his very grubby backpack and pushed past me on his way to the door. "Just a moment," I said, and that's all I managed.

He swung his bag round and faced me. As I already said he was a large boy. In fact he towered above me and was a prime candidate for WeightWatchers. He stared down at me and said, loudly "Fuck you!" as he launched himself down the stairs three at a time. He was surprisingly agile, and I got the impression that it perhaps wasn't the first time he had executed that manoeuvre.

I settled the by now quiet class to some exercise or other, and made my way across the corridor to ask my neighbour to keep an eye on them while I went to see the head. "Who was it?" Mr Casey asked.

"Sorry?" I squeaked.

"The runner," he said. "Who was it?"

I told him. I stood there humiliated, I had lost a child within twenty minutes of the start of the day. I'd be lucky if he didn't suggest me leaving right there and then. Instead, what followed is still clear in my memory today. Mr Casey said, "Oh, it was our Wayne was it? Don't worry, my love, he'll be back for dinner." He hadn't even paused for breath or looked up from his desk. Our Wayne did come back for dinner, and he stayed for the afternoon because PE was cancelled due to thunder and lightning and a steady downpour lasting all afternoon. We did some model making instead, and our Wayne was enthralled with the project. He came to school every day that week and I found myself looking forward to his bulky self arriving each day. He became my project manager for the week. He was good too. He may not have been the brightest bulb in the box but his interpersonal skills were laudable when he tempered his fruitful language.

I learnt a lot there, probably far more than I taught, and on reflection I know that Mr Casey was another one of those very human head teachers who influenced my long career.

Supply teaching was a bit like Russian roulette in those days. A school called you up, you had little idea of its reputation as there were no websites to check out so you relied on hearsay, or you took a chance depending on how much you needed the extra money, or a break from domestic routine. I used to fill my bag with art resources, fabulous books and audio tapes for dance and drama. There was choice you see. The great thing was that the National Curriculum hadn't been dreamt up. Teachers used their imagination to enthral the children and promote their curiosity. Being creative is such a gift, and I found that after a while I had regular work in a number of schools where my styles of teaching and growing knowledge of the complexities of learning were appreciated. Eventually, I had so much supply teaching that it felt as though I was full-time. I was running myself ragged with the driving to and from Bristol and fitting in the school run with Rebecca and John and the drop-off at my parents with Claire. By then I was teaching two or three days a week some weeks, and Claire was due to start school the following September. That was a wake-up call. Where was the time going?

I could see my glorious gap year coming closer and closer. For years I had promised myself that once all three children were in school I would stop supply teaching and take a well-earned rest. I would devour books, visit friends up north, go for trips with my parents and in-laws, get back to my sewing, have lunch with local friends whose children were also at school, and basically live the life of Riley for a while. My plans were scuppered though when one of my regular supply schools advertised for a five tenths teacher for the special needs class. How could I refuse? So it was that I found myself at St David's Primary School in the heart of Apache territory where, amongst other things, I learnt about familial child abuse. I was contracted to work with the special needs class for six months after which time I was encouraged to apply for a full-time post in year one. I watched my gap year wave goodbye.

I knew very little about teaching very young children apart from my own three, so it was with more than trepidation that I stepped into the year one classroom that year. My dad told me that teaching younger children would stand me in good stead for when I became a head teacher. I remember wondering what on earth he was thinking! The first thing I noticed in the airy classroom was a piano. I murmured a prayer of thanksgiving. The second and possibly most important thing was an adjoining door to a shared workroom with the year two class, and the very experienced teacher Mrs Singh.

Both of the above were godsends. There were days when the out of tune piano, with its rings of coffee mugs and beer tankard stains from another life, was the best diversionary strategy I had. If a planned activity proved to be finished in less time than anticipated, i.e. than the speed of light, I would feign delight and with a sinking feeling in the pit of my stomach I'd gaily call all the children over to the piano for a thirty minute sing-song while I dreamt up a follow-up activity to stretch them further. And, hopefully, for longer.

It was part of our routine in those days to have show and tell just before break in the afternoon. We're all familiar with these sessions I'm sure, but here's a *précis* of the structure. All the children sit comfortably, in a circle usually, and are invited to share any news or show any particular artefact they find interesting. Discussion then follows.

On the afternoon in question we sat together and the first few speakers, often the same eager children with little to say but with a desperation to be heard, shared the usual, "Our gran came over on Saturday. She took us to KFC. It was lush," offered by Charlene.

Next up was Jayce, "My 'amster died on Friday." Appropriate sympathetic noises all round despite the fact that Jayce's 'amster had died twice previously this term.

Troy's offering, "Our TV broke so we 'ad to go to bed 'stead of watchin' *Driller Killer*." I enquired whether or not the TV was fixed to which he replied, "It don't need fixin'. Our mum shouted at our dad an' 'ee threw it out the window." This almost got a round of applause, and several enactments of the scenario brought the house down as infant boys leapt about like mini Ninja Turtles.

Then there was Maddie. She began in a voice hardly more than a whisper, "My bruvver and 'is friends...my bruvver and 'is friends..." She stopped and looked around as if seeing us all for the first time. Her eyes brimmed over and silent tears coursed down her grimy cheeks. She was sitting close enough to me to take hold of the hem of my long skirt. She pulled it across her face and tried to make herself invisible.

I knew that coaxing her out would be pointless at this stage. I whispered in her ear, "Shall we sing a song?" Maddie nodded and I heaved her up with me to sit on the piano stool. For fifteen minutes, until break, we went through our meagre repertoire, "Bananas in Pyjamas", "Row, Row, Row the Boat", "Cauliflowers fluffy", then back to the beginning. We sang with gusto. Maddie squashed herself into my side as I tried to accompany the children on the piano. It wasn't exactly Gounod's "Ave Maria", but it was just what was needed. At 2.30pm the class went out to play. I stayed in with Maddie. What she told me, in halting phrases which I could barely hear, took me right out of my experience to date into the realms of the darkest, most evil behaviours imaginable. The worst thing was I *knew* there had to be some truth in it because it was highly unlikely that a child of her tender age would have this kind of specific detailed knowledge which she was doing her best to share with me. After ten minutes it was obvious that social services were to be informed and Maddie's family contacted. By now her tears had written themselves onto her puffy cheeks as she tinkered on the piano keys in her attempt at "Five little speckled frogs".

Two weeks later what emerged made Maddie's earlier disclosure seem like a walk in the park by comparison. Her brother, uncles and their friends had been sexually abusing Maddie and her ten-year-old sister systematically for two years. This was the first we had heard of it and nothing had previously been suspected. The behaviour of the girls and the rest of the family was fairly typical of most families on the estate. When I asked why the girls hadn't spoken to anyone sooner, I learnt that when children grow up with this type of abuse it is all they know, it is the norm. Maddie and her sister knew no other way. This was their experience of ordinary family behaviour. It changed when one of Maddie's uncles attempted oral sex with her and, at the age of five years seven months, she knew it wasn't right.

Overcrowded accommodation, unemployment, and serial relationships were the backdrop, or indeed the inheritance of their chaotic lives. Life was undeniably hard and yet most families retained some dignity and did their utmost to provide for their children. I remember one mum who was bringing up her son alone. She was often late in the mornings and would saunter up to the school gates, cigarette in hand, patent leather handbag slung over her shoulder, while Dan, her son, ran ahead. She always looked impeccable in an overstated way. Her make-up was immaculate and she sported a San Tropez tan which was topped up every six weeks by Shaz in the local massage parlour. She didn't engage in conversation with any of the other mums. In fact some of them could actually be seen turning away from her, or running to catch up with another gossiping group on the way home from school. She was a prostitute, she worked at night, usually in the centre of Bristol, although she had a regular gentleman who she visited fortnightly as she had done for a number of years. She was one of the most clued-in women I knew in Apache territory. Her life was sorted. Her son wanted for nothing. She spent quality time with him each day after school before dropping him at his grandparents while she donned her work gear and headed out for the night. She was a private person although her way of life was no secret. Despite the fact that the other mums gave her a wide berth, Dan was a popular young boy with plenty of friends.

Maybe the others envied her self-reliance. She could've taught them a thing or two about parenting. She truly was a tart with a heart. Sometimes I'd catch sight of her arriving at the gate. I'd wave to let her know I'd seen her and would watch out for Dan. She'd wave back.

At times there was an apathy nurtured through generations of low aspiration. The epidemic of benefit fraud was rife, violence on the estate was just a reflection of the frustrations felt, and drink and drugs were often a way of handling it. All kinds of scams and illegal activities made sure that there was always easy access to both, and the children were used to material benefits that could be got off the back of a lorry, or bought cheaply from a neighbour who had previous and still kept up his contacts. Almost overnight Sky dishes appeared and peppered the walls of the tower blocks. I didn't even know what they were.

Maddie's counselling journey began that year. I wonder how she is now? I wonder if the lives of her own children, if she had any, were different from hers or whether history repeated itself and the ruins of her childhood resonate still. At times I find myself humming, "Five little speckled frogs".

Chapter 11

The head teacher of St David's was suffering from agoraphobia. At least that's what we all diagnosed. He rarely left his office and avoided conversation with any member of staff. His communication with the children wasn't much to write home about either. He sneered at them in corridors, and barked at them in assembly. He backed teachers into the nearest corner if they dared approach him as he sprinted back to his office from *his* toilet. Once he made a child wash the boys toilet floor because he had supposedly been seen by another child attempting to overfill the sinks and flood the floor. The investigation was a perfunctory affair. The accused child was notorious for his challenging behaviour. Even if proven guilty, which he wasn't, the punishment did not fit the crime. He didn't tell his parents. He knew there would be little to be gained apart from a sound slapping and verbal onslaught. Mr Hillcrest, the head teacher, ruled with a rod of iron. He spat out orders and directives to all and sundry, then, like chocolate melting in a child's pocket, he morphed into Mr Nice Guy when parents were within earshot, his mellifluous voice lulling the young mothers into a stupor which had them forgetting why they had come in and what they ever had to complain about. They invariably left the building smiling, bobbing in mock curtsies and apologising for taking up his valuable time. Oh yes, he charmed the ladies all right. At a PTA meeting one evening I politely asked if there was any money to buy the children some furniture to create a home corner as it was called then. His mouth smiled. His eyes didn't. He chuckled. Did I mention this tack before? The chuckling was the precursor to some patronising comment so

I was prepared for what came next. "*A Home Corner?*" he leered, as he did a smirking sweep of the committee. His left eyebrow arched lifting the tramline wrinkles along his forehead in a shaggy half moon. Shaking his head in sheer disbelief he asked, "What *will* she dream up next?" Chuckle, chuckle, chuckle. The topic was dropped as his expression turned to one of distaste. I felt like a bad smell directly under his nose. As the crowd finally left after the meeting, darkness made monsters of the high-rise flats surrounding the school. I was eager to get home. I had marking to do and some prep for tomorrow, not to mention Rebecca, John and Claire to collect from my friend and sort out for bed, and dinner with Jeff.

I needed to collect my bags from the classroom so hurried along the deserted corridor so as not to keep the head waiting to lock up. I grabbed my bag, swung it over my shoulder, switched off the classroom light and found myself plunged into the pitch black corridor. Strange how schools change character within an hour or two of the children leaving. Tonight was no exception. It was eerie. The corridor light had been switched off, and the switch was at the far end just outside the girls toilets.

I paused for a second or two for my eyes to adjust and it was then that I saw him. He was in the doorway of the girls' toilets. He walked toward me slowly, and before I could make up some quip about the light going out he gently pushed me back against the wall. Not actually touching me, far too clever for that, no, he used his body to *cruise* me slowly, quietly, backward until my bag hit the wall, and I let it drop to the floor. We stopped. My heart was thumping. With his face far too close to mine, and one hand flat against the wall behind my ear, he raised his other hand and pointed his forefinger at me saying, "If you *ever* ask for *anything* at a PTA meeting again, you will be sorry."

I felt quite sorry *then* actually. To my annoyance I knew there was little point in trying to move past him to the foyer, front door and freedom. I'm five foot tall on a good day, and this wasn't one of those. I looked up to the ceiling to quell the tears I felt accumulating. "Sorry," I mumbled, sounding for all the world like a weary six-year-old.

I held my breath. He pushed off the wall with his flattened palm, nodded and walked off calling over his shoulder in the most genial of manners, having slimed into melted chocolate mode, "See you tomorrow, Miss!"

He pulled the wool over most peoples' eyes but his secretary and the staff had the measure of him. It was impossible to get to see him during the day or after school as he was always on the phone according to his secretary. This was code for let sleeping heads lie.

I listened at his office door once and there wasn't a sound from within. Phone? I don't think so. I pictured him cowering there, holding his breath, watching the door handle. He buried himself in books in there, he studied for his next qualification in there. He was collecting qualifications. They presumably gave him some sense of worth. His certificates boasted from the magnolia wall behind his desk. They framed his square physique as he feigned a glancing interest at a visiting LA advisor. Qualifications. He gathered them all up with a sly pride, and he hid.

One day he came shuffling into the staffroom in a stained, brown cord jacket without the distinctive elbow patches which at least would've given him some credibility. His once charcoal-grey trousers bagging at the knees, shiny across his also bagging bottom. What an apology of a teacher. Another youngish man promoted way before his time simply to get him out of the classroom. Damage limitation. He groaned under the weight of eleven A4 folders in a variety of different colours. He dumped them on the 50s coffee table and the splayed legs dipped a little closer to the threadbare carpet that was mottled with tea and vegetable soup stains, the badge of office in any staffroom. As he straightened up he flicked his unwashed black hair back into its Bobby Charlton comb-over. Who did he think he was kidding? Neither his hair nor his permanently closed study door fooled us. Neither adequately covered the reality. He was virtually bald and hopelessly out of his depth in running a school. "It won't catch on," he'd said. We knew what "it" was because we all recognised the folders as National Curriculum programmes of study. We'd seen them on *John Craven's Newsround*. We'd waited anxiously for this moment. Well, not exactly *this* moment, but we had anticipated some acknowledgement of the National Curriculum before now. We couldn't go on forever living in the Woodstock of creativity.

So it was with jaw-dropping silence that we watched his shiny trousers sidling out of the staffroom accompanied by nervous, dry coughing as he sloped off along the top corridor. Eileen, year six teacher, broke the silence, "We're on our own, girls," she said as she lit up an Embassy filter and crossed her stripy clad legs. "Tea anyone?"

I realised it was time to leave St David's after breaking the speed limit when leaving school one afternoon en route to pick up Rebecca, John and Claire. Although foolhardy (that's a word you don't hear much these days), the hair-raising journey was uneventful and I slid into the already crowded lay-by outside their school in good time easing the car up nose to nose with the school coach. I then dropped John and Claire at a friend's house and made the return trip into Bristol for Rebecca's violin lesson. I had a distinct feeling of *déjà vu* until I realised that the reason I *felt* as if I'd been there before was due to the fact that I *had* been there before, thirty minutes ago. We arrived with seconds to spare, that's all we needed, one wasn't late for the maestro. Parking was difficult but, not for the first time, I congratulated myself on my reversing skills. Why is no one around when one executes the perfect reverse parking? We just about made it to the lesson on time as the previous pupil, white at the gills, was wobbling her way down the mossy steps from the open front door. Miss Herbert, pronounced "Airbear", towered above us in the geranium-filled porch. As I gushed my apology, which wasn't needed but was part of the ritual, I had the distinctive whiff of cat's wee. I've since learnt that geraniums of a certain strain have this odour. Beats me why you'd want them gracing your porch. Maybe it was a deterrent to Jehovah's Witnesses. The apology was an attempt to get the maestro onside because Rebecca hadn't practised and I knew a reprimand was in order. I was simply trying to establish a congenial rapport prior to the inevitable roasting. I needn't have bothered. She cared little for my grovelling.

My body was in central Bristol but my mind was on the road, travelling at some ridiculous speed flying back from St David's, tempting fate with every overtaking manoeuvre. As a result I had successfully tuned out the abysmal rendition of whatever it was Rebecca was slaying via her violin. What followed wasn't pleasant.

I bore the brunt of the almighty telling off as Rebecca eyed the gallery of certificates adorning the walls, and Miss Herbert cautioned me about "wasting your hard-earned money on lessons for which there has been NO preparation!" I held my breath as we were positively launched from the front porch, forty-five minutes and thirty-five pounds later. I noticed an overweight tabby cat lurching between the maestro's bangled ankles. She's looking for the other cat, I thought, as she inspected the geraniums.

The return journey was also at breakneck speed. There was absolutely no need for that, but my anger needed an outlet and that outlet happened to be driving like a woman possessed. It was either that or murder. I was beside myself mostly because Rebecca didn't appear to be bothered in the slightest. How do they do that? Children have this capacity to take themselves off to another zone in times of duress. How I envy them.

We finally got home, all of us, safely. I allowed myself a cup of tea before even thinking about the evening meal. Raiding the fridge I found myself thinking that this couldn't go on. Not raiding the fridge, but the risking of life and limb due to my frazzled nerves at the end of the day. I was incredibly frustrated.

I loved St David's. I adored the children, they had so much grit. But I knew I could grow no further there. The head teacher, terrified of the world outside his office door, hardly capable of controlling his own emotions had absolutely no intention of developing his staff any further. The fear of them outgrowing his tightly controlled empire was making it impossible to for me to stay. I also feared the lack of training in the brand new National Curriculum which he clearly felt was a whim.

My leave taking was such a wrench, but we had a little party in the classroom at the end of my final day and sang "Bananas in Pyjamas" with verve. Maddie, sitting next to me on the piano stool, conducted the class with a chipped, wooden, thirty centimetre ruler and growing confidence. I envisaged her gracing the podium at the Proms in the esteemed Albert Hall, her past dissipated by years of healing music and emerging trust. I couldn't help wondering when I saw the blinds of the head's office twitch as I pulled out of the car park if he was, at that exact moment, having a melted chocolate ooze as he sniggered his fond farewell. I shivered, pointed the car in the direction of home and drove at an unaccustomed legal speed.

Chapter 12

It was around this time that Jeff was commuting several days of the week to London. He would leave early on Monday morning before the children got up for school, come back on Wednesday evening after they were all in bed, and then go back the following day. I looked forward to Wednesday evenings, but they inevitably disappointed. They were never long enough, and somehow the anticipation exceeded the reality for both of us. We put too much pressure on the middle of the week. The weekend saw us all under the same roof again. Finally the inevitable happened and he was offered a promotion which would mean a move to London. Thinking about it now, I wonder why, if it was inevitable, we hadn't discussed it much? I guess we were never in the same place long enough. Or was it simply a matter of time slipping by?

However, after a prolonged period of weighing up the pros and cons, we decided to forego the offer. In retrospect we agreed that this sounded the death knell as far as Jeff's career went. But at the time we had three children at different, important stages of their education, our ageing parents living locally and a respectable lifestyle. We had more than enough. This had coincided with my unrest at St David's and so it was with tremendous good fortune that I landed a teaching post nearer home at an improved salary scale. I also had responsibility for several of the arts subjects. It seemed as if all our ducks were lined up on the runway and facing in the same direction.

Comparing life at Notre Dame Primary School with life at St David's would be like comparing Eton with St Trinian's. The catchment area was upwardly mobile professional. People lived beyond their means, well, definitely beyond their neighbours' means. Keeping up with the Joneses wasn't the aspiration. Leaving the Joneses on the starting block was. It's important to understand that every child born into this social strata was expected to be brilliant by right even if the genes were not present. It necessarily follows that any child who failed to live up to parental expectations was the product of an under-achieving school. There was simply no room for any other possible reason for being less than average in any subject other than the following:

1   The teacher is inept/too old/too young.
2   The head teacher is a moron.
3   The child is being held back because he/she is brighter than his/her peers.
4   The child is under-stimulated/over-stimulated.
5   The child is bullied and no one cares.
6   The child is a bully due to his/her frustration, and no one cares.
7   The child is bored.

I realised this was the lay of the land after two weeks with year three. A child in my class was having difficulty with maths. She had been having difficulty with maths throughout her short career in school to date. Armed with the meticulous records from her previous teacher I added her to my shortlist of children for whom extra provision would be needed. I asked her parents to come to a meeting so that I could describe what I had in mind and show them my outline plans which I hoped would prove to be successful with their wee one. I think I also hoped there would be a sign of appreciation for the extra workload and long nights researching schemes of work which might promote a breakthrough. Almost before I could welcome the parents I was met with a torrent of frustrated diatribe from the mother. It went something like this. "We're sick of this. We thought *you* would be different. You haven't been here five minutes. How can you possibly have come to the conclusion that extra provision is needed? It's absolutely ridiculous! I have a MATHS DEGREE!"

Now, I believe I'm open-minded, I was even way back then, but I couldn't see the correlation between her maths degree and her little daughter's difficulty. I mean, being Mo Farah's offspring doesn't necessarily guarantee you a place in the Olympic Games does it? If that was how the gene pool worked we'd all choose our partners with a different set of criteria wouldn't we? Can you imagine it? Crushed by the reception of my carefully thought out strategic plan I dragged myself back to the surface, climbed the barricade of verbal onslaught, and countered by undercutting the shrieking verbosity with a chilling calm, itemising of the evidence leading me and previous teachers to the conclusion that extra provision would be necessary.

I thanked them both for giving up their valuable time to come and discuss how we, at Notre Dame, could continue to dedicate *our* time and diligence to ensure the appropriate progression of their daughter. They left. I opened my desk drawer, took out a handful of Jelly Bellies and wolfed the lot. Thank God there wasn't a revolver in there.

Illness was another excuse proffered when parents could find no other reason for their child's difficulty, or less than glowing achievement in every subject. This led to some bizarre behaviour. For instance there was a child in my year five class the following year who was late for school each and every day. He was an all-rounder you might say, good at sports and good academically. He was a very popular child who maintained his genial personality and humour without becoming in the least bit arrogant. He was even able to manage the embarrassment of each late entry to the classroom. At times the other boys greeted him with a round of applause to which he responded with a gorgeous self-effacing smile. At other times he attempted to slip into his seat with the least possible sound so as not to cause a stir. Because he was a bright child he was able to catch up with the missing ten minutes or so with little effort. He was proficient at it actually. After all, he'd had years of practice. His mother smothered him and was the main cause of his regular tardiness at the start of the school day. She didn't want to let him go. It was as simple as that.

She had insisted for many years that her son, we'll call him Ian, felt sick every morning and this was the cause of his slow start to the day. One morning I asked Ian how he was feeling because he actually looked peeky. He looked at me, excused himself as he burped, and replied, "Mum makes me eat breakfast every morning." I said that I thought this was reasonable and an excellent way to start each day.

I think I sounded a little like Mary Poppins if I remember rightly. I could see I had his attention even though his lips were white and beads of sweat were beginning to form on his forehead. To keep his attention I went on to tell him how I liked nothing more than to start the day with some cereal and maybe a banana. The colour began to return to his cheeks. I thanked God. For a moment there I thought his breakfast was about to put in a second appearance on the floor of the class library. I wasn't good with vomit.

"Mmm," he nodded. "Cereal would be ace. I have to eat bacon, eggs, sausage, beans, fried bread and tomatoes every morning." My cereal and banana almost surfaced at the thought! My heart sank. Not because of the enormity of his breakfast, but because his mother had the time to cook a heap of food with which to force-feed her son every morning, whereas we all rushed out each day after half a bowl of cereal each and half-eaten bananas for the journey! Wonder Woman I thought, while wishing the fleas of a thousand camels would crawl up her exhaust pipe and teach her a lesson for being so organised. Ian and John were good friends and I found myself hoping that John didn't get wind of the breakfast his classmate was having, if you'll pardon the unintended pun. He'd be ringing the equivalent of ChildLine to complain about his neglectful mother. Ian's mother also complained to me that her son was deaf and needed to be moved to the front of the class. I expressed some surprise as I hadn't picked up any problems with Ian's hearing so far. He responded well in class and was retaining information with remarkable acuity. He certainly wasn't deaf at playtime or on the football field either.

However, she was not to be gainsaid. The following morning she arrived late with a putty-coloured Ian making his way to the boys' toilets with anxiety etched on his face, and egg yolk congealed on his school tie. God love him, I thought. She rummaged in her handbag and extracted an envelope which she handed to me. "There," she said, as if we had just had a lull in conversation, "there…take a look at that!" I opened the envelope and picked out a piece of clear sticky tape with a large amber globule encased. Try as I might, I couldn't imagine what it was and looked to Ian's mum for clarification. "Out of his ear, this morning…wax that is…I got it out of his ear this morning." She smiled triumphantly, nodding at me like a demented dog on the back shelf of a battered van. I wondered if she'd extracted it prior to cooking his colossal fry-up or after. I thrust the envelope and its contents at her and made for the staff loo where my meagre breakfast did actually reappear.

At the end of a stuffy afternoon in the classroom the following week I closed the door behind me and felt a sense of finality. I put it down to dismal, wet playtimes and classrooms full of sweaty, pink-cheeked children in a riot of chess sets, sticky paper and comics heralding indoor play. The bane of every teacher's life.

I vowed that if ever I became a head teacher I would authorise outdoor play in all weather, barring a hurricane. Although, on some challenging days I could imagine that losing a few well-chosen children in a twister might be viewed as a godsend, but this "ain't Kansas" I guess.

That muggy afternoon I'd almost fallen asleep listening to Red Group reading, normally a time I treasured listening to one child at a time, hanging on their every struggling word and logging the progress made since the last session. I coveted this time as it was so much more than listening to reading. It's a privilege to look into the trusting eyes of so many children as they invite you to join them in their very individual learning journey. The pride shining out of their upturned faces as they struggled through a story of ten sentences length was wonderful to behold.

Today though, today was different. The corridor leading to the staffroom, an oasis at the end of such days as this, was cluttered with the fallout from an afternoon of artwork. Why is it that reception children are capable of clearing up after artwork, yet six years down the line their elders deem it an impossibility?

I watched Alison, a learning support assistant, shoving scraps of discarded paper into a recycling sack and muttering expletives to herself now that the children had long ago vacated the school. I smiled and wondered what it was that kept her motivated. Further on down the corridor, tea now almost in sight, I stopped by a new display outside of year six's classroom. It depicted a culmination of their learning about the ancient Egyptians. It was stunning, as was every display that had Alison's involvement. She walked up to me on cue pulling the reluctant recycling sack and clutching a dozen or so paintbrushes that had been misappropriated and used to apply glue. This was a mortal sin in anyone's estimation. To Alison it was a hanging offence. I waited for the verbal onslaught which began, "I don't get it, I just don't get it. They've got pots of glue spreaders but they can't be arsed to collect them from the friggin' cupboard in the classroom so what do they do?" I knew I'd be invited to comment and was desperately trying to think of something which would appease Ali. Making excuses would induce verbal abuse, commiserating would fall on deaf ears. But Ali stopped and dumped her sack, throwing the clogged paintbrushes into the sink and, folding her arms across her chest, looking up at the display she said, "Bloody brilliant that isn't it? Who'd have believed that those little shites could work together long enough to produce this, eh?" Oh how she loved the children.

She glowed with pride. I looked at her, looking at it. She looked at me, looking at her, looking at it and asked, What?" Sometimes she was a woman of few words.

It was then that I understood exactly what it was that motivated Alison. Her passion. Art was her passion. More succinctly, art with children was her passion and nothing was allowed to get in the way of her passion. Year on year she dealt with the whims and fancies of a succession of head teachers, faced the challenge of some truly wacky children, and even more wacky teachers, yet her work consistently reflected a supremely high level of expectation. The children in her art classes flourished, their experiences heightened by her talent, ebullience and wicked humour. The school classrooms and corridors sang out her skills and creativity. Yet we all took her for granted. "Oh bugger!" she gulped, dispelling my internal reverie. "I promised I'd get the hall sorted for tomorrow's assembly before I went home."

"Oh, leave it, Ali, there'll be time in the morning," I replied to her retreating back. I both envied and resented her dedication, her energy. I couldn't pull myself together to give her a hand.

Driving home I just had enough time to ponder again on what it was that Ali had and I didn't. Apart from an Oxford Concise volume of cursing, I figured it was that she was turning up for work every day pumped up to indulge and bestow her knowledge of art, her passion. Could it be that simple?

I decided to give it a try.

I began by asking what was my passion. Having ascertained that it was children, I then asked myself why I was feeling discontented.

The list surprised me. In fact it shook me to the core. To date I had given little thought to anything other than developing my knowledge and teaching skills to provide the best for the children in my care. Now my small world at Notre Dame was frustrating me. I couldn't indulge in creative management to the extent that I wished. Okay, I was now the deputy head, but I wasn't the head, the boss. Likewise I could only effect the school's curriculum coverage in the subjects for which I had responsibility, i.e. English, Music, French and RE, despite many futile attempts to the contrary.

And, at the very end of the list, thrusting its chin toward the finishing tape was this bombshell. I was beginning to lack the sort of energy that's necessary to continue delivering my best in the classroom. With successive governments doing *their* best to scupper any embedding of initiatives by feverishly concocting one strategy after another, there just wasn't the time to consolidate anything in our brains. Scoring, with the political football that education had become, was the primary target for each political party. I wanted more *say*. I wanted to be able to help colleagues to manage and develop and flourish in this madcap environment. I wanted children to reap the benefits of creative teachers despite the stranglehold of politicians.

Our own children were beginning to make the early decisions about the way their future education would shape up. Jeff was still away working an increasing amount of time either in London or elsewhere as more and more people were being made redundant, and he clung to his job with an enviable professional tenacity. At times I felt I was spinning a full dinner service of plates in an effort to manage at home and keep us all stress free. On top of all that I was aware that I couldn't run the risk of classroom burnout by expending so much energy every which way!

Emotionally I was all over the place. Working with the current head was pushing me to the furthest reaches of understanding and compassion. He was faltering, flagging and often ill. *His* passion had become his recently acquired Victorian house on the coast. All attempts at keeping to the agenda during staff meetings degenerated into a virtual black hole as one by one we all gave up while he ploughed on, shoulder to the grist, regaling his wife's attempts at matching the new parlour wallpaper with that which she had uncovered underneath the current Laura Ashley floral print. This was newsworthy indeed. In fact I can't imagine what kept it out of the school newsletter such was the excitement.

Their entire weekend had been a frenzy of mild hysteria which culminated in them finding a vintage décor emporium in an obscure village in Somerset. Not only did they buy rolls and rolls of replica Victorian wallpaper, they also found a forlorn antique shop cowering in a backstreet in town which just so happened to have the very taps they were looking for to complete the bathroom! Oh joy! Their return home was nothing less than triumphant. I pitied their four children. Jeff and I weren't too hot on decorating and I'm sure our children turned out the better for it. At least that's how I consoled myself.

His demise didn't go unnoticed by the parent body and, keeping them at bay, I was taking much of the flack aimed at him. Endless Friday afternoon meetings with him were predictable and non-productive as he whined about everything to do with headship and continued to list the latest projects he was carrying out at home. I was at screaming pitch with all things Victorian.

Introducing matters in need of discussion i.e. the budget, the newly qualified teacher who was struggling, or the refurbishing of the children's toilets which were also struggling, was becoming more and more difficult. He simply couldn't bring himself to focus on school. Sometimes he would sink with his head between his hands and quietly sigh while I sat not knowing how to help him short of suggesting he consider a career in home renovation.

Increasingly, I thought more and more about headship. I wanted his job. I wanted to be the one making decisions to improve the breadth of the educational menu at Notre Dame. I wanted to be the one nurturing young leaders to replace my generation in years to come. I wanted to be the one balancing out arts and sciences and astounding the children with the creative links between them all. I wanted to be the one who grew alongside the children and jour-neyed with the spirituality of each one, staff included.

Oh God… I wanted to be a head teacher.

Chapter 13

I realised that my dad's words were starting to make sense. He knew I had the ability, creativity, and strength, suffused with a smidgeon of insanity to lead a school. I began to think he was right after all.

The local education authority bulletin containing all the up-and-coming school teaching posts was about to slide onto the carpet as a plate of doughnuts shifted on the already laden coffee table in the staffroom. It being close to Christmas, generous parents surfaced and left offerings at the staffroom door. I couldn't help feeling that there was a hidden agenda lightly sprinkled between the tray of Chelsea Buns and the tin of Celebrations chocolates. Children were dropping like flies as nativity rehearsals cranked up and began to sound like a recurring Joyce Grenfell fest, but, with enough sugary offerings to sink several battleships let alone one, teachers countrywide would keep afloat and contain wilting children until the end of term, allowing parents all over the country to shop for Christmas in relative peace. Hence, the surfeit of cake and chocolate we managed to shift at break time. We weren't about to complain.

I caught the bulletin and flicked through the adverts for headship. To my surprise there was one there for my old school...the school I attended as a child. Not only that, it was the school my *parents* had attended! Jeff and I used to joke that when the headship for St Mark's came up I would apply, and here it was! You couldn't make it up could you? That weekend I pored over my application form with the diligence of a school swot. Then, at approximately 4.35pm, I read that the closing date for applications was... TODAY! I panicked. It was Sunday. Was this some kind of cruel joke? Was the position already stitched up? There was no post. I had no chance of getting my application in on time. Such a cruel twist of fate.

Rebecca came to the rescue. She was about to go into Bristol with her boyfriend so offered to post the form through the front door of the school. Relax. All was not lost.

Little did I know at the time that upon arrival at the school the front gates were locked, so access to the letterbox was impossible. Rebecca was not to be deterred. With a leg-up from her boyfriend she scaled the gates, popped the form through the letterbox, ran up the drive, executed an enviable hurdle back over the gate and slumped in the getaway car before any of the regulars from the pub next door noticed! Two weeks later I received an invitation to interview at St Mark's Catholic School. Suddenly it all became a reality. Where to begin? Shopping.

I decided on a mint-green suit for the interview. This was due, in part, to Claire telling me that every applicant for vacancies at her comprehensive school wore navy blue and subsequently you couldn't tell who was a pupil and who was an applicant for the job.

I thanked her for the compliment she hadn't intended! I would've loved the problem of being mistaken for a sixth form student, however, as I was advancing into my middle-years I was sure it wouldn't make a jot of difference if I turned up in the *complete* school uniform. No one would be mistaking me for anything other than what I was, a hopeful applicant. Just to err on the side of caution though, I splashed out on the mint-green. And new shoes of course.

On arrival at St Mark's I felt decidedly overdressed and began to wonder if I'd got the wrong day and had arrived for school sports day or, indeed, "dress-as-you-damned-well-like" day.

There were three male applicants attending for interview. I'll name them One, Two and Three. One resembled an estate agent, slick hair gelled into submission, yellow tie, (straightened by wife) sweaty palms. I envisaged his patter, "Oh yes, properties like this are flying off the shelves. *Bijou* residence (faux French accent), uninterrupted view of the Mendips, just beyond Asda and the skateboard park."

Two wore a thick, pea soup-coloured worsted suit and trainers leaving me, to this day, speechless. It was possibly the hottest day of the year for one thing. For another, *trainers* with a suit? Not in the early 90s. In fact, never!

Three was suited and booted appropriately. The perfect ensemble topped with an endless smile which made my cheeks ache in sympathy. I wondered if they were doing the same as me. Surreptitiously eyeing up the opposition, making judgements.

I wondered what they saw. Mint-green suit, ridiculous high-heels, cropped short hair, bright lipstick, probably bats for the other side, or maybe a nun who went over the wall. We were called one by one throughout the day and grilled. Interesting thing about governing bodies isn't it? There they were, the butcher, the baker and the candlestick maker, the checkout lady from the aforementioned Asda, the parish priest, and a couple of parents, reading their allotted questions at the allotted time and smiling awkwardly as they listened to answers they couldn't comprehend in a professional language which might as well have been Serbo-Croatian for all it meant to them. My heart went out to them. Possibly the only governor with any understanding and experience of education was the LEA advisor. The same would have rung true for any of us lifted from our normal *modus operandi* and plonked into unknown terrain. We'd all be clueless.

At the end of the day I walked out into the bright, beautiful sunshine from the confines of the parish office. Fresh air. I grabbed it gasping like a guppy returning to its tank after an unfortunate flip onto the kitchen floor. Encapsulated within the Bristol red-brick walled presbytery, it felt as if I'd breathed rarefied air for longer than was advisable. I've no doubt that an army of nuns equipped with beeswax, room freshener and a penchant for cleanliness were mounting an assault on floors, ceilings and furniture before I'd even been shown out by the flustered school secretary. I smiled as I conversed with my dad's spirit. "Well, dad, at least I got a drop-dead gorgeous suit and a day out! What happens now is out of my hands." Reaching home I showered and flopped onto the bed in the cool of the front bedroom. I did the usual post-interview exercise, I wish I'd said that... I'm sure they rumbled I didn't have a clue about finance. Maybe I was a little too outspoken with my answer about bullying when I replied by asking the parent governor, "How precisely are you defining bullying? I mean, are you perhaps thinking that teasing and children simply having a rough and tumble is bullying? Or are you actually referring to the dictionary definition which is a tad more explicit and significantly more disturbing?" She bristled, sniffed, looked at her neon toenails before firing the question back at me. I floored her with the dictionary definition of which I was proud, but it was clear to see that I had overstepped the mark as they say. Go figure. She rearranged her clipboard and scribbled viciously leaving no doubt in anyone's mind that she was dismissing my answer, and probably me too! I imagined her writing, *cocky bitch* as her pencil broke. Echoes of Miss Kirk. Oh well, too late now. I closed my eyes, luxuriating in the tenuous rays of the sun probing their way into the room. The curtains drifted in and out as the breeze played with them, and I found myself lulled into the bliss of almost sleep. As soon as the swirling thoughts in my head rounded for the third time on the day's carousel, the phone rang. Dragging myself up I answered drowsily, dropping the towel as I recognised the voice of the chair of governors. I scrambled to cover up and sat on the edge of the bed wrapped in a pair of jeans abandoned the night before, and a large T-shirt abandoned even earlier in the week. I'll never be known as a domestic goddess, that was my mum's undefeated title.

She seemed to be offering me the job. She *was* offering me the job! In my childhood school, the school where my parents met as children, the school where I met my first love, the school where almost everyone in my family was educated!

"So, would you like to join us at St Mark's?" I heard her ask for the second time, a little more anxious this time.

"Yes, yes of course, thank you!" My voice sounding too loud and far too fast. I gabbled on asking what happened next trying not to come across as totally ignorant of the responsibility being offered to me. Our conversation drifted on for several minutes before I realised that I hadn't actually taken in a single word. I was in shock. I was ecstatic. I couldn't wait to tell Jeff and the children. I put the phone down and fell back onto the bed. "I'm a head teacher! Oh God! I'm a head teacher!"

Leaving my class was something I could hardly imagine. We'd been together for three years and, as they were about to transfer to big school, I was facing a transition of my own. I remember my last day in fast forward mode. As all the celebrations were happening in school, my car was being adorned with balloons and crazy foam. Hanging off the back was a huge notice proclaiming "New Head Teacher" with an L-plate to match.

My personal adornment came next as multi-coloured balloons and ribbons were tied to every amenable and accessible part of my body. The children followed me out to the car. I was leaving early. We hugged like we'd never hugged before in an endless cuddle. I couldn't seem to take the final step to my car. Another teacher friend of mine came to the rescue gently detaching me and taking hold of the children nearest the car. They made a pathway for my exit. Thankfully, the drive home lasted only two minutes and the car knew its way by heart. Tears and smiles combined as I took the turn into our road to the echoes of a cacophony of bursting balloons and shouting children. "Good luck, Mrs C!"

Chapter 14

I felt very much at home with the prospect of working near the city centre. After all, I was born there. My earliest memory from that time happened when we lived with my grandparents in their terraced home which teetered on one of the steepest hills in the city. I think I was almost three-years-old. We moved after my third birthday to the outskirts of the city and a new housing estate considered posh by comparison.

Sitting in the dim light on the flagstone kitchen floor where my nanny had left me playing with some pots and pans I saw a mouse run out from under the table. Being a toddler I had no fear of it, but my gorgeous mum screamed and literally leapt on a chair gathering up her Doris Day gingham skirt and apron round her knees frightening the life out of me. The ensuing chaos as my cries joined the screams of my mother's brought everyone in the house running into the kitchen. By now the mouse was nowhere to be seen. I didn't blame it, if I'd been able to keep up with it I would've fled too!

Although we left the inner city before I started school I knew enough about life in less advantaged areas, as they came to be known, to feel passionately that the entitlement for *all* children should not be defined by their socio-economic status. Most importantly, I had a total intolerance of the notion some teachers held that began with the words, "Well, what d'you expect?" when talking of the challenging behaviour or slow achievement of any child who happened to have been born in the inner-city. It was a favoured opting out clause. It meant they didn't have to make an extra effort to understand or reach any child who didn't learn with the speed of the majority. In fact any child who might think differently and cause staff to pause, and wonder, and thus deter them from "getting things done" with the rest of the class. Even in the early 90s the pressure was mounting and it took courageous and dedicated teachers to ensure a balanced curriculum in their classrooms.

I remember the first time I heard this opt-out clause as an excuse at St Mark's. It was during a meeting with my leadership team. I paused just long enough to take in what had been said before I replied, "Well, I thank the teacher who decided to have higher expectations of me when I was a pupil here." I never heard the opt-out clause again. However, I was aware that for some teachers this had been a mantra for many years exempting them from meeting the needs of generations of children. Children who, with their rowdy footfalls and unabridged thinking, left school disillusioned and with little self-esteem. These same children grew quite naturally into engineering, computer programming and the other skills upon which the twenty-first century has become reliant. Untethered learners. If you know such a one, be in awe, you walk on hallowed ground!

All that was to come later but, for now, here I was picking up a school which had languished in the comfort zone of out-of-date educational philosophy from the previous century for well over twenty years. It would take time for me to understand the best way to discover and optimise the pool of the staff talents and to enable them to come gently into the new world which was leaning, exhausted, at the main doors to the school, trodden over for years, unnoticed for even longer, a kind of homeless educational reformation desperate to gain entry to St Mark's.

The community was a miniature version of the United Nations with families settling in from Jamaica, Italy, Poland, India, Ireland and, most recently, lured by BUPA and NHS proposals, the Philippines. My appointment prompted a varied mix of responses from the parent body. They were used to the old ways. They were used to male head teachers.

I was, however, welcomed like royalty during the summer holidays before my first term began when I'd been invited to open the school summer fair. I dressed suitably in a floral print, Audrey Hepburn-style dress and appropriate stilettos. I thought, foolishly in retrospect, that I'd be able to park on the drive of the school. I arrived to find others had parked there before me and the drive was jammed with queues of bag ladies and baby buggies. When I eventually found somewhere to leave the car it was round the back of an enormous block of graffiti-spattered flats.

By now I was late. I grabbed my bag from the passenger seat of my convertible, and headed back the way I'd come with far less confidence and *joie de vivre*. Where the main road met the side street was a patch of land similar to any abandoned, pot-holed strip in the developing world. I could see a group of young lads hanging around drinking. There were empty beer cans rolling disconcertedly away toward the gutter or into the path of the oncoming cars, accompanied by jeers of unrepeatable slang. It was a hot day. Hot and dry and I would've given over the odds for a cold beer. As I approached the huddle I began to feel uneasy. I realised I was sweating and my bare feet were sticking to the soles of my ridiculous shoes as I panted toward the school. I was about to navigate around the lads when they suddenly parted to let me through. A real Red Sea moment which I found quite unnerving. There was a silence as I hurried on and I half expected a can to come flying past my head accompanied by raucous laughter. Instead a young teenager with spiked up red hair yelled out, "Nice legs!" Without a nano-second pause this was followed by "Shame about the face!" from a John Travolta lookalike with sleeked black hair with an unbelievable quiff. I couldn't help myself, I giggled. I know, I should've treated it with a dismissive shrug, but the comic timing was brilliant. I had to admire it! I guess they knew where I was headed. It wasn't the norm to get all dressed up to shop locally in the equivalent of Albert Square, and the only other possibility was the school. I gasped my way through the crowded drive squeezing past chattering mums and fidgeting children, and was met by the chair of governors who thrust the microphone into my hands and nodded at me like an over-excited, parcel shelf puppy.

I cleared my voice and got as far as thanking everyone for inviting me to open the annual summer fair when, from somewhere in the jostling mass, a voice with the clarity and volume of Brian Blessed boomed, "Open the bloody gates, woman!" I did without hesitation, flattening myself against the nearest wall as the tide of humanity thrust its way through like the running of the bulls in Spain, clearing the path with swerving buggies tilted with flying carrier bags toward the bargains.

I'd never seen anything like it and I imagine that was as plain as the nose on my face as I tried to apologise to the chair of governors for my late arrival. She beamed and explained in hushed tones, while steering me toward the sun-soaked playground once the stampede passed, "Take no notice of them. Professionals they are, always here, every year grabbing the bargains and anything else if you look the other way." Throughout the afternoon I was paraded around and introduced to parents, children, and the professionals still lingering on the off chance that price-slashing would happen before the end of the day. Good luck with that, I thought, this is Bedminster. I felt clammy and overdressed and wondered how royalty managed to remain so cool and unruffled. Maybe their salary helped. By 4.00pm, most of the visitors had left, satisfied that they had got all they came for, and probably much more. One young man sporting a matted Rastafarian hairstyle swung his bulging plastic carrier bags onto the rack balanced on the back of his rusty bike and tied a child's scooter across the handlebars before flinging his leg over the saddle and peddling off somewhat precariously to join the main road. "He comes every year, buys up enough toiletries to last the year and leaves. Must be a new baby in the family this year. He had enough Johnson's to equip a maternity ward. Three children, maybe four soon."

The chair of governors filled me in. My thoughts went back to the early years at my grandparents home. No matter how little we had we children were always loved, and we were always spotless. My mum saw to that. Ms Davis, the chair of governors took my arm and led me over the melting tarmac to the marquee on the school playing field. From inside I could hear singing belting out and swelling as lounging parents and roly-polying children began to join in. Gradually the parents and grandparents seated on the sloping bank began to sing too. It was an Irish folk song, particularly well-known it would seem. Children hurled themselves into roly-polies down the steep bank as the singing grew with the enthusiasm of the flowing beer. I wasn't aware that the school had a license for alcohol so I brought it into the conversation we were having with a group of parents. It brought the house down. Guffaws of laughter echoed out over the playground. I sat, bemused, wondering if someone had cracked a joke that I'd missed. "License? Jesus! We're a Catholic school, we've a license for everything, Missus." This from Micky, yes, he really was called Micky, a ruddy-complexioned, larger than life character, swaying at the edge of our group.

"Shut up you daft eejit!" This accompanied with a slap from Mo, his long-suffering wife, who cackled and wheezed her way through a cigarette. "Don't you know you're talking to the new headmistress?" That was my cue to leave. I was no one's mistress. I was a head teacher. A head teacher with a headache. Besides, no one would notice, they were all too busy trying to shut up our Micky.

I turned to take my leave only to have my arm grabbed by Tyrone, Micky's teenage son. "You can't go yet, Miss, I got you a bevvy." He thrust a pint glass at me.

"I hope this isn't alcoholic," I said as I smiled my thanks at him.

"Ah no, Miss, not so's you'd notice," he winked and turned to stagger back to his girlfriend. It was clear that I wasn't going to get away that easily. It was also clear that I was going to have to ditch my pint without anyone witnessing it!

By nine o'clock someone suggested moving to the pub next door and, thankfully, the mass exodus began with Micky like a latter day Moses leading his people out of slavery and into the promised land of St Mark's Catholic Club's skittle alley.

I slipped through the crowd, and when I knew I was out of sight of the school I kicked off my shoes and felt the still warm pavement beneath my bare feet. Hobbling back to the car I found myself wondering if it would still be where I'd left it hours earlier. To my surprise I found I wasn't in the least bit worried whether it was there or not. The half pint I had downed was obviously much stronger than I thought. I remembered Tyrone's cheeky grin and wondered whether he'd spiked my drink with a drop of the hard stuff which was passed round the crowd earlier. Thank God I'd slopped most of it onto the grass when the dancing began…did I tell you about the dancing? What a day! Catholics sure know how to party!

Chapter 15

The madness of the summer fair was relegated to a file somewhere in my subconscious as now, on the first morning of the first term of my first headship, I was about to meet the children. As they tumbled into the hall for assembly I noticed the complete lack of energy demonstrated by the teachers. And I mean by the *majority* of them. You would've been forgiven for thinking it was the end of the school year, not the beginning. Not a smile to be found. Snarling appeared to be the order of the day apart from one male teacher who showed signs of being human as opposed to just being another lukewarm body in the room. I wondered what was wrong. Had I missed something before school? I didn't think so as I was the only one present in the building apart from Mrs Walters the school secretary until ten minutes before the bell rang, unless I include the caretaker who I met propping up a bookcase outside the boys' toilets. For a moment I mistook him for an ageing, discarded mannequin as he was leaning, motionless, with an expression resembling a pickled walnut. More of that later, not the boys' toilets, the caretaker. And possibly the toilets too come to think of it. I smiled at the gathering children. They whispered behind cupped hands. At last the youngest children filed in and sat at the very front of the hall close to where I was standing. I bent down to speak with one or two as they settled. The smell of barbeque flavoured Monster Munchies was ripe. I soon found the muncher. His cheeky round face was peppered with the salty flavouring which coated the crispy shapes he'd clearly demolished for breakfast. One of his eyes was green and the other was blue and they were both as bulbous as newly fallen raindrops. He was sitting cross-legged with his hands threaded through each leg of his Thomas the Tank Engine pants. Yes, threaded through and out the other side. Having achieved what I suspected was a well-practised manoeuvre, he then attempted to join his hands together. Unfortunately, I could see the effect this would have on the aforementioned pants so intervention was the name of the game. I leant across and whispered, "Don't you just love Monster Munchies?" He looked at me and slowly withdrew his hands while holding my gaze in a vice-like grip. His stained tongue slid out of the left side of his salty lips and he smiled and nodded. Words weren't necessary, his expression said it all.

As I stood a child with knotted, mousy hair was looking me up and down, and then up again. I smiled. He didn't stop the up and down staring as he said, in an accent as sturdy as the cliffs on the Avon Gorge, "Miss, I likes your tights." I thanked him for his observation. I'm sure he meant well.

One teacher affectionately named "the folk singer" slumped in her chair chewing gum. She was in her fifties. Her hair was in its fifties. Her clothes were younger and perhaps originated in the 60s. Opposite her at the end of a row of year five children sat another teacher with a dismissive snarl on one side of her face and a smirk on the other. I wasn't sure which side of her I would choose to sit at given the choice. She lounged in her seat, arms folded, facing slightly sideways on to me so I had almost the full benefit of the snarl/smirk expression. The two women resembled a pair of bookends…the kind that would cause you to hesitate before reaching for a coveted book.

Encouraging, I thought, and with a wry smile I launched into my introduction.

Assembly went well and then the folk singer stood and shrieked at the children to "Open your hymn books at page 487, and NO TALKING." This, of course, was the signal they needed. From around the hall conversations started up and gained volume as page 487 was sought amidst a growing rumble of "page 487, page 487, page 497, 487 stupid!" She strummed a chord and the hubbub subsided like the lazy outgoing pull of the River Avon at the top of the road. Same slow speed, same inevitability. She strummed the same chord again and pitched into "Autumn Days when the grass is jewelled…" Then she stopped. By now I was wondering what could possibly be coming. Whatever it was it couldn't be any worse than her previous rendition surely. "THIS TIME I WANT TO HEAR ALL OF YOU!" she screamed through clenched teeth. I found myself wondering when her last professional development had taken place. Clearly there was only one way to get the attention of two hundred children, and this bellowing hysteria, worthy of a less than friendly BFG, was it. Children in the front row blanched. I walked over to a couple who were huddling in disbelief at the screaming spectre before them. I sat down with them and smiled. She resumed her banshee-like wailing. I had never heard the actual banshee wailing, but was sure this insane screeching was as close as it got outside of Irish folklore. She rocked back and forth on her flat shoes... FLAT SHOES? her knees protruding from her mini-skirt. MINI-SKIRT? If she'd worn mini-skirts the first time round she would've been too old even then. Her greying, dispirited hair, hanging lifeless as the woollen top-knot of a rag doll fell forward to hide her face on the forward rock, and then (Oh God!) limped back to reveal her strained face as she rolled back. I wasn't sure whether to laugh or cry. The situation called for a response of some sort, of that there was no question, but my emotions were a cocktail of early morning euphoria at the thought of my adventure, warmth as I chatted to the children, puzzlement at the apathy of the teachers and fear of this woman. Yes! Fear! She scared me. Not for any personal reason, but I was fearful for her life! How could anyone who was clearly frustrated with children, and lived in the abyss of let-down that she didn't make it in the 60s folk era, *sleep* at night. More worrying why was she still coming to school? There were plenty of well paid jobs on the outside. She could've been a checkout person in Asda or even shop assistant in the local Sound as a Pound, the difference in pay would be negligible and the responsibility far less. She'd even have spare time too. Time to practise her guitar, time to join the other folkies standing hunched over a beer in the pub, or singing some jarring lament with left finger in the ear and right thumb tucked into the top of corduroy jeans. Time for a hairdresser perchance!

I could picture it now. Not a page 487 in sight just a throwback from the 60s folk scene perishing behind a pint of cider in her favourite rural watering hole, and entertaining with a "Whack-fa-the-daddeo, there's whiskey in the jarro".

Meanwhile she spread her angst and gloom. It emanated from her. You could smell it mingled with cloying cigarette smoke and spritely nicotine chewing gum. She needed both in order to function. I supposed I should be grateful for her musical enthusiasm, if nothing else.

As the children left the hall, mayhem was the order of the day. I had never witnessed anything like it. The deputy head stepped in, contorted his face, which turned puce, and spat out the command, "Shut up, the lot of you, or you'll all be in at playtime! This is *your* time you're wasting." (Do people STILL say that?) His accent took me way back to my student days. He was from Gateshead. As he turned his back on his class of year six children, they sniggered and mimicked his prune-like face brilliantly. I chose to pretend I hadn't seen, but I don't think I fooled anybody.

I walked back to my office and sank into my overlarge faux leather chair and realised that my feet didn't touch the carpet.

Within seconds my secretary Mrs Walters came in to let me know that one of the Italian families had arrived to see me, and did I have time now? "How thoughtful of them," I said, making the assumption that they had come to welcome me and wish me luck. I stood to invite them in. They didn't need an invitation. The grandfather was first through the door catching me off guard as he backed me up against the spearmint-coloured wall. When he could get no closer to me he stopped. The grandma, mama, Uncle Alphonso and an overbearing lady in a faded black crepe dress, which my mum would've called "poor black", and an alarming shade of red lipstick all piled in behind him. The whole thing was like an excerpt from an early Laurel and Hardy silent movie. Except the silence didn't last. With his index finger perilously close to my nose, and the rest of the cast bobbing up behind him to catch a glimpse of the action, he whispered a torrent of Italian/English abuse beginning with, "You are the woman and shoulda be at the sinka ina the home…" and ending with, "We are froma Sicily, froma where the Mafia isa coming, you willa do wella to remember this." With that, and a final gesticulation of his index finger, they turned as one and stumbled out leaving me to wonder what that was all about. Was I to worry about a horse's head turning up in my bed? I made a mental note to tackle some research on Sicily.

Mrs Walters, a wonderful Irish lady, came in smiling with a cup of tea. She gestured to the departing Mafia, "They're Italian for God's sake," she said, speaking with her soft Irish lilt as if that explained everything. I nodded as if it made perfect sense. It didn't. As a young teenager I had worked for a wealthy Italian family selling ice cream in their coffee bar in town. The large family was handsome, gregarious, flattering and stylish, and I loved every minute working for them. It was unlikely that I would ever travel as far as Italy, but every Saturday Italy came to me in the centre of town. I dreamt of marrying a Mario of my dreams and settling in Venice where we'd cruise up and down the canals selling ice cream and singing opera.

Mrs Walters placed the tea carefully on a stained, slightly curved cardboard coaster sporting a greying picture of Bristol's suspension bridge, and went back to the school office. She proffered her parting shot over her right shoulder as she left the room, "The travellers will be next." Her words hung in the room like mist over the peat bogs. I could hardly wait.

They were *almost* next, but not before I met "Our Beckay". Our Beckay (Rebecca) was four-years-old and determined not to come to school without putting up the mother and father of a fight. Her mother dragged her in through the back door, stumbling over abandoned wellies of the reception class, amidst a string of blue language of which it would appear there was no end.

Our Beckay screamed in protest, fists flailing, as she planted herself on her bottom in the doorway in an attempt to stall her mother's progress. It didn't work though. Her mother simply dragged her along like a baby Barbie she'd found left out in the road, or tied to the back of a refuse lorry. She literally dumped her at my feet, flicked her unruly hair from her face and, turning to me while trying to take a decent breath, said, "She's all yours. Oh, nice to meet you, Miss." With that she turned on her heels, gave her hair another flick, dismissive this time, and left the building…and her loudly protesting daughter.

I turned to Our Beckay. "Hello," I said smiling.

"Piss off!" she yelled.

Okay, I thought, that's how we're going to play it. I reached down to help her to her little feet. Bless her. She stood slowly, and with her steely brown eyes looking up at me she took a hefty swing with her right foot and kicked me on the shin. She got me twice more before heading for the front door in a sprint which I hadn't foreseen. I followed her, half hopping, worried that she'd make it to the busy road outside. Luckily she was too short to reach the door handle. I picked her up, kicking and yelling and cursing, and sat her on a bean-bag in the office. While I dealt with the post her sobs grew further apart and she fell asleep. I was under no delusion that Our Beckay would return to school tomorrow a reformed character. I had a feeling that school was the least of her worries. I was right. With an alcoholic often absent father, a younger brother, and a mother with the parenting skills of Caligula, Our Beckay was old before her time. If that wasn't enough to cope with it would appear that their high-rise flat had a revolving door policy through which a constant flow of uncles from a selection of continents came and went.

By the end of my first day I had been welcomed by the following: Travellers, "So you're the missus they're talking about."

Social Services: "We need a meeting, or rather a series of meetings, soon as you settle in."

The community police: "Welcome to the funny farm," was offered.

The younger officer sniggered and rolled his eyes as if to say, "He's a one mind!"

And finally, the landlord of the club next door who was cleaning up vomit deposited by last night's revellers on the school drive. (Why didn't he do that BEFORE school started? The foyer reeked!) "Hello, darlin', you'll brighten up the place eh? Give us a shout if you need anything mind!" I'd like a vomit-free drive for starters.

The staff meeting at the end of the first day was sabotaged by the folk singer who arrived late, smoke swirling round her lackadaisical hair, gum pushed from one side of her mouth to the other in a kind of rhythmic motion. I couldn't help thinking she looked rather like a ruminating camel. "Hymn books," she said. I wondered if this was code for something.

"Hymn books?" I replied.

"Yes, bloody hymn books...falling apart. I'm sick of 'em. We need new ones."

"Okay, perhaps we could begin with each of you making a wish list of resources so that we can..." that's as far as I got.

"Sod that!" she said as she spooned coffee into an enormous mug which proclaimed, "Best Teacher" round the grimy, chipped rim. The mugs obviously weren't personalised in this staffroom then. "Soddin' things are falling apart!"

We finally moved on from the "Soddin' hymn books" and by 4.45pm I closed the meeting. I sat in my office staring at the spearmint-coloured wall opposite, and determined that St Mark's School was going to undergo a change. A change of revolutionary proportions. Appropriate in a Catholic school, I mused as I made my way to the car at 7.15pm to the cat-calls of the guys hanging over the wall demarcating the boundary between school and the club, their pints balanced precariously like toby jugs on the top shelf in a charity shop.

I joined the motorway, and as I left the city behind, speeding toward another beautiful sunset, I thought it was like the end of a crass movie. Except that this wasn't the end. It was the beginning, the beginning of something amazing. I decided I loved my new/old school, and the entire community.

As the year progressed, hymn books were recycled and replaced by overheads much against the folk singer's wishes. I had an issue which would've had the nuns on their wool-clad knees offering novenas every first Friday of the month until the end of the millennium.

It began with the recruitment of new staff who came through the front doors of St Mark's like the first breath of spring air after a seemingly endless series of arduous winters. Actually, it didn't begin there. It began with a number of teachers deciding that, as things developed during the school year, it was time to move on to pastures new. The folk singer was leaving at Christmas to become an undertaker's assistant, and Sister Imogen who taught in the infants was recalled from her dismal classroom and spoon-fed children to the "Mother House" of her order in France. Her move also was to take place at Christmas.

I was stonewalled by almost all of the Irish community as the news spread, like an oozing puddle at the feet of a frightened child, that Sister Imogen was leaving. I was delighted she was leaving. It was nothing personal, I rather liked her round smiling face and starched beige habit, but we differed in our understanding of the length of the school day amongst other pretty fundamental things. Sister Imogen told the children to stack their chairs at 1.45pm, go out to play for half an hour, and come back in for story time and napping which lasted until the bell announcing the end of the day at 3.30pm. I felt she'd be happier in the Mother House where it was okay for her to take a nap after 2.30pm. It wasn't just the shortening of the school day though. Unfortunately her passion for teaching had faded long ago like her fading beige, double-knit cardigan. I had no doubt of her love for the children, but her teaching style (there was only the one teaching style) was limited to the talk and chalk of her own childhood in Limerick. At SATs time in year two where she taught, the wee ones were required to write a story. Hilarious. The majority of the children could barely hold a conversation of even the simplest kind let alone write a story. So, to avoid the proverbial hitting the fan as it were, Sister Imogen wrote the stories for them. Simple solution, private, secure. The outcome? Ecstatic parents, congratulatory local education authority, extremely puzzled head teacher. I found myself echoing the words of "Mary" when given the news of her impending motherhood: "How can this be?" I asked myself.

The most articulate children in year two could probably manage a couple of sentences written in dialect. The others, bless their hearts, were still struggling to spell their own names correctly let alone write a story of any length requiring imagination. I thought I'd begin my investigation with the most readily open source, a group of year two children. They were more than eager to dob on Sister Imogen, and eager voices were in competition to dish the dirt. "We never writ they stories, Miss, Sister did 'em." Out of the mouths of babes.

We were well into the school year and the children were slipping into inertia which could, if left untreated, develop into an epidemic of disaffection. Hence the return to the Mother House with much weeping and gnashing of teeth from the disgruntled Irish families and several loyal parishioners who, themselves, had been taught by Sister Imogen and, "It never done them no 'arm mind."

I was eventually blessed with some newly qualified female teachers, young, energetic, creative teachers who chose to wear trousers. Perfectly understandable when spending your days surrounded by budding Van Goghs with fully loaded brushes and all the directional prowess of the proverbial blundering bull in a china shop. Trousers weren't the problem, but the low waistbands were and, as crop tops inched away from the waist, waistbands dropped to the hips and the resulting exposed centimetres of flesh in between often sported a back view suitable for pole dancers only, *not* for teachers. Diamante hearts, lacy bows, even saucy Minnie Mouse wedged in between bottom cleavage, all clearly visible whenever a teacher bent to listen to a child or wipe a dripping nose. After hoping against hope that the fashion would change, discomfort would prevail resulting in the choice of sensible underwear from M&S, or even someone else would notice and say something, I had to face up and address the issue. What I failed to do when I called an extra staff meeting for the purpose was to tell the three male members of staff they wouldn't be needed. The ensuing embarrassment as I launched into, "thongs are fine for the weekend, however I don't wish to see any more of the black lacy number, or the satin-sky-blue version with the sparkly heart winking out from a sagging rear end that we've all glimpsed this week..." worked for me better than any rhetoric. Thongs became a thing, or a thong of the past. I guess I won't be sued for discrimination on the grounds of gender in *that* particular meeting. The showdown did more for the dress code of the teachers than any policy document. Men smartened up and crisp white shirts brought an air of purpose to the classrooms. The caretaker remained the only staff member untouched by the initial changes. I think he probably had a thing for the folk singer. They were both heavy smokers who enjoyed the complicity of the boiler room to indulge the habit. In fact, the only time I saw the caretaker shift from his sentry position, propping up the bookcase in the foyer, was when he doggedly followed the folk singer round to the boiler room at break time in the morning ferreting in his jeans pockets for his Benidorm cigarette lighter.

Having a stationary caretaker did have its positive side though. I always knew where to find him should I need anything. He could signpost all manner of tools from his semi-prone position which meant that his leaning could continue without disturbance while I chased around the school delving into long forgotten cupboards for the even longer-forgotten screwdrivers. I must've been soft in the head back then. I felt obliged to leave him as he was. He was happy enough I assumed, but as he rarely smiled it was difficult to judge and, like the rusted toolbox I eventually found in the darker reaches of the caretaker's cupboard underneath a nibbled cardboard box containing Jeyes tissue toilet paper, if disturbed too much would give up the ghost and disintegrate. He was the flaky-pastry man as far as I was concerned. If I left him long enough he would be the author of his own destiny, his own crumbling destiny.

Chapter 16

As we approached Christmas in that first year, the phone call I'd been expecting and dreading came. I confided my fears to Mrs Walters. By now we had realised we shared a similar sense of humour. She had a dry wit and a priceless knowledge of every family in school. The cause of my anxiety? We were to have an OFSTED inspection – soon. There were two ways of looking at this my colleagues suggested. Firstly, if the school was put into special measures (failed), blame could be attributed to the previous head teacher. Secondly, I could claim staff changes and general upheaval hoping for a reprieve or at least a Satisfactory judgement. Friends tried to reassure me but I gradually learnt to switch off the platitudes and decide how to prepare in time. We had three weeks or so before the inspectors arrived and they would be with us for four days. I remember pondering to what extent I could blag enough to keep us out of trouble. There was no way we would be judged Outstanding, the highest accolade, but I was determined we would keep far enough away from the other end of the spectrum to hold our heads high.

The weeks leading up to the inspection separated the sheep from the lambs or, to be perfectly clear, it sorted out staff with balls from those without. There were no surprises. The folk singer continued to live in a kind of misplaced, *blasé* world where she delivered perfect lessons day in, day out. She was obdurate and openly thwarted any offers of assistance declaring that, "any inspector observing my lessons can take it or leave it. I do what I do, end of. AND, I'm on my way out of here remember?" Not one to mince words. The deputy head led the headless chicken dance with aplomb and was only slightly more useful than a paper colander. I dreaded the first morning of the inspection as I had a strong feeling that he was saving his cream linen suit for the occasion. I was concerned on two counts. One, the inspectors may mistake him for an ice cream man. Two, whenever he wore it I had an overwhelming urge to tear it off him and iron it!

My leadership team, I'm being kind, consisted of the deputy, the maths co-ordinator and the folk singer. Sounds like the beginning of a Michael McIntyre joke doesn't it? Meetings with them were never that side-splittingly funny though I can assure you. Pre-inspection meetings took on a sombre air as we looked at what data there was and the trends shaping up over the last few years. In this area my deputy came up trumps...figures being his strength. It didn't make for an encouraging read, so we had to do our best to spin the information as best we could. I must admit I was pleasantly surprised at some of the suggestions offered. Several of them lacked even a whiff of the truth, and were thrown out despite being plausible. Eventually we composed a pre-inspection report for submission. We were slightly liberal with the truth describing a strategic plan which, to date, had only been the stuff of dreams. We would also play the new head teacher card if necessary.

I decided that the game was to keep the inspectors moving and ply them with coffee and cakes at every opportunity. I must've lost a couple of pounds in weight that week just sprinting up to the corner shop and back every day to replenish stocks, and Mrs Walters almost ran out of embroidered tray cloths. The other important plan of campaign was to entice the inspectors into classes where good lessons were taking place once their own schedules eased up, and herding them away from any classroom where there were early signs of pandemonium. At times I felt like Disney's Road Runner.

The statuesque caretaker was galvanised into action. Buckets and mops careered through the school whisking up chips and children in their wake. Light bulbs were replaced, shelves were put up, floors were scrubbed and carpets vacuumed to within a centimetre of threadbare. I became anxious for his safety. I'd never seen him move with such purpose before. In fact I'd rarely seen him move at all but, give him his due, he was not about to let the school down. I drew the line when he suggested taking the hall curtains down for a wash though. Not that I was too worried about him by this stage, but the health of the curtains was dubious, and I wasn't convinced they would survive the dry cleaners.

Mrs Walters and I took a critical look at her office and decided that a few leprechauns had to take a break on the top shelf of the medical room in order to restore a touch of professionalism. The map of our fantasy island was also relegated to a filing cabinet under "W" for wishful thinking. The island had become a focus of interest for many visitors to the office, but we had sworn each other to secrecy and promised not to tell a living soul what it was all about. To the north of the island was a list. Mrs W's wish list of males of the species she'd like to get on a desert island. She'd add to her list regularly and would then make derogatory comments about the men to the south of the island where my captives were held. Amongst the chosen few were Richard Gere and Mr Williams, a local undertaker who made me laugh and sometimes brought doughnuts into the staffroom. Our lists were as different as chalk and cheese. We were nothing if not compatible. She'd peruse with a dreamy look in her eyes sighing, "there'll be no need for seven discs, a Bible or a book of my choice... just leave me my gorgeous men." Terry Wogan was her favourite. I had no problem with that. Terry's always been a tad too beige for my more exotic taste. The map peeled off the wall leaving smudges of Blu Tack behind as a reminder that this was purely a temporary measure and normal service would be resumed as soon as possible. Meanwhile an A4 poster of the Sacred Heart took its place.

A swathe of inspectors arrived early one Tuesday morning and sidled through the foyer, clipboards held aloft purposefully. I'd heard of the strange behaviour of course, but part of me didn't quite believe it. Here it was though, before my very eyes. Initially they moved as one like a shoal of tropical fish, then, without warning, they dispersed going their separate ways, investigating this unchartered land, this unknown terrain called St Mark's.

At the end of day two, Mr Watchet, principal inspector, edged toward me in the hall where I was reprimanding a child who had left his lunch box behind the water feature a while back. We had turned the school upside down to find it as his mum said it cost her a bloody arm 'n' leg. The previous night a curious aroma had led one of our cleaners, who actually *possessed* a sense of smell, to the water feature. Behind it she found the lunch box and its abandoned contents. After taking a closer look I had every sympathy with the child who had ditched it there. Tuna and tomato sauce sandwiches which had seen better days, yoghurt with a wonderful mould specimen making its way along the side of the carton, and a gristle-ridden sausage with one bite taken appeared to be attempting the great escape. The lunch box and its contents left the building. It would be a day or two before the smell followed.

Mr Watchet tapped his pencil along the top edge of his clipboard. He inhaled and pointed the pencil in a sweeping gesture around the hall as he said, "The hall is too small. It doesn't meet requirements." He wasn't telling me anything I hadn't already spotted and I found myself wondering what possible reply there could be other than, "Well, go figure", or "What an outstanding observation", and after just two days. I decided not to dignify his remark with a verbal response but simply looked at him, smiled a tight-lipped smile, and raised an eyebrow, a trick I'd learnt while studying drama at college. I knew it would come in handy one day.

He wasn't satisfied with that, oh no. He wanted me to speak. "Yes, Mr Inspector, thank you, I'll pop into Asda on the way home and buy another hall". No, that wouldn't do. I looked him in the eye, luckily I was wearing my FM heels that day. "Well, if you make enough of a fuss about it in your report, maybe the government will fund the extension so that it *does* meet requirements." I smiled and turned on my heels almost executing a classic Dick Emery trip as I strode away. Maintaining my confident stride and enough dignity to get me out of his sight I imagined him standing there, marooned with his clipboard and sweaty hands. In my mind I heard Mrs Walters pronouncing "Do one"!

The following day the parish priest from a neighbouring church came in to head up assembly with the infants. The theme was "Peace" and I thought one of the inspectors would appreciate being present. Father Riley began by asking the children to offer a sign of peace to the child on either side. This is part of the Mass and something the children are familiar with as they attend school Mass regularly. They duly obeyed amidst giggles of embarrassment as several of the children bum-shuffled across the floor in the direction of the inspector, who had not a single clue as to what was going on, to offer him the sign of peace, in this case several sticky handshakes and a half-hug.

Calm finally settled once more and Father Riley asked how grown-ups might make peace if they'd had a disagreement. "Our ma and her Billy snog!" was offered by Tanya amidst screeches of laughter and stifled guffaws. I must admit I found it difficult to remain unmoved as I thanked Tanya for her contribution and remarked how lovely it was to kiss and make up after an argument.

Father Riley was looking as if he wished the theme had been something less provocative like vandalism in the area, or the recent suicide in the block of flats behind school. Something a little less contentious. He would be sure to get plenty of less embarrassing responses from the former, and perhaps one or two culprits amongst older siblings. He continued with, "I wonder if any of you know the sign for peace that was used during the Second World War?" I thought that was pushing it a bit. After all the children were aged between four and six and several of them were challenged to name their transitory grandparents let alone have any knowledge of World War II. A child volunteered an answer and sure enough demonstrated the V for Victory his granddad had shown him. "Thank you, son, that's absolutely right," beamed Father Riley. Douane shot his hand up. My heart sank. Douane could always be relied upon to come up with something controversial and I hoped that he would go unnoticed by Father Riley. No such luck. Father Riley jumped straight in with "Ah, Douane, what have you to say, my child?"

Douane stood and clocked his audience. He sensed the anticipation. I held my breath. "That's the sign for victory," he said raising his two fingers toward the other children. "And," he smirked as he turned his hand around with the fingers facing him now, "that's the sign for fuck off!" Dear God, please let the floor of this teeny, tiny, less than regulation size hall open and swallow us all NOW! I prayed as all hell let loose amongst the infants and the inspector grasped his clipboard close to his chest and beat a hasty retreat. Father Riley blessed the children and left.

"Let's sing, 'Cauliflowers Fluffy'," I bellowed, while pounding out the introductory chords on the liquor-stained piano donated by the Dew-drop Inn in Bedminster. Oh the joys of headship.

The next criticism fell into the human resources category and was brought to me by Mrs Smyth-Clay. Double-barrelled names eh...why would you bother? She had already gained the rather harsh descriptor of "the iron fist in a velvet glove" from staff experiencing her feedback after lesson observations. Now she presented herself in my office and I was awaiting the treatment. She began asking me, in a soft voice, about the longevity of many of the staff. There was little I could say about that. They weren't going anywhere, at least not in a hurry. Next up was this corker. "You don't appear to have any staff members from any cultural background apart from White British. Is there an explanation for this?"

I thought long and hard before replying, "There's a perfectly simple explanation in answer to your question, Mrs Smyth-Clay, and it's the same reason we don't have any one-legged, partially sighted staff at St Mark's either. No one from those particular categories has ever applied to work here."

Call it intuition, but I have a feeling that wasn't the answer she had in mind. She dropped her voice to a hard baritone for the next question. "There appears to be a lack of ethnic role models visible in displays around the school also."

It was then that I began to wonder whether *she* was actually partially sighted. I had brought with me, from my last school, a series of posters depicting the life of Christ which were displayed all over the school with a handwritten, child-friendly text beneath each one. Without saying a word I motioned to Mrs Smyth-Clay to follow me into the foyer where there hung a one metre by two metres poster of the *Last Supper*. Each disciple looked like the burly fishermen they were. Each one was also black. They surrounded a black Christ at the table. "I'm so sorry you missed this beautiful picture, Mrs Smyth-Clay, I expect you were concentrating on negotiating the baby buggies in the foyer each morning. Never mind, you have one day left to point it out to your fellow inspectors. Oh yes, before I forget, you will find Martin Luther King on the wall opposite the boys' toilets, Gandhi on the right hand side of the corridor just before the cycle rack, and Mother Teresa is usually in the library corner in year five." For heaven's sake, how long can this go on?

The meeting at the close of play on the penultimate day of the inspection did not go as I had expected. I was dismayed to learn that the lesson observations were perilously close to landing us in deep shit. Basically we needed a few more lessons to be judged Good or Very Good, as was the terminology at the time, to keep us out of the mire. I spoke with the teachers and explained the unenviable situation. I played down the drama of a potential failure to achieve a Good or even Satisfactory overall judgement, and encouraged them to recall past lessons which they knew had been fabulous and perhaps revitalise them for tomorrow. I wasn't that surprised to see them all but rub their chins in deep concentration as they tried to come up with a lesson, any lesson, meeting that description in the memorable past. Then I asked them to go home, dig out the pertinent plans and revamp them in time to come back the next day and wow the inspectors. I even said in the hiatus of team enthusiasm that I'd teach a dance lesson too. The following morning we were all in school before the inspectors. I dusted off the *Last Supper* in the foyer and suggested that someone check out the demise of Martin Luther King et al. There was an air of excitement and camaraderie, there really was! I decided that I LOVED OFSTED. It was bringing about a sea change amongst the staff who busied themselves making last minute adjustments to resources and themselves.

I was pleased with my dance lesson. Not only did it have everything the programme of study required, it was based on a tribal dance I had joined with during my time in rural India when I was there helping with teacher training in the mission schools. After a while I turned my attention to Tyrone, a child with Asperger syndrome. I asked if he would be my partner. We'd already spent a lot of time together this term as he was experiencing difficulty settling with his new teacher. We did some low level movement mirroring each other. Progress was slow but, to my astonishment, Tyrone began to respond affably enough. We eventually made it to a standing position, stretching toward the vast expanse of blue sky we had conjured up in our imaginings. As the music stopped and we ended the lesson with the usual performance element I knew the lesson had been a success.

Later in the day I had feedback from the inspector who had observed my lesson. "Of course it can't be judged Excellent because not every child progressed enough." Here we go again I thought. The old children as commodities not humans factor trotted out for the umpteenth time. I couldn't let it rest.

"What would have had to happen to warrant a higher judgement?"

He checked his notes. "The child you partnered hardly moved from floor level movement." My heart sank. The euphoria I'd experienced when dancing with Tyrone had been matched by his massive smile and vigorously nodding head as we stretched up to the sky. How did the inspector not see that? How did he not realise that for a child with severe Asperger syndrome this could've been a major milestone this term? I looked at him and held his gaze for longer than was comfortable. I hope in that gaze I managed to convey exactly what I thought of his judgement. I decided to maintain my dignity. Nothing was going to detract from the exhilaration of dancing with Tyrone.

Chapter 17

We survived our first inspection and celebrated. I must admit though that when the report was published I wasn't exactly ecstatic. The overall judgement was that we were a Satisfactory school. I knew the judgement was as good as it could be given the previous twenty years head in the sand style of management, but I was disappointed. I felt we had let the children and parents down, and I made a secret promise that our next OFSTED would be much better. God willing.

The morning after the report was sent home to parents I was apprehensive. How would they respond? After all, I was the new head teacher so it would automatically follow in some minds that I was to blame. I had no idea what to expect from them. During assembly I congratulated the children on their role during OFSTED. For the most part they behaved impeccably. Okay, maybe not Douane although he had demonstrated an admirable confidence. As I headed for my office after the children had returned to their classes looking extremely pleased with themselves, Mrs W told me there was a group of parents waiting to see me. I knew it was too good to last. I reapplied my lipstick, straightened my white shirt and stretched my skirt so that it almost met my knees. I didn't wish to appear cheap, did I? The group had a self-appointed leader known for her lack of diplomacy and loud, clear voice. Her expression was stern and I braced myself for the worst.

"We knows our school," she began, in her broad Bristolian accent, as the others nodded encouragement. Oh God, it's a lynch mob! I thought. She repeated, "We knows our school and we wants you to know we don't give a toss what they inspectors said. They can sod off. We loves our school… Yeah…an' our kids loves our school."

Much nodding of heads and, "Yeah…that's right, Shaz, you tell 'er. Yeah…sod off the lot of 'em." With that they turned and left, lighting up cigarettes as they pushed buggies and lugged sticky toddlers and shopping bags up the drive.

Mrs Walters popped her head round the door. "Didn't I tell you they'd be fine? Let's have a coffee." I couldn't refuse any more than I could stop grinning, or prevent the tear coursing down my cheek. It was at that moment that the fondness I had for the parents transformed into love.

OFSTED didn't reappear for another four years by which time I was growing my own team. During the honeymoon period working in the city, my brother-in-law, who was also a head teacher, warned me that you have to be prepared to work with the team you inherit. True enough. However, if the team you inherit isn't fit for purpose, it isn't long before desperate measures are called for.

With the folk singer amongst the dead men, literally, and Sister Imogen resting in France, it wasn't long before one or two others fell away from the ranks. My team was being picked carefully. I was only looking to recruit for the premier division after all. Around the same time my wonderful Mrs Walters decided to concentrate her efforts on enticing Terry Wogan to leave the current Mrs Wogan and move to the island. I pictured her grasping his hand and his Blankety Blank cheque book and pen and heading into the sunset. The country was experiencing a mass exodus of administrative staff as the technological age swept them all off their feet in a tsunami of new systems which was far more efficacious than the grim reaper.

I had no idea how I would cope without Mrs W. She was my rock, my *confidante*, we were like Morecambe and Wise, inseparable. We had enviable comic timing and had become expert at feigning control when school threatened to overwhelm us.

I lost sleep pondering school without Mrs W. She held my innermost secrets, my lapses in self-confidence and she was utterly safe. I pictured the office without her. It resembled the non-negotiable, long, straight line of a hospital monitor registering death. It was almost unbearable until the day she came to my rescue yet again. Mrs W confided in me that her daughter, Glenda, was about to leave her job as a PA in an import company in Bristol. As we talked, idly at first, it became apparent that Glenda might consider applying for her mother's old job. I hardly knew Glenda, but I knew enough to know that apples don't fall far from the tree. She interviewed and was immediately taken on. As Mrs W left we vowed to be in touch. Glenda had a quicker, sharper wit than her mother. She didn't suffer fools either. The parents loved her and were wary of her in equal measure. Perfect. Without shifting her gaze from the computer screen she would reprimand a passing parent with the misfortune of being tardy with dinner money payment with all the charm of Anne Robinson disposing of the weakest link on her TV quiz. The miscreant would burrow into her Asda carrier bag and deposit the money in loose change, while giving Glenda the evil eye. It was water off a duck's back. No one got past Glenda.

Around the four-year-mark, I knew most of the issues facing the majority of families in school. It wasn't a steep learning curve, it was more like conquering Everest. Financial challenges faced approximately two thirds of the parents but most managed to keep afloat and remain positive. Yes, unemployment was pretty bad, but worse still was a growing apathy amongst many young couples. It spread like some kind of silent, progressive, terminal illness. There was almost an audible, collective sigh of resignation whenever a group of them got together to swap tales of misery.

I used to ponder how parents could claim that money was tight when it came to funding dinner money or a school trip and yet found enough to feed an addiction. A boisterous, tattooed dad made it perfectly clear to me, and half of the estate, that I needed to get my priorities sorted out. This was in response to my mention of a substantial debt accumulating due to lack of payment of his children's dinner money. I stood facing the parent in question. His unruly hair had seen better days, his eyes functioned independently, he wore designer threadbare jeans spattered with what looked like red wine stains, and his T-shirt boasted "Guns N' Roses 89". As he left school with three children in tow, his partner met him just beyond the school gates. She was pushing a shabby buggy with the latest addition to the family screaming in protest. She stopped to link arms with her man and wander into the club next door leaving the older children outside to "mind the babber". It didn't take much to fathom out *their* priorities. I began to learn that a contributor to the anger and aggression demonstrated was poor living conditions. Lots of families lived in tower blocks overlooking the idling River Avon. Unknown to me, living in the soulless flats meant adhering to a timetable of sorts. For example, there was a launderette in the basement of the tower blocks. Due to the sheer numbers of families living there each one had specific laundry days allocated. If this was missed for any reason, you simply lost your laundry day for that week. So, while washing piled ever higher, and children wore the same clothes day in and day out for an extra week, tempers frayed. The most accessible outlet for the head of steam was school. After all, no bank manager, doctor or landlord would see you without an appointment, but teachers, especially head teachers, presented an easy target. The open door policy has its downside.

I remember one mother storming in to the office with Glenda in hot pursuit berating her. There was no doubt as to her opinion of anyone breaching the barrier of the front office to reach me.

"It's okay, Glenda, thank you," I said, in an attempt to quell the storm. "I have a minute or two before my first appointment." I asked the parent, we'll call her Mrs Maggs, to take a seat. First mistake.

"Take a seat? I'll fucking take a seat! I'll take a seat and wrap it round the neck of that kid in our Justin's class who stole his Pokemon cards!" *Sacré bleu!* I thought, anything but the sacred Pokemon cards.

This was a hanging offence. Pokemon cards had been banned two weeks ago after the first accusation of theft. It turned out that the child in question had swapped his and then decided he wanted them back because the water pistol he swapped them for wouldn't squirt. At the time it brought forth a barrage of similar complaints mostly unsolvable as the children bent the truth to fit their needs. At times it was rather like solving *The Times* cryptic crossword, with clues seemingly leading nowhere except up a blind alley.

I began by commiserating with Mrs Maggs. She was having none of it. "Get the bugger round yer. I'll sort 'im out. 'Is mother's as bad. She wiv the pink fuckin' hair-do. Stupid mare. I'll 'ave 'er after school too, mind!"

I recalled the "pink fuckin' hair-do" and indeed the neon purple hot pants, vivid orange crop top and platform shoes which completed the ensemble. Oh, that's the bugger's mother, I thought, and made a mental note to 'ave 'er after school too, concerning the bugger's unsavoury behaviour in general.

Mrs Magg's toddler, Milo, having escaped the confines of his tired pushchair had shuffled his rather overladen bottom to the electrical lead of the printer behind my desk. He was about to sink his teeth into it when I noticed him. I stooped to pick him up and rescue him from potential harm when his mum pushed me out of the way, hoiked him up by his right arm and plonked him on my chair. "That's elfinsafety that is."

"I'm sorry?" was all I could come up with.

"Elfinsafety, you knows elfinsafety? It's all over the news. I could sue you for that!" She appeared to have forgotten her original reason for coming in as she grabbed Milo for the second time, virtually threw him into his crusty pushchair and turned to me brandishing her leopard skin bag saying, "Don't think you've 'eard the last of this mind!" She left, cursing and swearing about the lack of "elfinsafety" in this "fuckin' school".

I sat down to record the incident, good practice if you want to survive for any length of time in almost any school. Gradually, I began to feel an oozing dampness seeping around my bottom. I stood up, alarmed, only to find that the force of "Our Milo's" plonking onto my chair by his anxious mother had prompted leakage of the aforementioned overladen nappy. Oh God, is there no end to the joys of this job? Glenda held the fort while I changed into my trackie bottoms, stuffed my knickers and skirt into a plastic bag from the school kitchen and drove home to shower and change. The following morning Mrs Maggs came back. I was ready. Boy was I ready! She knocked on my office door which made me suspect that she'd brought a solicitor with her to pursue the elfinsafety claim, and was trying to impress. I took a deep breath and was preparing to quite enjoy the next couple of minutes when her hand came around the door clutching a Spiderman lunch box. I couldn't believe her audacity. After yesterday's fiasco she was going to ask me to take a lunch box to her son's class. Her bulk followed the proffered polythene box. Our Milo crawled from behind her clutching a handful of sour cream and chive flavoured crisps. "You've got kids 'aven't you?" she asked.

"Well, yes I have..."

"Give 'em these. I made 'em last night, once the kids were abed an' the old man went out. Rockie Road they're called, your kids'll like 'em. All kids likes 'em. I missed me laundry day see." There was a pause as she looked down at Our Milo. I thanked her and took the Spiderman lunch box she held out. She left mumbling, "Yeah, me bloody laundry day…fuck…no socks nor clean pants for Our Bev… she'll kill me later…missed me bloody laundry day…" I lifted the lid, cautiously. There, sure enough, were half a dozen Rockie Roads Did I detect a faint whiff of sour cream and chives? The unexpected was the only constant at St Mark's. This day was no exception. I had a phone conversation with a lady calling from Canada whose husband had been offered a terrific career move. You know, the sort which defines your future and that of your family. After protracted discussions regarding moving their children, leaving friends etc. they had decided to grasp the offer and move to England for four years. They had two children she told me, a son of secondary school age and another son who would be year two in primary school. She particularly wanted a church school and, while researching the area near the city centre, had read that St Mark's had a good reputation for caring for children with special educational needs. Music to my ears. She went on to explain that Gareth had Down's syndrome and was attending a special school in Ontario. The family and his teachers felt that he would progress well in a mainstream school, and she wondered whether we could discuss the possibility. After a series of such transatlantic discussions we agreed that my special needs co-ordinator, Sadie, would spend a week with the family in Ontario to assess Gareth's needs. On her return we would gather all the records and actual experience with Gareth together and make an informed decision.

I couldn't have predicted the height of excitement and volume of paperwork presented to me by Sadie later in the term as she returned from spending an exhausting week with the family in Ontario. Despite this she punctuated her verbal reports with, "We can take Gareth, we really can, Mrs C. It won't involve much expenditure to make the necessary changes". The pound sign popped into my mind followed by the not too healthy outturn statement of the year's budget. What had she said? "It won't involve much expenditure to make the necessary changes." I dismissed the morbid financial thoughts ticking over in my head now on a screen the size of a financial floor in Wall Street. I looked at Sadie and saw the eagerness in her eyes. In the week she'd spent in Ontario she had fallen hopelessly in love with

Gareth and was fired up with an enviable zeal and project plans for furniture replacement, signage etc.

"We will need to hit the ground running when Gareth arrives." Oh my goodness. I'd said it before I engaged my practical brain. We began to plan for the changes to accommodate the specific needs of one little boy travelling halfway round the world to St Mark's.

We would do everything in our power to welcome Gareth at the start of the new academic year. Little did we realise just what a huge difference this little boy would make to our school and our lives.

Chapter 18

The Woodworth family arrived. It was delightful to meet them and interesting to put faces to the names after all this time. However, prior to their arrival we were stretched to the limits of patience as we battled with the local authority (LA) to obtain funding so that we could prepare with the basics necessary to help Gareth settle, and to keep him safe. We met with bureaucracy at its most ludicrous. The argument was that funding could not be provided until a full assessment of Gareth could be made in school. Reports, video footage of Gareth at home and in his current school made during Sadie's week in Ontario, plus her own extensive observations had to be confirmed by the LA's own assessment team sometime in September. I wearily lifted the phone to yet another department in the LA in a last attempt to plead our case. "Please just listen," I began, quietly, "Gareth has Down's syndrome. As you know, it is a permanent condition. His difficulties in September will be those he experiences on a daily basis right now coupled with the adjustments encountered when moving home and school from one country to another. There must be some way the LA can fund basic resources before he arrives next term." I waited for the reply to which we'd all become accustomed over the past few weeks.

Then, chirpy as you like, came the reply. "Oh yes, of course. There's emergency funding." You're familiar with the expression, "You could've hit me down with a feather", well, the feather wasn't necessary. After the call I laughed, cried and jumped up and down with Sadie. We also swore quite a bit. Quite a lot actually. Well, the exasperation had been suppressed to date. It was a lid we had both clamped in place in order to retain some dignity, while at the same time wanting to yell from the rooftops how innocuous and incredible bureaucracy can get. I believe we had reached explosion point.

The following September Gareth arrived in a flurry. He burst through the front doors of St Mark's with his mother in hot pursuit, her Canadian accent causing more than a little curiosity. "Gareth, honey, wait for mommy! Gareth, honey, WAIT FOR MOMMY!" as they flew past in a blur of uniform, school bags and desperately smiling faces.

This was to become the routine for the next couple of months as Gareth led a chase of teachers, support staff and other children as he charged about the school seeking an open door. We must've resembled an illustration from a children's storybook, possibly *The Gingerbread Man* or *The Enormous Turnip*, as we all joined the chase behind a beaming Gareth.

In no time at all Gareth became the friend everyone coveted from reception to year six. He was swamped on the school field where he learnt to make daisy chains, was swung up in the air by year six girls, raced and tackled by the boys, and maintained his broad, infectious grin throughout the continuous rough and tumble. He giggled and led us all on a merry dance! Talking of dance...he fell through Glenda's office door one afternoon, greeted us both and disappeared head first into the large cardboard Asda box containing spare PE kit. He resurfaced with a pair of garish lycra shorts smudged with neon flower heads. Not a typical choice perhaps, but Gareth had struck gold. He viewed them from every angle as if he couldn't quite believe his good fortune. He abandoned his school uniform with the speed of a stripper desperate to get the whole thing over with, while Glenda grabbed his airborne pants and wrestled him back into them. Trainers were next. But no, Gareth had seen the footwear he wanted and was heading straight back out into the hall where his learning support assistant, Zena, was setting up the music CD having left her own shoes on a bench nearby. Gareth made a beeline for them. They were gorgeous, Italian, high-heeled sandals. Zena had great taste in clothes and Gareth knew an expensive pair of shoes when he saw them. With renewed dexterity he slipped them on and began wobbling around the hall to the strains of "The Runaway Train Went Down The Track..." How apt I thought! What a sheer delight Gareth was.

Inspired, Glenda and I kicked off our shoes and joined the cavorting Gareth. He was impressed by our shapes and whooped with vigour as the runaway train gained momentum, and the adults in the room collapsed with laughter and exhaustion. For the two years Gareth was with us he taught us all so much. The children at St Mark's at that time experienced his unconditional love and responded like with like as if it were the most natural thing in the world. Which of course it is...for children.

Chapter 19

You know how you sometimes allow yourself to sit back and survey your surroundings and perhaps once in a blue moon a glimmer of satisfaction seeps through? Well I was experiencing something similar when my past caught up with me. I'd been caught out like that before, and since if I'm honest. Just as you are about to sigh with relief something unexpected happens to reign you in again, and set you back on your tip-toes as if to remind you not to take too much for granted. During a relatively calm period at St Mark's my days at the labour exchange caught up with me in a way I could never have dreamt. And they say lightning doesn't strike twice.

There was a child in year six, Hans, a beefy child built like a WWF wrestler. He had a singing voice like liquid silver. Smooth, clear, fluid and he was pitch perfect. I had mentioned this to his parents on a number of occasions because it was one of his few redeeming features. In retrospect, maybe his most redeeming feature. He wasn't popular. He used his strength to terrify and was rarely seen playing with anyone in particular. I knew that with the quality of his voice life could be very different for him. I think I almost made headway with his mother by suggesting that Hans apply for an audition at a private school in Somerset where they offered bursaries for musically talented children. I felt that Hans had a chance. She was a frail, gentle soul with natural blonde hair and large blue eyes. She had appeared in school recently at the end of the school day with a large bruise which was making its way from her right eyebrow toward her upper lip. It held all the colours of a threatening sky. She said she had "walked into a door"…that old chestnut. It was such an old chestnut that it was accepted as a given for domestic violence, and prevented having to say the words, "my husband hit me", thus breathing life into the situation, making it real. When I mentioned Hans' voice her eyes shone and she smiled knowingly. She looked around to see where her husband was and continued our conversation in muted tones as though we were plotting his upcoming unpleasant demise like a couple of gangster molls. Yes, she was aware of Hans' voice, though he rarely sang when his father was in the house. His father was a builder by trade, and would take little truck with anything other than outdoor, physical work. Mrs Wenger wanted Hans to have singing lessons but realised there was more chance of hell freezing over than Mr Wenger ever agreeing to that. She looked around again, furtively, and seeing her husband approaching with Hans smiled briefly and hurried off to join them. As they walked up the school drive it was clear that some altercation was taking place between them. Hans cleverly positioned himself so that no physical contact was possible between his mum and dad. She looked over her shoulder back to where I stood in the doorway, her eyes no longer shining. I wondered what she had been about to tell me.

Hans had been reprimanded several times for wrestling a certain child called Cauley. Hans had perfected a manoeuvre which began with an unannounced leap from behind on any unwitting child, progressed into a headlock, and then the grand finale comprising of slamming the victim into the ground before jumping on them. I believe it's called a pile driver. His favourite victim was Cauley who was skinny by comparison. What he lacked in stature he had in spades when it came to verbosity. He was also bright and had a sense of humour, all of which made him the more popular young lad of the two. All of which made him infuriate Hans.

There was an ongoing feud between the two boys. They sought each other out and sparred, often before an audience of idol-worshipping younger children who goaded each boy to fever pitch. One rainy day in October a situation blew up. Hans had pulled the dining chair out from under Cauley at lunchtime and, in retaliation, Cauley had grabbed the knife from his plate and threatened Hans. There was no imminent danger. Anyone who has used a school knife will know that they are harmless. Useless, in fact. Cutting through mashed potato is about the limit of the implement, but the underlying menace was unpleasant and needed addressing. After sorting out the two lads, thankfully without too much opposition, as Hans was twice my size and need not have complied if he had been really angry, I called both sets of parents to a meeting.

The meeting began with the boys explaining what had happened and then I read out the eye-witness accounts of which there were many including those of the ladies on duty and the deputy head teacher.

Both sets of parents agreed that their sons were equally to blame. Cauley had provoked Hans by taking his place at the table, and Hans had dealt with it by whisking away Cauley's chair. The rest is history. Suitable punishments were meted out and the families left the school comparatively okay with things, if a little shame-faced. I should've realised then that it was too easily settled. Something unnerved me about the swift outcome.

An hour later, Hans' father, Mr Wenger, came back to school. It was almost 5.30pm, it was early evening and dark outside, and the caretaker had prised himself away from the bookcase to walk the five metres to his home in a flat above the club. The one remaining teacher was in his classroom at the other end of the school. Glenda had just left. I sat at my computer finishing off some long overdue emails when there was a soft knocking at my door. This was unusual.

I called "Come in," and in came Mr Wenger, smiling. I remember thinking what an uncanny resemblance he had to Jack Nicholson in *One Flew over the Cuckoo's Nest*, a resemblance which I find to have its disadvantage as I have, to this day, instant recall of his face. Mr Wenger took one step into the room and stared at me. He was breathing noisily and I wondered whether he was a smoker. His round, reddening face was sweating profusely and seemed to be fixed in his Jack Nicholson leer.

He took another step, this time to face me across my desk. He leaned in and placed both his hands on the desk top, fingers chubby and splayed, boasting filthy, chipped nails.

"I don't like the way you dealt with Hans." I believe I got as far as drawing breath to reply when he whispered, "You'll be sorry." His sweaty fingers left cement prints on the desk top as he left as quietly as he had arrived, nodding his mole-speckled, balding head.

As I shut down the computer my hands were shaking. I wanted to go home – now. I walked round to the end classroom to let the remaining teacher know I was leaving in ten minutes and would be locking up. I thought I'd done a pretty good job at covering up my trembling persona, but he asked if everything was alright. Bright as a button, I replied, "Yeah…just tired that's all," as I turned on my heels and went to collect my briefcase, desperately trying to regain control of my quivering bottom lip. Fifteen minutes later, driving home in the pitch black, I replayed Mr Wenger's visit and wonder today why I hadn't simply called the police then and there. Head teachers think they should be able to rise above these things, quell racing hearts, and return to face another day without residual damage. They can't. Travelling down the motorway the following morning I succeeded in relegating last night's incident to the far reaches of my subconscious. It settled, momentarily snuggling there with hundreds of other unexploded improvised explosive devices.

After assembly I turned to have my morning briefing with Glenda. It was an excuse to catch up on the latest crack, rewind the previous evening's social misdemeanours and put our world to right. This morning was no exception, and as we were recovering from our first bout of hysterical laughter we spotted a late arrival attempting to sneak in unnoticed by performing a limbo under the window. It was Miley, a gorgeous, if unruly child. He was one of twelve children from an Irish traveller family, the recent additions being twin girls, born six weeks ago. How lucky can one lady get? His freckled face just about cleared the window sill of the sliding glass panes to Glenda's office. "Morning, Miley, how's your mum?" Glenda asked.

"Alright thanks, Miss."

"How about the beautiful new twins. When do we get to see them?"

"Don't know, Miss," he answered, shrugging and looking in the opposite direction. In an attempt to get him to open up a bit more, I asked how they were all getting on at home.

"Ah, sure not good, Miss."

"Oh, I'm sorry to hear that, Miley, what's wrong?"

"They're dead, Miss. The twins. Sure they're dead."

He stood there, forlorn, tired, obviously grief-stricken. I rushed round to where he stood on the other side of the window and bent down to be level with his face. Glenda was in shock, clucking round her office like a mother hen who'd just caught sight of a fox making

142

a meal of her eggs. "Oh, dear God...Jesus, Mary and Joseph...your poor mum...is she at home? Where's your dad? How did it happen?" the litany went on as I gazed at the saddest face imaginable.

"Oh, Miley," I began, "I'm so very sorry." I searched for the right words knowing full well that there *were* no right words. Time, indeed, stood still, without even a request for the clocks to stop. Glenda joined me where I stood with my arms around Miley. Slowly, he looked from one to the other as we struggled to find words with which to comfort him.

Then I noticed the stirring of a smile as it curled the corner of one mucky lip and he said, "Ah, Miss...only jokin'!" With that he grabbed his second-hand PE kit and headed at full pelt toward his class. I heard him hollering like Tarzan as he leapt the three steps from the hall to the junior corridor...at speed.

"The little toerag..." Glenda muttered through clenched teeth, as I leant against the wall trying to assimilate what had just happened. Glenda motioned toward the staffroom, I followed and, once safely behind the closed door, we corpsed with laughter as curses spilled from us both. You couldn't help loving Miley. I have no doubt he, and possibly his eleven siblings, will go far.

Later, as I sat to go through the vetted post which had made its way past Glenda's sifting scrutiny, I couldn't help wondering what Mr Wenger had meant the night before. Perhaps it was an empty threat intended to frighten, but with little substance like some 50s sci-fi film. This time, though, hiding behind the sofa wasn't an option. The best case scenario was that he'd feel I'd been sufficiently terrified the night before, and that would temporarily satiate his bullying appetite. I didn't allow my mind to go to the worst case scenario.

As it was I didn't have long to wait before Mr Wenger raised his sinister face again, but not before his frail, ash-blonde wife came to see me once more. She'd made an appointment. I hoped that she had given some thought to Hans' singing potential and I was ready to give her any help she might need to apply for a music scholarship in Somerset where his talent could be cultivated, and he stood a chance of escaping the iron grip of his already disappointed father.

Glenda showed her into my office while attempting to give me some sort of non-verbal warning by screwing up her face as if in pain. Before I had time to glean what the attempted charade was all about

Mrs Wenger, arm sporting a neon pink cast, apologised her way into my office. She stood there picking the fraying, grubby corner of her sling.

"Oh my goodness, Mrs Wenger…" I began.

She interrupted me with, "Yes, I know, the colour's dreadful isn't it? The boys chose it. They said it was cool. Who am I to argue?" I wondered how many times she'd heard that from her husband.

"How did it happen?" I asked, already guessing the answer.

"I missed the last two stairs and landed badly." I gestured for her to sit. Of course you did, I thought. I said nothing. She couldn't meet my gaze. She shifted around in her chair and turned her attention to the strap of her handbag. I left the silence floating with the dust moats in a meagre ray of sunlight. She had come to see me, so I left her to fill the silence. She didn't, not immediately. When she finally broke the silence, what she said was chilling.

"My husband isn't happy, and I just wanted to come and see you…to…to…" She couldn't go on. I waited. She composed herself and continued. "He is likely to come in to see you to…to…" Again she stopped as a tear navigated its way, falling like a thin silver droplet along her high cheekbone to her chin. I looked at her, eyebrows raised in enquiry, although we both knew she'd said enough already. She stood up to leave. At the door she turned to look at me apologetically. I thanked her for coming and decided that should I ever "fall the last two stairs" and break an arm, I would opt for the traditional white cast and collect autographs from friends and well-wishers.

I sat daydreaming trying to imagine, yet trying *not* to imagine exactly what Mr Wenger could have in mind. Would he write to the governing body? Unlikely. He wasn't so much reflective as active. He wouldn't waste time writing. Would he decide to transfer Hans to another local school? Also unlikely. His wife was a Catholic and moving Hans to a non-Catholic school might just be the Jenga brick which toppled the already precarious structure of their sham marriage. Maybe he would pay me a return visit, in which case I would be sure to enlist the support of one of my male teachers, although I doubted whether he would feel physically intimidated by either of them, but might at least serve as a deterrent for any verbal abuse.

I must admit to being relieved when the day ended and the scuffling of children raiding the cloakrooms heralded a vestige of some peace and quiet. From the window I could see children chasing each other as they coursed around in the fading light playing tag and emulating Power Rangers as they positively flew across the playground swinging their bulging bags and catching each other unawares. Mothers stood around in groups holding the same conversations they held every day at this time. Gate gossip we called it. It's a kind of one-upmanship in terms of who can "diss" the school/teachers/the head teacher the most. We drew an imaginary graph once and plotted the peaks and troughs of gate gossip. The start of the year was always going to be a peak what with new teachers, pregnant teachers, teachers on the move from one year group to another, parking, lack of parking, rise in price of school dinners, that kind of inevitable thing. There was a lull, with maybe a few blips for in-service days and the inconvenience they caused up to Easter, when the gossip turned to couples getting divorced, DNA tests to determine parentage, recently divorced spouses resurrected, new partners, transitory partners, useless teachers, gay teachers, teachers they'd like a night on the town with, right on through to SATs results…always good for hot gossip, and, of course, the threat of OFSTED. In the event of the latter everything would take a shift and, like herding buffalo turning as one, everyone would talk of how wonderful their school was! Today it was just background babble, the muzak behind a cannon of children's voices. I turned my back to the window and faced the computer, satisfied that all was well.

The next few seconds still cause the hairs on the back of my neck to stand on end after almost twenty years have passed.

A thunderous banging on the windows behind me brought me into the present with one hell of a shock. I spun my chair round and there stood Mr Wenger with his Jack Nicholson grin. He slowly raised both arms without blinking or losing eye contact with me. Grasped firmly between both hands was a gun. Once level with my face he stopped and adopted the pose of an LA cop. Behind him the playground spectacle was one of hysteria as mums grabbed children and trampled toddlers in their panic to put as much distance between themselves and Mr Wenger as possible.

He stood stock still.

I froze. His leer stretched. He was getting such a buzz. There was a fraction of a pause before he laughed, turned and ran off. I guess the time this all took was approximately ten seconds, but for me it was endless. I couldn't move initially, then I was aware of Glenda's voice behind me where she had come to a standstill in the doorway. "The police are on their way…any time they friggin' like. Are you okay?" I insisted that I was fine and went outside to see if there were any children or parents left on the premises. By now there weren't. Thank God. Although a sizeable group had gathered outside the club next door. I resisted the urge to join them and instead walked twice round the deserted playground, with Glenda watching my back like a re-run of *Cagney and Lacey*. I don't recall thinking of anything in particular except the fact that Mr Wenger had gone and everyone was safe.

Walking back into school I found myself at the open door of my office. I went in, leant against the door until it clicked shut, my legs buckled, and I slid slowly down to the ground and sat crying tears of relief, rage, and fear while reciting a mantra, "Bastard! You evil bastard! Bastard! You evil bastard!" I felt the door pushing into my back as GIenda tried to wedge a cup of tea round the door, and let me know the police had arrived. The police had indeed arrived and, after a tea-fest, others came to give an account of their interrogation of Mr Wenger. The gun was a replica. He said it belonged to his boy who'd had it in school all day. Strange nobody had seen it during the day. This alone confirmed it as a lie. Hans often brought screwdrivers, hammers and drill bits into school which he bragged about until they were confiscated. Could this be an exception? I doubted it. Mr Wenger maintained the whole incident was a joke. His little bit of fun. The man was a monster. He sickened the entire community. During the course of the next week or so, police presence, covert and overt depending on the time, was the order of the day. I was also assured that a patrol car would "do the rounds" outside my home as Jeff was working away. It helped. Mr Wenger was also served an injunction which kept him away from the school premises. His "fun" continued, however, via the telephone. Several sinister calls prompted me to inform the police. The turning point was the day that Mr Wenger let me into his little secret. He knew the whereabouts of my children. Two were still at university and college, and Rebecca was touring with a dance company in her first experience as a professional musician. He knew where they were. He *told* me where they were. When I informed the police I felt I should warn them that if Mr Wenger came anywhere near my children, he would be the one needing police protection. He really brought out the mother hen in me and I had four brothers-in-law and a ripped husband who would need restraining if any harm came to our family.

As with most good crime thrillers there were no threats or details of impending proposed action, simply a calculated dropping in of the all-important fact that he had a little secret which meant that he could be assured of my living in constant fear and anxiety. Is it any wonder that my original mantra took up residence in my mind? "Bastard! Evil bastard…"

Precautionary measures were taken and the police were brilliant. All my personal details which Mr Wenger could've used were removed from any school related paperwork. We changed our private phone number and went ex-directory. One could be forgiven for thinking it was a tad late to be "shutting the stable door" however, what else could be done? Eventually, on moving to another school, I was advised to continue to withhold personal details from the school's database and not to have my name printed on the school noticeboard on the main road perhaps making it slightly more difficult for him to menace me in future.

At the end of the year both Hans and his younger brother transferred to other schools. I felt a sense of loss actually. We could've supported Mrs Wenger, maybe even have helped Hans work toward his music scholarship, possibly even prevented his younger brother from following in his footsteps. But it wasn't to be. I don't know what became of the family, but I did see Mr Wenger many years later. Jeff and I were walking along by the harbour and there he was sitting facing the murky river, cradling a cup of something steaming. As we approached my heart crept up into my ear-drums, and seemed to be pulsing with the verve of the distant cathedral bells. He didn't look up. When we had passed by and were out of earshot, I heard someone repeating, "Bastard! You evil bastard!" It wasn't till we were getting into the car that I realised it was me.

Chapter 20

It was around this time that the most horrific event occurred in the small town of Dunblane, Scotland, which put Mr Wenger's incident into perspective. I remember watching the BBC news that evening and feeling the angst of every parent and teacher there as they waited to hear whether their children were alive or dead after the carnage created by one man. One man, as he opened fire on innocent children throughout the school. I found myself wondering what I would have done had this horror hit us at St Mark's. The assembly hall was in close proximity to the front door of the school. Access could be easily gained early in the morning as parents came in to pay dinner money or drop off forgotten swimming kit. What would I do? Throw myself at the gunman? Doubtful. How would I gather all two hundred children into the safety of my arms? Oh God, it was beyond rational thought. Going into school the following morning I rehearsed assembly as I drove along the bypass. It wasn't a usual assembly day but, as with most head teachers in the UK, I wanted to be prepared to respond to questions and the inevitable sadness and shock triggered by the monstrous events of the previous day.

What I wasn't prepared for was the surge of parents about to arrive. Some were openly weeping as they stood clutching the hands of the children they were often only too glad to see run off into the safety of St Mark's. Over fifty stayed for assembly sitting behind the rows of their innocent, living children. There was a reluctance to leave as assembly drew to a close with one of our favourite songs, "This is our school, let peace live here…"

The words were never more poignant.

Several parents lingered in the hall and I decided to ask if they'd like a coffee before heading off. They didn't want anything but the space to sit and be together. We talked about the devastated community of Dunblane, of the anxiety as parents watched little bodies lovingly carried out to ambulances while longing for a glimpse of their own child running toward them.

It seemed the only place they wanted to be today was school. It wasn't that they couldn't leave their children...they simply couldn't leave each other. I assured them that they were welcome to stay as long as they felt it helped them to be together. Gradually, as the morning crept toward midday, they left, and an uneasy quiet took up residence in the hall where they had been.

Throughout the day children came to see me with pictures they had drawn for the children and teachers of Dunblane. Often they had written their own prayers too. Precious offerings depicting flowers, doves of peace, candles, angels wearing school uniform, parents crying, Jesus comforting. One class after the other brought their pictures and cards to the office.

We opened a memorial book for all to sign in the weeks to come, and I shall never forget the heartfelt sentiments expressed and lovingly posted to Dunblane. At the end of the day two mums came to see me as I stood on the playground. They asked if they could all come in to the hall again to talk and perhaps to pray together. Within five minutes the playground began to clear as parents and children called everyone to meet in the hall for the children of Dunblane. The hall was jammed. Everyone was standing and staring expectantly toward the stage where I had arranged some candles. Soft music was playing as we gathered. The sense of a common grief, an unfathomable sadness, touched us all, from the youngest baby to the oldest grandparent. I invited spontaneous prayer, and before long a murmur of hesitant voices, minutes before bellowing across the playground to call us all to prayer, began to flow. I can only describe the whole event as an outpouring of love and shared grief. Parents reaching out to parents they would never meet. Children holding angel-children in their hearts.

Chapter 21

It's true the school is the heart of the community. To be enveloped in that community is quite remarkable and provokes an obsessive desire to make everything perfect. So it was with the appointment of our new deputy head. Having spent many years with a deputy whose self-image was so low it could only creep after him like a reluctant shadow everywhere he went, it was with much joy and relief that the governing body received his resignation. It had to happen. Counselling, courses, disciplinary procedures, gardening leave all pointed toward a meltdown just as sure as an ice sculpture at a beach party in Malibu. An embarrassing number of years on leave of absence left us all in little doubt that we were more effective without the additional tension created by the deputy in school. His return was not anticipated, it was simply a matter of time. So it was that I was without a deputy head for a number of years. Without a deputy but not without the money-frittering process which lingers like some debilitating disease in the world of education. One can have a sustained period of time on leave of absence with full pay reducing to half pay after six months or so, then, simply by returning to school for a week when the money runs out, one can restart the whole crazy cycle! However, the current deputy finally saw sense and called it a day. Although this heralded a long-awaited change, it was sad to see his career ending after over thirty years punctuated by disappointment and rejection.

After advertising we had a good field of applicants which is always a bonus. The day for interviews came around quickly and we were well prepared to put each candidate through their paces. By the end of the day it was clear who was our new deputy. He was a young rising star in education complete with references from those numbering amongst the great and the good. He was articulate, an interesting teacher, energetic and able to use his initiative. His knowledge of the many ways in which children learn was enviable and I knew we would all benefit from his expertise in this field. There was, seemingly, nothing he didn't know about information technology in education too. As we were about to build our own computer suite, this was a fortuitous bonus.

What I hadn't reckoned with was his ego. Oh, I know, ego is often the fuel for high-flyers, but it sometimes leads them too close to the sun and, before the first year was over, his wings were singed to within a feather of disaster.

Our morning meetings began to resemble counselling sessions as Mr P, the new deputy, sought answers to the meaning of life. Questions such as, "Why can't I commit to a long-term relationship? Why is there no one out there with my intellect? Why do the parents laugh at me on the playground? Why don't the children listen to me?" In fact any questions with "I" as the subject were mulled over before school began. In an attempt to engage Mr P in some downtime, I suggested a shopping spree at the weekend. I've never known a straight man get so much pleasure from shopping. He had good, but expensive taste, and I found myself wondering if he had some private funding from his parents. His shirts were all bespoke.

I invited him to dinner with my family. I even went to an evening class one-off session at his request on something weird to do with Karmic energies. I think I tried my best, some might say the Karmic activity should've been a warning, but I didn't see it coming...the nervous breakdown that is...at least not at that time. However, several months into the school year Mr P's behaviour was becoming more than a cause for concern, but I guess I was hoping that he would overcome his current anxieties and refocus on helping to develop St Mark's.

One afternoon I was on a Learning Walk around the school. It was almost time for the bell signalling the end of the day, bringing with it a huge sigh of relief that another day had passed without major incident! Never rest on your laurels.

There was an inordinate row coming from Mr P's classroom and it wasn't the type of sound indicating the glee of exploration. It was more akin to a scene from *Lord of the Flies*, but it wasn't immediately obvious who held the conch because the noise was deafening.

What met my eyes as I opened the classroom door was beyond *Waterloo Road*. You know the show. It's the only comprehensive school I know of with thirty-five children in total, and a staffroom the size of a family dining room. Anyhow, there they were, thirty-two rowdy, sweaty year four children all attempting to make themselves heard. All apart from Denny who sat in the reading area with his thoughts immersed in *The human body*. This was his cave, his territory, where he had control over who came in and who went out. Usually it was nobody. The other children found him strange but most of the time he was oblivious to them. His reliable companion, last week train timetables this week *The human body,* was always his latest passion. I was tempted to join him on a number of occasions. We spent time in the office researching planets or playing. There are such gifts accompanying autism.

I cast my eyes around taking in the shambolic scene before me and seeking Mr P, the supposed adult in the room. He was pacing up and down like a caged lion, appealing, in a high-pitched whinge, for order. He might as well have whistled up his own Barcelona for all the affect he was having.

I noticed a gaggle of concerned parents staring through the windows. At the same instant so did Mr P. He strode to the playground door and flung it open. Did I mention his dramatic aptitude? By now some children had seen me and were attempting to alert the others. Gradually quiet descended as the dejected children returned to their seats. The unexpected calm coincided with an outburst from Mr P who yelled at the assembled parents, "This is what your bloody children have done to me!" He stood there, reddened face glistening as droplets of sweat rode the roller coaster of his Adam's apple and squeezed their way under his bespoke collar. His words spat across the group of mums who stood gaping at him. "I can't sleep, I can't teach them, they're uncontrollable, they're YOURS! For God's sake take them home!" It was a performance worthy of Hugh Grant who Mr P resembled in a foppish kind of a way.

I realised in an instant that this was not a situation for glossing over. By now the parents were incensed and had begun to close in around Mr P, sharks sensing blood. I made my way over to the shuddering playground door, gently took Mr P's arm, and led him, backward, into the classroom. I sat him down on the first available chair belonging to a child where he resembled Gulliver surrounded by the Lilliputians. The noise outside was reaching a crescendo as I told the children to stand so that we could recite our end of day prayer. There's a lot to be said for routine in this kind of situation. We stood and thanked God our Father for our families, friends and the day. When it got to the part, "thank you for my family and all the friends you give to me", I couldn't resist a sideways glimpse at the family and friends gathered outside like baying wolves. Establishing some kind of decorum I then dismissed the children in an orderly fashion to their awaiting parents. As the remaining few children left I followed them onto the playground to apologise to the parents. I explained that Mr P wasn't feeling too well and, although this by no means excused his behaviour, I hoped they would cut him some slack and forgive his outburst. Some parents nodded and shuffled their feet as if embarrassed by their own anger a few minutes before. Others, the majority, began to express their thoughts in different ways as one after the other they gained confidence. The first to speak was Mrs O'Brian who had an on/off infatuation with Mr P. "He'll be feeling worse when I get hold of him…blamin' my son for his feckin' illness…he couldn't organise a piss-up in a brewery, stuck-up prat that he is." Nice one, Mrs O'Brian, I thought. That's really going to help calm things down. This was followed by a hurling of venomous insults heading my way. If I had been in any doubt as to who was to blame they were quick to obliterate any doubt. I, of course, was to blame. I hadn't seen this disaster on the horizon.

I invited the parents to a meeting the next morning explaining that now was neither the time nor place. Space was what we needed. Space, and a chilled Pinot Grigio. Tomorrow, after having slept on it, we would manage an adult conversation, a rational exchange of opinions held in a calm setting. I found myself praying that between now and then no one would miss their laundry slot!

Returning to Mr P, I found him gently sobbing. He blubbered an apology as he swiped the back of his hand along his upper lip then down the outside leg of his perfectly pressed trousers. Such a child at heart. His public schoolboy mop of mousy hair fell across his eyes. He made no attempt to push it back. I think he needed his security blanket fringe.

An hour later we had planned the perfect meeting for the morning. A balance of contrition and futures thinking which would include an invitation to the parents to come into class and work alongside Mr P. We knew the latter was unlikely ever to be taken up as a viable option, but felt it was important to float the idea. Ownership was very popular then as a universal panacea. Six parents turned up in the morning. Once they'd got their pound of flesh by way of an apology, and compensation in the form of a cup of coffee and a broken custard cream biscuit, they left.

I had a supply teacher in for the day so that Mr P could re-establish his equilibrium. The following day was a Friday. Mr P didn't turn up for our morning briefing, although I'd seen his car in the car park. I found him in the staffroom, asleep across four chairs. Miss O sat marking a heap of maths books, slapping them down one after the other when completed like a beaten dominoes player. Without looking up she greeted me by saying, "He's been like that since he arrived. He made it to the loo, threw up and collapsed right there." I decided the best course of action was inaction for the time being. He needed to sleep, I needed to get to assembly. I left Miss O to watch him.

At 10.25am, a dishevelled and bewildered Mr P woke up, staggered to the loo, and repeated the earlier performance. The staffroom smelt of the morning after the night before. What our daughter Claire used to call, "stinky-boy-smell". He needed to go home, that much was obvious, but he was in no fit state to drive. He would still have registered over the limit if breathalysed. Miss O offered to drive him home in her car, then he could pick up his own car tomorrow by which time he would be sober. This episode was to bite me back the following year during Mr P's employment tribunal. Bear with...it's worth reading.

His week of gardening leave turned into six months on full pay, then six months on half pay during which time I believed that Mr P would either seek counselling and return fit for purpose, or leave. I had a strong and unwelcome sense of *déjà vu*. He didn't return. He didn't resign. Instead he set his sights on a pay off from the school and local authority and he determined to do this by proving disability discrimination. Initially I thought it was some kind of joke, but stopped laughing long enough to double-check his original application form and references in trepidation that I may have missed something vital. All was still as glowing as ever and I could find nothing to indicate that he was disabled in any way. In fact his medical record was enviable. He'd obviously had a good work ethic in his previous existence too.

So we continued to pick up the pieces left in Mr P's substantial wake. The senior leadership team had supported him as he settled into school and he had appeared relaxed and diligent in managing the subjects for which he held responsibility. His record keeping was good, his lesson plans were sporadic but sound, in fact, on the surface, everything seemed hunky-dory. Digging deeper, however, a different story began to raise its ugly head.

Parents who hadn't made it to the meeting began to come in with their stories of bullying, verbal abuse, and tales of inappropriate behaviour directed at them – stories for which we were hard-pressed to find any evidence. Mr P had kept the more gullible mums on side through flattery and a well-polished charm offensive. He partied with them and made them feel special and had accepted a number of invitations to family events. Although all perfectly above board, it appeared he was unaware of where to draw the line between personal and professional life. All the unturned stones were beginning to yield quite a murky crop, added to which he had a large unpaid bill outstanding for items he had purchased for himself from a company we used for RE artefacts. The company was chasing me for a settlement. Throughout the year his colleagues kept in touch with him from time to time, but mostly they concentrated on ensuring that the children in his class didn't suffer, and the subjects for which he held responsibility were kept current. Working in schools there is no time to throw a sickie or sneak an extra crafty tea break to nurse a hangover. No matter how cheesy it may sound, teaching is a vocation. School is not a place for shirkers, and I was blessed with a staff who supported and covered for each other in times of need, such as this one.

At Christmas I sent him a card. He had called school a couple of times, and I always made sure that my phone was put on loudspeaker so that a second person could witness the conversation and record it. There was nothing untoward about his calls. He apologised for the problems he felt he had caused, and I assured him that all we wanted was for him to get better. I was concerned for his well-being and wished him a full recovery. Reading between the lines I think we both knew he wouldn't be coming back. There was nothing further to be done until he resigned.

I don't believe I had ever heard of an employment tribunal apart from on the national news once many years ago in a case of alleged abuse. But Mr P must have already had wheels in motion, running almost concurrently with his contrition for the mess he'd stirred up and which was now muddying the waters for the rest of us at St Mark's. I was soon to learn all about employment tribunals. Solicitors were called in and the tedious process began. Minutes of meetings, records of concerns, absence, parental reports, local authority meetings, well-being activities, all formed the bundle of evidence for the defence. This involved the monumental task of trawling through all of the above to be sure that we omitted nothing of consequence. It was no mean feat and I couldn't help resenting the time and effort it took. As a learned priest friend of mine from Ireland once eloquently commented, "You can spend so much time raking over your shit, but at the end of the day it's still the same shit." He had said it in the softest Irish lilt you could ever imagine. It was as if he were reciting a W.B. Yeats poem, he gave it such reverence. The inevitable tribunal date arrived. Jeff had been brilliant in preparing me for it as I had absolutely no idea what to expect. He explained about the likely row of officials sitting in an elevated position in the small courtroom. Apparently they had varying tasks. One would observe and note body language, one would keep a watchful eye on consistency and the other would listen out for contradictions, or seemingly hesitant responses to questions, or possibly too much repetition. It made me think of a Radio 4 quiz show, *Just a Minute*, where contestants are asked to speak on a given subject for a minute without hesitation, deviation or repetition. Seriously though, despite Jeff's brilliant preparation, including a sketch of the tribunal room, nothing could've prepared me sufficiently.

Mr P took to the stand. He scanned the court and, with visibly shaking hands, took up the Bible and swore to tell the truth, the whole truth and nothing but the truth. What then followed was astounding. Mr P spun a yarn that would've stretched from here to Neverland and back by the scenic route. I didn't doubt his sincerity, but was astounded by what I was hearing. It was hard for me to disguise my incredulous expression. Jeff and Rebecca had been able to take time out to support me. They sat either side of me, with my solicitor next along the row, entrenched in whispered conversation with my chair of governors. In fact they almost sat on top of me on a number of occasions when the aforementioned truth pushed credibility to the max! Looking around at the few spectators, they all appeared to be in sympathy with Mr P. A couple of young mums sat puppy-eyed as he waxed lyrical about the "unreasonable workload" I had given him considering his disability. Two older ladies sat together looking for all the world as if they couldn't wait to spirit him off, feed him up on home-made chicken broth, and smother him in a choice of ample bosoms. The officials sat expressionless like the vultures in *Jungle Book* perched along a creaking bough.

He maintained that I knew he was ill and had done nothing but make demands of him expecting him to take on mammoth tasks such as sorting the musical instruments kept on a trolley in the cupboard. It would've taken any other member of staff half an hour or so, but I thought it would be good for him, as music co-ordinator, to get in there and organise, then come up with a proposal for new instruments to boost the rusted, chesty-sounding sleigh bells, clapped-out tambourines and chordless, three-string guitars. He almost broke down as he told of this and other such trivia.

His *pièce de résistance* was harassment. Let me explain. If a colleague is ill for any length of time and is unable to come to school, it is customary to send them a card to wish them well. All the staff sign the cards in question and, on the whole, the absent colleague receives it with pleasure.

I had made the mistake of sending Mr P such a card from us all, and a Christmas card from me and the family. Okay so far? Good. DON'T EVER DO IT! In the twenty-first century it is classed as harassment. After forty-five minutes he was asked if he'd like a comfort break. He accepted and we adjourned for the time being. Returning after lunch, Mr P was not recalled. I was asked to take the stand. Smoothing out my skirt, I walked toward the stand. I must admit I felt unsettled. I knew that there was nothing to do but tell the truth and anyone with half a brain would toss out Mr P's claim with the carafes of stale oxygenated water gracing the oak desks behind which sat m'lord.

But swearing on oath is not for the faint-hearted. Certainly, as a cradle Catholic my childhood memories resounded with the possible punishments for lying, which included years in Purgatory flying around with nowhere to land. Lying under oath was tantamount to kissing any eternal life goodbye. Have I mentioned post-traumatic stress disorder at all so far?

So, I swore. Hand on Bible. The drama graduate in me came to the rescue. My voice surprised me. It resonated around the room, carried along the oak panels behind the officials, and prodded spectators in the small of the back so that they sat up and damn well listened. They wanted the truth? Well hold tight 'cos here it comes!

The first hour and thirty-five minutes were spent revisiting key issues arising in the bundle such as meetings, procedures, minutes, actions taken/not taken, resolutions etc. Not much of a problem there. Explanations as to Mr P's responsibilities in and out of the classroom were accepted as reasonable. I think I even detected a slight twitch of possible amusement as I listed the paltry contents of the music trolley which Mr P had found so overwhelming. Then came the crunch. The senior barrister, sitting as the rose between two thorns, leant forward seemingly to achieve closer proximity to the stand, where, by the way, I had been ensconced for almost two hours by this stage.

He cleared his throat and proceeded:

"Mrs C, you were aware of Mr P's disability, were you not?"

"No, I *was* not aware of any disability, and *am* not aware of any disability."

"Is that so? Yet on 9th September, Mr P states he arrived at school where, due to the pressures levelled at him by your good self, he felt so anxious that he was rendered incapacitated. Furthermore, Mr P maintains that this physical and emotional trauma was the situation he found himself facing on a significant number of mornings. He states on page 256 of your bundle that you showed little sympathy as to his physical state, or gratitude that he had managed to get to work at all under the circumstances." Pause. "To what did you attribute this incapacity if not to a specific disability caused by unrealistic demands in the workplace?"

Unfortunately this was like a red rag to the proverbial bull. I took a swig of stale water – wishing it was a G and T – pulled myself up to my full height of five foot one inch, in kitten heels (new shoes), and began.

"Today, women all over the world are arriving at work feeling disoriented and often vomiting before fulfilling a focused and productive day. This is known as pregnancy. It isn't a disability." I saw Rebecca sinking down in her chair while Jeff slowly shook his head from side to side with a curious warning look on his face. None of it made any difference. In my mind I was on course to checkmate.

I continued:

"Mr P was certainly suffering on numerous occasions on arrival at school due to an over-indulgence of alcohol the previous evening. I believe that his sickness was due to this. We use the vernacular term for this disability. We call it a hangover. Unfortunately, Mr P suffered with this disability in epic proportion."

There was a titter around the room. Hardly the man the barricades response I'd hoped for, but better than nothing. There then followed a cross-examination by Mr P's solicitor. He didn't spare the punches. I didn't blame him because it was around this time that the pendulum began to swing a little in my direction. The women in the room had certainly changed allegiance. Fickle. It takes more than foppish hair and a Hugh Grant stammer to sustain loyalty.

Hymn practice was the next subject. Apparently I had asked Mr P to lead hymn practice and he felt it was too much of an ask. Bless him. I thought. I'm sure this registered on my face which Jeff had cautioned me to control as I tend to wear my heart on my sleeve. Hymn practice was a doddle and was something I had led, sometimes unaided, to give the teachers a short break and to polish up on some new songs with the whole school together. By now I was warming up and replied, "Saint Mark's is a Catholic school. Mr P is a Catholic deputy head teacher. Mr P is also the music co-ordinator. I would appreciate clarification on what specifically is untoward or onerous about the head teacher asking the deputy head teacher/music co-ordinator to carry out this task."

One glance at Jeff and I could tell that I was in danger of overstepping the mark – again. But honestly. Get a grip everyone! Employee rights are fair and just when applied judiciously, but this was becoming a witch-hunt and I needed to go to the toilet, or hop on my broomstick and launch myself from the high-rise block in which I felt incarcerated. I noticed that equal opportunities were sadly lacking in respect of the toilet, or in fact my general well-being. Mr P had been let off the hook after forty-five minutes. I was into the third hour of questioning and no one had even *asked* if I'd like a comfort break! I made a mental note that should we be recalled tomorrow, I'd wear less make-up and aim to look a little more pale and wan to illicit a touch of humanity or compassion. After all, it worked for *him*!

Finally there was an adjournment. We slumped in the tiny room allocated to my solicitor, chair of governors, Jeff and myself. Rebecca had already returned to work. She was gutted. She absolutely relished the drama of the whole thing.

Apparently the two solicitors had had a discussion regarding a settlement. This was as good as saying we had won. The pipe dream £60,000 compensation pay off disappeared into the sunset of reality as the sum of £3,500 was agreed. I was still angry but the euphoria of the solicitor and everyone else soon had me jumping up and down in a frenzied Mexican wave and silently squealing "YES!" Leaving the tribunal that day the injustice of the whole process began to kick in. Why was I the one feeling mangled and pegged out to dry? Jeff tried to assure me saying that in his experience, vast as it was, this was often the way things went.

And that was it. No debrief as such, just the drawing of an invisible line, and business as usual.

Chapter 22

Business as usual meant unpredictability each and every day. Some days Glenda and I would begin the morning saying, "Let's hope we have a normal day today," although if asked to describe what that might look like, we'd have been hard-pressed.

Two days after the proverbial guillotine fell on Mr P, I walked purposefully into school hoping to knuckle down with some futures thinking. I had been looking forward to this moment for the last couple of months, so it was with a skip in my step that I opened the door to my office. What confronted me was a singing fish. To be precise it was a shiny mackerel singing, "Do Wah Diddy", a la Paul Jones and Manfred Mann.

It's not often you see a singing mackerel. Actually it was my first. It was mounted on a wooden block and was gyrating as if its life depended on it. I turned to see Glenda and our gorgeous new caretaker standing there doubled up with laughter. Business as usual? OH, YES PLEASE! That mackerel restored my equilibrium and tickled my sense of humour. On a more serious note, First Holy Communion Day was looming. For every Catholic school this is a very important event on the school calendar. It can also be every head teacher's nightmare. I defy an events manager to cope with the variables of this glorious day. One morning a parent of a little girl who was receiving her First Holy Communion arrived at school to clarify a couple of things. To say this lady, Mrs B, was flamboyant wouldn't do her justice. She walked into the foyer and lifted up her head so that her gorgeous, round, ebony, heavily made-up face was larger than life on the camera relaying to the screen in Glenda's room. She took a deep breath and began singing, "It's Raining Men". What was it with everybody? This was one of her more "out there" numbers comprising her impressive repertoire. On other days we were treated to a variety of songs from *Sister Act* and neither Glenda nor myself would've been in the least bit surprised to find a swaying gospel choir accompanying her in the cramped foyer. Without batting a copiously long eyelash, Glenda buzzed through to say that my appointment with Whoopi Goldberg was on. She'd arrived. Did she think I was deaf?

The purpose of her visit was quite straightforward. She was enquiring on behalf of a friend, naturally, as to whether she could reserve two pews in church for her family visiting from Camden Town for the big day. This may not sound much, but bear in mind the fact that First Holy Communion was almost a three-line whip for families. Whether your family was from around the corner, Italy, the Philippines, Ireland or India, the call was out. Space was at a premium. Aside from Christmas it was probably the only other day of the liturgical year which would command a full house in church, and inevitably a prolonged homily from the parish priest making the most of a captive audience.

Ms Goldberg left ten minutes later wondering which of her fifteen relatives would be occupying the church porch on the day.

Seats were allocated equally to each family. We did our best to accommodate everyone, but each year there were still hordes of relatives propping up the pillars of the church, or hanging over the balcony of the choir loft brandishing video cameras to record the big day. Seating was the least of my worries on the actual day as the children began to congregate in the school hall prior to processing into the church. Picture the scene as seven-year-old little girls pitched up looking like Jordan on her wedding day (the first one). Voluminous, multi-layered dresses with hooped underskirts swayed across the polished wooden floor of the school hall. Mini high-heeled shoes clacked along as mini Jordans tried their hardest to walk normally. As if that wasn't enough to cope with, there was an epidemic of long lace gloves and Swarovski crystal-studded handbags and matching tiaras, or "tararas" as Glenda and I called them. The entire ensemble was crowned with heavily embroidered veils and arms hung with rosary beads. Oh God, I thought, where to begin? The point being that all over-the-top accessories were to be left in school to avoid distraction, tripping, choking or garrotting others. It wasn't so much a health and safety thing, it was more a plea for reverence of some kind. Gloves had to come off so that the Communion host wasn't dropped as it caught in the lace. Handbags were simply excess baggage, and one set of rosary beads was ample. We weren't at Lourdes for heaven's sake. Previous years' experience had taught me not to attempt this with families in the vicinity. Oh no, you didn't make that mistake twice. Last year I got into what may only be described as a brawl with a grandmother as she wrenched the mother-of-pearl rosary from my hands in an attempt to adorn her Francesca. At the same time Mrs O'Gormley threatened to flatten me if I so much as touched her Maeraid's gloves. She would've done it too. I'd seen her in action at the school disco the year before last when she decked another mum for "eying up my Dessie", her nineteen stone man, who sported a tattoo of a cobra writhing from the base of his rugby player's neck to the arch of his right eyebrow where its flicking tongue protruded in a most menacing manner.

Parents preened and wiped lipstick smudges off their children's faces, while grandparents wept silently or snuck a wee swig of something undoubtedly alcoholic before leaving to get into church ahead of the procession.

Once they were gone, Glenda and I set to work. We perfected a pincer movement. She went for handbags, while I went for lace gloves and rosaries. One of my young teachers set up a table in the hall and labelled every item as we coerced each child into parting with family heirlooms the like of which wouldn't shame *Cash in the Attic*, the Catholic version.

Leaving the table heaped with unnecessary trappings, we swiftly got the children into line to avoid the possibility of a rising hysteria. Thank God for the boys. Beautiful little scrubbed up seven-year-olds proudly wearing white crisp shirts, red ties and their school trousers. No fuss, no frills or fancies. Fabulous.

Anyone watching the procession into church could be forgiven for imagining that they were at the Oscars. The congregation parted like the Red Sea as the children walked down the centre aisle with hands joined in prayerful pose and the choir sang "Immaculate

Mary". I wondered about the choice of hymn, but then remembered it had fifteen verses. Even the slowest of processions would not reach the finishing tape before the hyperventilating congregation gasped its way through the last verse. Perfect.

Flashbulbs flashed, video cameras videoed, while mobile phones managed both. Great, I thought. All pleas from Father McMahon to refrain from photography at this most blessed of moments had gone unheeded. That's what I call consistency. Year on year, same old same old.

Mr Giordino, resembling a tick-tack man at Chepstow races, gesticulated wildly to family scattered around the humid church as his daughter walked by minus accoutrements. Consternation triggered a female frenzy as, one by one, the women of the family got to hear of the stripping of Angelica. The grandmother, "mama", in black lace diamante from head to toe almost ululating in her grief. I chose to believe the criticism was not *all* directed at me, but the tension mounted and emotions were beginning to escalate as parents from all over the church joined in. If it hadn't been for Father McMahon I may well have finished the day pinioned to the bus stop outside the local Pizza Hut with a horse's head cowering under my duvet back home. The rest of the service went quite well considering the dramatic *entrée*, the only two miscreants being Joe Marny and Alex Grey. Joe walked back from receiving Holy Communion with his tongue sticking out showing the host to all and sundry, and Alex almost had to be prised away from the chalice containing the Communion wine as she attempted a third gulp.

The service over, the celebrations began. The club next door to school overflowed with rheumy-eyed adults and screeching children by now reunited with their holy accessories and less holy siblings, and charging around the car park. Again, I remembered thinking we Catholics know how to party.

Arriving at school the following day I caught sight of something shiny in a puddle against the wall of the club. Further inspection revealed a blue plastic rosary partly hidden under sodden cigarette butts. I wrapped it in a tissue and realised I was saying a swift Hail Mary to apologise.

Marcie, older sister of Miley, dropped the children into school that morning. One of the twelve children having made their First Holy

Communion the day before, her parents were "sleepin in this morning, Missus." As she was here, I asked her why Miley hadn't been in school the previous Wednesday. Quick as a flash she replied, "'Twas Bank Holiday, Missus... Bank Holiday Wednesday." I remember seeing the funny side of it later on. You couldn't fault her ingenuity.

Spared the wrath of the Mafia, I decided that eight years at Saint Mark's was probably enough. It's said that it takes eight years to create a good business with a sound team and effective management systems well embedded. Well, this was my eighth year at St Mark's. We had recruited some of the best young teachers the local authority had to offer as the old guard threw in the towel, gave vent to their feelings and drove out of the school gates for the last time. My talented aspiring leaders left to become deputies or heads of other schools, and each time one of them left I felt such a mixture of sadness and pride. It was like saying goodbye to family. After all, I had watched them grow and we'd helped each other survive some tough times. We'd even survived a couple of OFSTED inspections without resorting to physical violence when presented with a couple of crazy judgements. The paper copy of the *Vacancies Bulletin*, by now mostly accessed online, was buried in one of my in trays, the one marked non-urgent. In my head this translated to that which will never see the light of day again. I tugged at it from under a pile of paper nothingness. As I flicked through the pages and spotted an advert for a head teacher to open a new school, St George's. To be more precise, it was an existing school moving to a bigger site and a state-of-the-art building.

I was tempted by that. The challenge of successfully moving the school community with all its renowned traditions, while introducing developments across the curriculum and beyond was too enticing to resist.

New suit time again. Not that I'd waited eight years, but I always feel that it's a part of the application process, don't you? A kind of reward after dragging up your CV and updating it. Why we don't ever do this as a matter of course I'll never know. Then, the imagination required in creating an application which stands out from the rest. That's exhausting enough to warrant a bit of a splurge at the mall.

The interviews took place in a hotel overlooking the Bristol Channel. It smelt of damp, distant wedding receptions, except when the mottled glass doors swung open at the behest of the channel breezes. I sat looking out at the murky brown water swirling in unpredictable curves and currents just offshore, and imagined slave ships making their way up the coast to Bristol, or weighing anchor and waiting for the tide to turn in their favour. Maybe this hotel had once been the home of a rich Bristol merchant keeping watch out to sea, bewigged and snuff stained.

My daydreams were soon cut short as I spotted a school governor heading toward me, hand outstretched and a welcoming smile. So far so good.

The interview took place upstairs in a slightly less musty room with large windows offering a superb view. After the pleasantries came the questions. And they were thorough. Interviews rarely phased me. After all, performing was something I was good at and I was enjoying the banter. During one round of questions the parish priest, giving his best shot at a spot of role play began, "My children are aged five and seven. We are moving into the area. Describe what you would promote about your school during our first visit." I couldn't resist it.

"First of all, Father, I think we need to establish whether or not the bishop is aware of these children."

The teacher-governor guffawed expelling a very loud "PAH!" I can only imagine the majority had left their sense of humour at home. Father Gregory saw the funny side of it, nodded his head to governors either side of him, and muttering, "very good, very good, funny," as if waiting for confirmation.

However, it all came to a sticky end when my religious practice was questioned. Initially I felt that the question was not permissible, but I gave an honest answer. An honest answer leading to a phone call later that same evening. It was the chair of governors. She was speaking in almost hushed tones verging on conspiratorial. She said that unfortunately I was not being asked to go forward to the next round due to my relaxed approach to Mass attendance. I've heard that people react in a number of ways to the breaking of unexpected news. Some may feel a crushing weight descending, for others the physical response is a primal scream or collapse. I was struck as speechless as the expectant father of John the Baptist.

Jeff was waiting for the news. I tried to speak, but uttered a strange sound of incredulity over which I had little control.

Another candidate had been asked the same question regarding his religious practice and had been liberal with the truth. That's me being kind. I had been honest about my Mass attendance and was not being recalled.

What followed was possibly the most upsetting couple of hours Jeff and I had experienced in the context of my professional life.

We analysed, we sought answers to so many questions which would never find a voice. Questions aimed at no one in particular shot out as we recalled the many roles we'd taken on within the church over the last twenty years. Presumably they counted for nothing, obviously not substantial enough in terms of evidence of my commitment to the church. Both our families were known in the diocese for their own active involvement in the church over the past forty years when, as children, Jeff and I had felt that we lived and breathed in musky, freezing parish churches in various parishes. Our fealty toward the Catholic faith, even when our own consciences were pulling us in other directions, was faultless. Apparently nothing could erase the blot that was indelibly printed on my poor soul. The blot which, writ large, spoke of relaxed attitude toward Sunday practice. The tissues lay shredded on the carpet next to an almost empty Kleenex box. This was karma. Karma of the worst kind. I had played the nuns, this was my comeuppance. I guess I always knew it would bite me back one day. Then the phone rang. This time Jeff answered. He came into the room nodding and saying, "Yes, she's here, I'll just pass you over." He handed me the phone with one outstretched hand, and a sheet of soft, pink loo roll with the other. I wondered what else they were to throw at me. Oh God, what is it now? Excommunication? It was the chair of governors again. This time she was animated and gushed,

"I've found a loophole." No need to seek out the nearest priest's hole hidden within the walls then, I thought. There was a reprieve.

I was being asked to attend for a further day of interviews tomorrow, including a religious education lesson with a group of seven-year-olds. I took a deep breath. It was too late now for any preparation, it was way past midnight. I was emotionally drained and had also managed to demolish two rather large glasses of gin and tonic.

I accepted on condition that I could have five minutes to tell the panel of governors, the local authority advisor and the diocesan advisor why I, currently, was not attending Mass on a weekly basis.

I could hear muffled voices on the line and finally came the answer I was waiting for. The governors had agreed.

Next morning I was in fine fettle. I love a challenge and Jeff and I had perfected a brilliant, so we believed, five-minute clarification for the interview panel as to my current status as a Catholic. It may only have been five minutes, but it took a couple of hours to prepare because I was fired up with questions for them, and Jeff realised the importance of giving me free rein to aid in my catharsis. I wanted to ask how many head teachers of Catholic schools were practising Catholics and how they policed this. Jeff suggested this was perhaps not a great idea. I wanted to ask them their opinion on Jesus and his fraternisation with sinners. Again, Jeff suggested this was perhaps not a great idea. I wanted them to tell me what they knew of Jesus's interaction with hypocrites. Again, Jeff... *Oh I wanted so much*, as I wallowed in self-pity and the need for retribution. The injustice of it all. Jeff stayed awake throughout and was a perfect counter to my ego-motivated blabbering. After an hour or so we settled to put my thoughts into some kind of pragmatic order. I don't recall how the day went in detail, but I do know that my case was heard with respect and an acceptable level of understanding, coupled with further in-depth questions. I finished by telling the governors about one of my favourite instances in the life of Jesus. It's when he turns to the thief strung up on the cross next to him and assures him that he will be with him in Paradise that very same day. I asked the governors whether Jesus had enquired as to the thief's attendance in the synagogue before he uttered those words of unconditional love. I blanch now as I recall my parting shot. In retrospect it was unnecessary. It was purely self-indulgent...but it still gives me such a BUZZ! At 4.35pm I found myself experiencing *déjà vu* as I sat staring at the swirling tide of the estuary. I wanted this job more than I'd realised at the outset. I had bared my soul in the attempt to convince the panel that I had what it took to complete a successful move and invigorate an ambience of spirituality and learning in the new building, while developing the many traditions nurtured by the sisters of La Sainte Union for the previous ninety-odd years.

I wasn't sure what I'd do if the job was offered to the only other candidate left. In a sense I felt my fate was sealed. If the panel decided that due to my lack of regular Mass attendance I could not be appointed, then how could I possibly continue in my *existing* role? I wondered whether I was too old to become an air cabin crew stewardess. They didn't seem to be so fussy these days. I found myself practising "Chicken or beef?" as I imagined sallying up the aisle of a 747.

I don't suppose I'll ever know what it was that swayed opinion in my favour on that eventful day. The chair of governors bustled toward me with arms outstretched. "Oh, *why* are you so contentious?" she asked as she hugged me and continued, "We're offering you the job." Relief, the like of which I cannot adequately describe, flooded through my entire body and psyche as she led me back into the interview room where the governors waited to offer congratulations. All except one. We'll call him Mr Pound. Heading swiftly toward my car in the hotel car park, I caught sight of Mr Pound struggling against the onshore wind as his gabardine mac got caught between his legs threatening to topple his not insubstantial self as he groped for his car keys.

"What a day!" I said cheerily. My guess is that my voice was carried off to Newport via Redcliffe Bay as the response he fired back was this.

"I didn't support your appointment, you know."

"Oh...okay. Well, I hope we'll be able work togeth—" The rest of my sentence didn't make it. Mr Pound was already in his car and firing up the ignition. I noticed his mac was trapped in the door, and was secretly hoping for an Isadora Duncan moment.

Chapter 23

The first couple of years in the new build which was St George's more than qualified me for a career in snagging... No, it's not a typo. It's what happens after a beautiful new building complete with all manner of cutting edge fixtures, fittings and facilities begins to settle and show its faults. I'm not talking about the inevitable tell-tale cracks, or even the dripping taps which seem to be par for the course. I mean important stuff like the doors to the children's toilets which were so heavy that the children, who would invariably leave it to the last minute to go, were physically unable to pull open without adult assistance. I'm talking about the automatic hand dryers in the children's toilets which sounded rather like landing aircraft approaching the tarmac at Bristol International Airport each time a child so much as looked at one sideways. The result was often a pile-up of terrified children throwing their weight against the aforementioned door to escape the monster! Talking of toilets, let's not forget the back up we experienced in the first heavy rains of autumn. I have fond memories of teachers standing forlorn, fighting to control unwieldy umbrellas as they attempted to stop parents driving their four by fours into the school car park before spilling children onto the pathway, in order to give them the news that school couldn't open. You wouldn't believe the number of parents who felt that we *should open* despite toilets belching effluence because they had an important meeting in town today. That was the autumn we were told the heating system had been put in upside down, with wires crossing, valves blocking and switches tripping, leading to areas of the school feeling like a tropical rain forest, and others like a cowboy-built igloo. I finally got the reason straight from the horse's mouth when a young apprentice sidled up to me in the corridor after a protracted and dismally ineffective meeting with the heating engineers. Looking up and down the corridor he leant in close and, from the corner of his mouth, whispered, "We knew they plans was all upside down when we put in them radiators mind."

I asked the obvious question. "Why did you install them then?"

"Well," he paused before continuing in his broad Somerset accent, "we don't *make* the plans. We just follows 'em."

Oh, that's alright then, I thought. Actually, I didn't think that at all. I thought, You complete knob-head! Then I looked at him and saw the child he had only just grown out of. "Thank you," I said, and almost reached for a gold star as a reward for the information.

The worst snagging item was the hall floor. One morning I walked into the hall before school and noticed that there were little hillocks appearing all over, rather like the mole hills we were experiencing on the sports field. Weeks after reporting this hairline cracks began to appear too. I wondered whether there was a particularly Herculean strain of mole attempting to stake a claim. Again the builders returned and tried to convince me that the children were responsible. They felt this had to be the only credible reason. Why? Because this type of flooring was used in hotels across the country without any problem, so it followed that the children must be mistreating it somehow. Thoughts of children planning the great escape via a tunnel dug under the school hall made me smile. I had visions of them assembling on the playground on one of those crisp Jack Frost mornings, and standing in height ascending rows with pockets dribbling soil down the legs of their charcoal-grey trousers. It was a coping mechanism and, along with my inner scream, prevented me from hurling abuse in every conceivable direction.

Other snagging issues included:

1   Windows opening horizontally outwards at the height of the average five-year-old's head.
2   Inadequate ventilation in the IT suite which housed thirty computers and thirty children – equally warm and glowing!
3   Fire doors leading nowhere.
4   Push-button flushes. Definitely NOT designed for four-year-olds with tiny thumbs and even tinier bladders.

A disproportionate amount of my time was spent in and out of toilets during those early years rescuing little ones (children), and plunging big ones (not children) due to inadequate water pressure.

Several years slipped by in the *Brigadoon* that was snagging land. Just when it seemed everything was at last normal something else would appear out of the mist. On a parallel journey was the head teacher of a sprawling comprehensive school in a neighbouring town. We had met in Bristol several years earlier, albeit briefly. We were propping up the bar at a head teachers' meeting both cradling long, cold drinks and staring into the chipped mirror behind the counter. Sometimes inertia takes over after hours of listening to people directing the course of education from a vantage point which is Buzz Lightyears away. His name was Matt. We got talking with an ease that is rare and I suppose we didn't stop talking for the next six years during which we became good friends and partners in crime.

We were soul-mates. There's such a wonder in that isn't there? Around soul-mates there's a frisson in the air. It's true. It's to do with the chemical reaction that is taking place between them. It's invisible but tangible, unstoppable. That's how it was with Matt and me.

Every head teacher should have a soul-mate. One with a shared sense of humour, one who doesn't take them self too seriously, one who could balance the huge responsibilities of running a successful school with realism and fun. We did that. Thank God we did that, or we'd be occupying adjacent beds on a psychiatric ward by now.

He had time for everyone. He rescued colleagues from distress. I mean major distress such as threatened school closure, or suing parents. He always paid compliments when due, and noticed things like earrings, or nail varnish, or new glasses. You know, the kind of things that men aren't renowned for spotting. Sometimes I wondered if he was gay. It wouldn't have mattered a jot.

We often sat together and wickedly took the opportunity to quietly compose defamatory verses about local authority speakers, some of whom were lovely people with difficult messages to convey to us all. We would've been every teacher's nightmare had we been at school together as kids. Matt was my champagne. He never failed to make me feel fabulous, feminine and above all, valued.

There were many times I needed his humour and stoicism. For instance, after a particularly frustrating meeting with the governing body, I would rail against one of the governors in Matt's sumptuous car for the ten minutes it took to get to the pub. He'd swing his car into the pub car park, switch off the engine, turn to me and say, "Have I told you, you look gorgeous today?" I would dissolve into laughter or tears and suddenly the world was restored to its equilibrium. My erstwhile bursting head space instantly emptied of school matters.

Male and female colleagues opened up to him. He had a way with women, he was a charmer I guess. But he was also invariably surrounded by men, possibly hoping for some of his charisma via osmosis.

Occasionally we would take a day out on the pretext of working on one leadership initiative or other and drive to the Gower Coast or somewhere away...just away. We'd pack our play clothes in the boot of his car and escape to spend the day walking, discussing books, favourite music, school, families, life. All the big issues were rolled out and we laughed our way through them, reducing them to the insignificance of a squashed milk cartoon careering round the playground. I have since recommended this day out to younger head teachers. It's invigorating, cathartic, fun, and throws you back onto the shoreline with renewed energy levels. I think it's called well-being in today's vernacular.

On a sparkling October morning we drove to the National Conference for Head Teachers in the Midlands. We stayed in an average hotel with colleagues from all over the world, not just the UK. The atmosphere was charged with expectancy. Groups of heads shared animated thoughts of what was to come during the next couple of days. Looking back I smile at the unshakeable optimism of that time. We had taken a record number of hits from the government during the last ten years, but we all bounced back endlessly with the same smiling faces armed afresh with initiatives of our own with which to wind our weary way through the midden of effluence presented by the Secretary of State. Do you remember the children's programme featuring Weebles? Well, that would've adequately described us. As they used to say, "Weebles wobble, but they won't fall down."

Day one was designed to motivate and it didn't disappoint. International speakers included the director/conductor of the Boston Philharmonic Orchestra. He was the man of my dreams. What an inspiration. He spoke, played piano, joked, and brought us to the verge of tears and back. He was no spring chicken either, but his age did nothing to slow him down either physically or mentally. Not for him the index cards of memory-joggers or autocue. His passion and humour swept us up on such a tide of enthusiasm that we left the centre buzzing with renewed purpose and brimming with the "art of possibility" which was his strapline for the conference.

Day two came and I guess we all knew that the euphoria had a terminal prognosis, although we still basked in the afterglow of the previous day. A procession of exuberant speakers from every world imaginable kept the balls of possibility in the air and showed us so much blue-sky thinking that we were longing for the shade of a transient little cloud. Then came the crunch we had all suspected, delivered impeccably by the well-pressed Secretary of State for Education. There we were, thousands of us, high on futures thinking, with our visions revised, dusted down, primed, ready for the countdown, trembling fingers on the buzzers of opportunity, revitalised and waiting to be sent forth to take the good news to all when, from out of nowhere, all our Christmases left at once. The cause? There was to be another major shift in education, more lumps in the school custard.

The NEW CURRICULUM served as the main course, rehashed onto the conference menu. Taste buds recoiled, diverting to default, as when presented with school broccoli, boiled to distraction and plopped on an unamused, pale green plastic plate.

I'll talk you through it. In the pause between the introduction and to the accompanying strains of Vangelis, reminding us that we too have a place in the 2012 Olympics, I scanned the audience. What a representation of UK and global head teachers. Every age there from the youngest, looking hardly old enough to have *left* school let alone be running one, to the most experienced, often care-worn, older, fading stars of headship that the country and the world had to offer. Within that vast spectrum I noted the facial expressions and body language. If asked for a run down I would say the categories varied from excited, confused, morose, confused, disconcerted, confused, accepting, confused, bemused, confused and the overwhelming category of "Did he really say what I think he said, or is it April the first?" His back-up team had anticipated our responses, and what followed was rehearsed and polished to a level comparable to a West End musical. Volume increased as Vangelis achieved gold and power points swung in from every conceivable direction and lit atmospheric spotlights. All that was missing was a Bruce Forsyth lookalike giving it, "Nice to see you...to see you...!" and, on the crest of the wave, we most probably would've bellowed back "NICE" with all the programmed hysteria of studio-audience enthusiasm.

Following the razzmatazz, the boiled broccoli, or rather the dried-up rationale was served. Drained of taste, bereft of a single vitamin, here's what we were supposed to swallow. "Something has to be done to address the failure of UK schools to achieve their targets." Mutters became audible declarations as colleagues turned to each other, and, with mounting fury, a cacophony of indignation spread like a Mexican wave around the auditorium as reasons for this "failure" ricocheted from wall to wall. Raised voices, then loud shouts were heard, "Over-inflated targets! Imposed, unrealistic percentages! Local authorities' face-saving initiatives! Doctored league tables! Borough interference! Governing body pressure! Unrealistic expectations! No time to implement new imposed initiatives!" All spewed forth from the upper circle, exploded across the plush, raked seating and flooded onto the stage, pooling at the foot of the podium where the least envied man in the room stood. The blanched face of the Secretary of State for Education was a sorry sight. I almost felt sorry for him as he looked toward the wings where it was easy to imagine conference facilitators facilitating their getaway cars. Returning to the presentation the poor man ploughed on. The finishing tape was in sight and he made it, gasping, red-faced, took a long swig of water, thanked everyone and stepped down. One could imagine him wrapped in turkey foil in the wings to restore his adrenalin levels, equalise his temperature and quell the shakes.

By now the atmosphere was electric. There was considerably more action than at the post-dinner disco the previous evening which had been a frenzy of poorly executed 60s moves and ineffable dad dancing as over-fifties threw some shapes. Groups gathered and surged toward the exits grabbing their freebies en route for one of the many bars alongside the canal. For a while I allowed myself to become excited by the demonstration of disapproval and looked forward to listening to Matt's thoughts on the way back down south. It's not often you see head teachers venting their collective spleen. Usually we're like the committee charged with designing a horse which eventually comes up with a camel. So yes, I was encouraged by the unanimity. In a moment of sheer fantasy I even felt the stirrings of a rebellion. Then I remembered last year's fiasco when there was a call to boycott SATs. Talk abounded. Colleagues bragged about how they were going to break the news to their governors and parents, and there was a distinct possibility that we could win this one if we stood together. Motivational pleas at local conferences were met with plenty of affirmation and promises but, on the day, few were there to man the barricades as embarrassed, empty promises swirled in the dust by the unhinged, playground gate.

So many excuses, all plausible in their own context. "I'm a new head...my governors will go ape-shit...the parents will be up in arms...the children ENJOY SATs," and perhaps the most depressing of all, "We've worked all year toward SATs results we can be proud of." My worst fears confirmed.

SATs came and went with seven brave head teachers making a stand in the local authority. The Magnificent Seven! God bless you for your courage and commitment to education. The rest? I wished them well and wonder to this day how they sleep at night.

But now my gin and tonic was a mere footbridge away from the conference centre. It seemed to me that the world of education that I had walked away from a few minutes ago had absolutely nothing to do with the world I now approached. It wasn't a spiritual experience, there was no moment of enlightenment, no trauma on the road to Damascus, but a calm settled over me. I chose a bar near the footpath running alongside the canal and ordered a gin and tonic, although it was only 4.30pm. Don't you just *love* residential conferences? The anger and sheer frustration which had been coursing through my every pore minutes before seemed to have dissipated into the drizzle. I watched a family of ducks enjoying the rain, showing off manoeuvres as they negotiated with barges and the inevitable supermarket trolley, vying for a place on the crowded canal.

I sat there hoping that the rest of our group wouldn't turn up for a while. It wouldn't be difficult to find me. I wanted to watch busy people strutting by. I wanted to listen to snippets of their conversations, normal conversations. Normal, meaningless conversations. My own thoughts wouldn't wait though, and began arriving at breakneck speed.

Words sprinted, gasping around my mind circuit...targets,

failure, percentages below the national average, failure, catch-up programmes, one to one tuition, targets, failure, boys' achievement v girls' achievement, failure, percentages of level fives etc. The perpetual carousel...the organ grinder grinned while his monkey danced a dervish, and underpinning each thought was the question, "Where are the children in this?" It repeated and repeated. I found myself clinging to it, and the gin and tonic, lest I should spin away into the grey mist hovering over the canal and miss my lift home. The return journey was quiet. Unusually so. To say the stuffing had been knocked out of us is rather cliche, but I struggle to describe the deflated atmosphere accompanying us like some uninvited guest crouching unseen in the back of the car.

Chapter 24

Another reluctant Friday dragged itself up from the coast with all the enthusiasm of a dry stone wall. I quite enjoyed Fridays though. I had another brilliant assembly up my sleeve involving lots of participation from the children. The kind of assembly that cranked up the week and the teachers, and left the hall humming long after the children had walked back to class. The kind of assembly dreaded by staff, firstly because it would include some follow-up activity which they hadn't planned, and secondly would require some homework from them to ensure they got the God bit right. Shouldn't be too challenging I know. After all, we are a Catholic school, but sometimes we need to research the church's stance before answering questions from inquisitive children and sometimes even more inquisitive parents.

Strangely the assembly didn't hit the spot as well as I'd envisaged. Unusual assemblies were a strength of mine. I remember one particular assembly when I introduced the children to the notion of *Obstacle/Opportunity*. This was something I'd learnt from a gospel preacher in America. It was simply a notion that whatever misfortune comes our way, there is an opportunity for growth therein. We explored several possibilities which the children offered and, at the end of each scenario, I asked them, "Obstacle?" and they all replied,

"Opportunity." The phrase and I hope the practice became part of life at St George's. If ever something didn't go according to plan, Obstacle/Opportunity became the catchphrase to move the situation on. Today's assembly didn't strike the right chords though and left me feeling if perhaps I was beginning to lose my touch. Later, as I drove to St Benedict's school for a lunch time meeting, the thought took up residence in my head.

The sun was shining on the wet road as I took the motorway exit for St Benedict's Catholic Comprehensive School and this term's Catholic head teacher's meeting. I remember thinking how I'd enjoyed the otherworldliness alongside the canal after the conference in the Midlands. Realising that out there, in the world that is *not* education, there are people, places, new ventures, and a certain enigmatic freedom. A *potential* world not totally governed by the whims of politicians.

The meeting was in full swing by the time I parked my car at St Benedict's Catholic Comprehensive School in a space reserved for the deputy head teacher. I figured that if he wasn't in school yet he wouldn't expect his space to be waiting for him. I locked the car, decided against taking an umbrella, and ran the fifty metres to the school lobby. Damn shoes! Someone needs to design a pair of running shoes that are elegant, with a heel of course, and possibly even with some comfort in mind for occasions such as these. By now I was feeling flustered, almost stressed perhaps. I hated being late for anything. I didn't mind the late entrance, in fact I could almost enjoy being the focus of attention for a second or two, but it was the anticipation of the mood which got to me. There's something which defies adequate description about opening the door to a meetings room and seeing sagging, drab colleagues barely able to lift their equally sagging, drab faces from the wodge of paper in front of them to acknowledge the late arrival. These days there seemed to be so few *colourful* personalities in headship. As I opened the door the warmth assailed my nostrils. The smell of stale room and stale conversation almost clamped me to the spot. A morbidly obese primary school head teacher (he had told us all at a previous meeting that his doctor had described him thus. His doctor was correct) dropped his A4 diary in an exasperated attempt at non-verbal communication. He was one of the few who clung to paper as if committing notes to a laptop was tantamount to tossing them into the deepest fathoms and mildew of a medieval well. He swivelled his seat turning away from the speaker, and sat with morose head in hands. Next to him was a new head teacher from a local primary school. Pert, and pretty, but with an unmistakeable expression of OMG, *what is everyone talking about?* while attempting to remain unflustered. She would learn that it didn't matter. We knew who got it and who was guilty of not reading the latest fiction from the government. The current speaker, the head of St Benedict's Catholic Comprehensive held court. She always did. It was assumed she lived alone, partied hard and worked equally hard. She drove a fabulous black convertible, played a mean game of golf and wore designer shoes. Am I beginning to sound envious? That's because I was! I'd never heard anyone cross her. It would've been foolish. She was an intellectual goddess. Opposite her sat Poor Stuart. I called him Poor Stuart because he was clueless, but it was okay. He had *never* had a clue. His school was going down the tubes at a rate comparable to that of the country's banks. He fiddled with his watchstrap.

Two women colleagues sat giggling, while reaching for another chocolate Hobnob from the paper plate sporting Mr Men in the centre of the tired, wooden table. One was notorious for telling the most filthy jokes and I hoped that she would repeat this one loud enough for the rest of us. Heaven knows the atmosphere needed a lift as much as the sagging breasts of her colleague. I noted who was missing and remembered that a head from our cluster was in hospital after suffering a major stroke which had rendered him partially paralysed just last week. I made a mental note to get a card and send flowers. A couple of others had sent their apologies, apparently one was too bogged down with an impending OFSTED inspection to attend, and the other was dealing with a violent incident which had occurred at lunchtime.

I plonked myself down on the nearest hard, plastic seat and realised that I'd missed out on lunch. It didn't matter, I had little appetite, and the leftover wraps, unwrapped and adorning centre stage on a creased sheet of aluminium foil, looked as limp as school spider plants in draughty corridors. There was one remaining Hobnob amongst the crumbs, but before I had time to decide whether I wanted it or not morbidly obese stretched out his pale, puffy hand and lifted it delicately to his mouth where it disappeared, whole. I didn't much care. I guessed the biscuits had done the rounds before gracing this particular meeting. They looked second hand.

The topic was Academies. Was it a good idea to go for academy status or not? An interesting one this. Not so long ago under-performing schools became academies in an attempt to raise standards by throwing money at their flagging attempts to improve. So we all did our utmost *not* to be offered academy status. Then, all change, schools judged to be outstanding by OFSTED were *invited* to become academies. There were plenty of head teachers gagging for the status that would bring, to say nothing of the funds which accompanied the status. Then, all change again. *Any* school could become an academy provided it was prepared to oversee a less successful school. Hey, great idea, I thought with a tinge of cynicism, even more work for the already overworked head teachers. I didn't envy the comprehensive school heads though, the financial carrot dangling to encourage them to become an academy was very tempting. After all, it could facilitate the building of a much needed science block for example, or the purchase of masses of new resources. Laptops for all!

I found myself tuning out. Not a good thing for me. I didn't have the intellectual prowess of some of my colleagues and couldn't be relied upon to contribute much unless fully alert. And fully alert was the last thing I was. I stared out of the window to the sports field in the middle distance. I could just about hear the thwack of the ball on hockey sticks and the occasional muffled whistle from the ref. I remembered my own school days. I loved hockey and played right inner as it was called then. As I continued to watch, I realised that some things hadn't changed much. There were still reluctant participants lurking along the edges of the pitch avoiding the herd mentality of the other girls and the eagle eye of the games teacher. PE kit was still adjusted to show as much leg as decently possible, and sometimes a whole lot more! Girls still fussed about their hair even after a breathtaking sprint down the centre of the pitch when everything paused for a moment. The game was suspended, sticks were dropped and hair was repositioned before the match resumed.

Back in the drab room I registered that someone was making their apologies and heading for the door. I grabbed the chance to escape making the excuse that I needed to speak with my colleague who had just left. No one believed either of us of course, but we'd taken our chance and left, and they hadn't. *C'est la vie.* She who dares and all that.

I caught up with my fellow escapee who had turned as she heard my footsteps. "I knew you wouldn't be far behind," she said. "You zoned out about twenty minutes ago didn't you?" I was alarmed that

I'd been rumbled. Normally I could fake interest quite well, raising an eyebrow here and there, coughing and reaching for the fizzy water, looking like a panel member on *Question Time*. At least that was my perception. Maybe I wasn't fooling anybody. That was quite a disconcerting thought. If I *wasn't* maintaining a professional *façade*, what exactly were my colleagues seeing?

I must admit I felt a little embarrassed. Maybe they were all sitting there thinking, Oh bless, she's lost the plot. God…maybe they were laughing at me behind my back. It all began to fall into place. They felt sorry for me. They knew I was only half-present. Paranoia or what? Get a grip, girl! We walked to our cars sharing her umbrella and snippets of diocesan gossip, until a gust of wind took her and her inside out brolly to her car.

The school buses had pulled up along the pot-holed road outside, blocking the car park exit. That's all I needed to begin to feel claustrophobic. Children spilled out from every available door like water from a burst pipe gushing toward the buses, laughing, pushing, swinging bags, linking arms and shouting across the road to friends disappearing along the congested footpath. The mobile phone chorus, as regular as the dawn chorus, began. Hundreds of children walking together but conversing with some absent person deemed more important than the one by their side.

I reached for my laptop, flipped it open and buried my head in some meaningless MSN celebrity news, not wishing to make eye contact with the herd jostling past my car. The last thing I wanted was to invite conversation from a past pupil. Who was I kidding? I was beginning to doubt that anyone would initiate a conversation with me. After all, I couldn't maintain concentration at meetings, everyone knew that. Surely I would be considered "way un-cool, innit" by any self-respecting teenager. I don't think *I* would've talked to me at that age either!

The rain had gone into overdrive. It pelted the windows and provided a welcome screen between me and the outside world. I felt overwhelmingly tired. I put it down to the seamless grey sky. I'd always suspected I had seasonal affective disorder (SAD) and claimed that it was due to my Portuguese heritage. I flicked the switch for the wipers to come on and didn't like what I saw. One or two buses were pulling away from the parking bays in front of the school gates as children pushed through the already crowded aisles and fell into vacant seats, squashing up against steamy windows. Others stood waiting for someone to pick them up while chewing gum, mouths wide with pink, bursting bubbles. Astonishing how many of them weren't wearing coats, their shirts clinging to soaking shoulders. I don't suppose it's cool to wear coats any more. I pulled mine closer around my neck. I was cold, not cool but dismal, just like the weather. There were hoards of children coming in waves, and I wished they'd all disappear. I made a mental note of the time and decided that in future I would make my getaway either before 3.15pm or after 3.45pm when, hopefully, the way would be clear to beat a hasty retreat and head up the motorway back to school.

As it was I was trapped, an unwitting prisoner in my own cell, with no time off for good behaviour to restore my sanity. No J2O in a warm, empty pub somewhere even. No fun, no warmth, no worth. I wasn't ready for the tears, though at my stage of life they never seemed further than a hair's breadth beneath the calm I maintained as my public face. I sniffed, pulled a tired tissue from the side pocket in the passenger door, started the car and headed for the motorway faster than intended. Before I realised it I had taken the turning for home which was in the opposite direction to the exit which would take me back to school. Well, I rationalised, it was Friday, and traffic would be hell heading south. For some inexplicable reason I pulled over into a lay-by near the equestrian centre. The view from there was great on a clear day, right across to Wales. I was in the minority who didn't actually mind seeing Wales in the distance, but today the cloying mist and wistful clouds wafted undecided toward the coast limiting the view. Today the fields resembled a watercolour painting left out by a forgetful six-year-old. Colour, draining from the leaden sky, blended into green-grey sodden fields. I felt the pull of the downpour. It was as if I too was dissolving and could do nothing to stop it happening. I was grey-green, without power, without energy, without light. It was Friday, but my Friday feeling wouldn't surface. I searched for my phone. It had slipped out of my bag and was lodged somewhere in the recesses under the passenger seat. I grovelled around, found an apple core and my sunglasses, both of which had undoubtedly lodged there since last summer. Swearing under my breath I finally located my phone, threw the apple core into the hedgerow, and tapped in the school number. The battery needed charging. I found myself grateful that the five per cent battery left notice didn't pop up on my forehead, like the screen of the phone, highlighting my flagging demeanour. Wouldn't it be great though if we could simply plug in and charge like all our commodities, and emerge in fifteen minutes fully functioning. I should've realised that at this time on a Friday all available office staff would be manning the front desk finding lost coats and lost children for impatient parents and glassy-eyed toddlers already well into their pre-tea nuts and raisins snack. The call went straight to answer machine "if you would like to report an absence, key one. If you would like to speak to a member of staff, and know their extension, key in their extension now. For all other enquiries…" Inwardly I formed the words, I'd like to speak with a friggin human being actually! Whose idea was it to have that litany on the answer-phone? Oh God, it was mine. "Hi, it's me," I chirped, after the beep. "I'm not coming back this afternoon. Any problems please give me a call. Have a great weekend. See you Monday!" My cheerful voice, belying my internal angst, would be recognised immediately and all would be well. I didn't anticipate a call.

The ensuing silence wasn't good for me but I couldn't seem to make the right moves to start the car. I didn't want to go home, yet I didn't want to sit in my already steamy car, but neither did I want to go back to school. Gazing out at the flimsy morphing shapes as mists wafted by I recalled how, on Fridays sometimes, Matt and I would meet up for a drink and mull over the week. It wasn't quite a ritual as our days were so unpredictable, Fridays more so than most other days. Anything might kick off at his school and, if it did, he would call and let me know that he would be later than planned, or that he was involved with some parents, or perhaps the police or social services and we wouldn't meet up at all. If all was well we both looked forward to this downtime together. It was an end of week reward. Sometimes we didn't speak for a while, just sipped fruit juices and gazed into the nothingness of a local pub. Too tired to talk much.

Sometimes the weekend was the topic of conversation. Matt and his partner might have friends staying over. He enjoyed cooking and we'd talk about food, and whether they'd barbecue or not. For me it was never a question of whether to barbeque or not as

184

I don't do barbeques in England. I claimed never to have enjoyed a barbeque here, and it was a legitimate claim. I found the range of food as depressing and limited as the new curriculum the government was about to cook up. The weather was guaranteed to surprise even in the height of summer. Even if the sun was forcing its way out heroically between gathering clouds, within an hour I'd be shivering and wondering how others were able to withstand the cold while wearing T-shirts, jeans, and false smiles. I gave up persevering and frequently got my North Face jacket from the car while summoning up all my will power in order to manage a blackened sausage oozing pink stuff from its centre. Despite my lack of practice I could drop a sausage into a laburnum bush simply by shifting my balance from one foot to the other, while maintaining eye contact with whoever was talking to me. To this day I haven't been discovered, and have never suffered from post-barbeque projectile vomiting. The same cannot be said for most of our friends. I can't speak for the laburnum.

I'd wax lyrical about barbecues at my brother's place in California. He was passionate about food, at least about cooking it, he didn't eat much. He consumed tinny after tinny of Bud, while passing round a spliff and pouring honey over every sizzling surface of the meat on the griddle. His speciality, fresh salmon, the length of the griddle, melted in the mouth. His salads resembled Covent Garden veg markets, a riot of colour and textures composed with lavish attention and every conceivable vegetable, fresh from the "Salad Bowl" region of California. Needless to say the dressings were all home-made and transported us all to the Mediterranean. What I also loved was the notion that, mid-week, you could invite friends around for the barbeque and know, beyond a shadow of doubt, that the weather would be perfect. Not a North Face, a Shake and Eat lettuce, or an apologetic, half-cooked burger in sight. Now *that's* a barbeque!

"Enough wallowing," I chastised myself, in the mock Irish accent I saved especially for self-chastisement because it wrapped the warm comfort of Mrs Walters, my first secretary at St Mark's, around my drooping shoulders,

"Get yourself home, girl...go on."

Backing into the drive at home, I narrowly missed the wall. I swore, levered myself out of my little soft top, opened the boot and lifted out my school bag. It was so heavy that there and then I decided to fling it into the lounge and sit quietly sorting it out. It would be a couple of hours before Jeff came home, so I figured there was sufficient time to upend my bag and sift through the residue accumulated and unnoticed since the beginning of term. Most cathartic.

For almost forty years I had lugged different bags between home and school. First of all a giant PVC carrier from Sainsbury's supermarket. It was colossal, designed to hold family-size loo rolls and bottles of on-offer Chablis. Then a more trendy beach bag, striped and clean, sporting wooden handles and reminiscent of beach holidays reflecting the fresh start as we moved to Bristol in the 70s. This was replaced by a proper briefcase when we moved to Somerset and I became a deputy head. Jeff bought it for me as a congratulatory gift. I thought the case gave me an air of credibility. It looked the business, I looked the business, but apart from my planning file, lipstick, tissues, half a dozen paper clips and a selection of pencils from WH Smith, it could hold little else. I was forced to revert to a canvas Bag for Life for carrying children's books to and fro for marking.

Jeff made a comment one day that I never actually got to the bottom of any bag, and that I was probably carrying an unnecessarily heavy load. I scoffed at his observation while secretly knowing he was absolutely right. I remembered tipping it out one Sunday afternoon before beginning my planning for the week. This was a delaying tactic I hadn't used before. I promised myself it would only take half an hour and made a mental note of the time. It was 2.35pm so I reckoned I'd make a cup of tea at 3.00pm – another delaying tactic – before spending the next four hours or so planning. At 3.50pm I came up for air, or rather a loo roll for my streaming nose. Paper always did that to me. It had the same effect as light summer breezes transporting pollen had on a child in my class. The poor child streamed over any available surface for a couple of months each year. I stood up to go to the bathroom and had a bird's-eye view of the mountain of rubbish I'd created. Old worksheets, so popular then, erasers, broken pencils, a sharpener, one half-sucked polo mint with a hair clinging to it, two hymn books with matching turned up corners, six rulers, several computer discs, some aged audio tapes (one which I had sworn I didn't have last Christmas when questioned by the reception teacher), perfume, too many used tissues to count, a collapsible handbag-umbrella, a small china hedgehog and a copy of the songbook, *Merrily to Bethlehem*. I was ashamed of my capacity to hoard. But actually it wasn't that. I was appalled that I had trundled this hefty dross underneath the thirty-six exercise books I threw in there every day term after term in the vain hope that I would catch up with my marking. I made a resolution there and then that I would only bring home what I intended to work on and leave everything else behind. It went the way of all resolutions, however, and pretty soon I was back in character as the bag lady.

I promised myself that today's exorcism would be different. I settled with a cup of tea and lifted the first of several A4 files out of my bag. It was Health & Safety. I recalled that I was going to sort it by ditching all out-of-date policies and risk assessments, a sort of paper detox, and return it in its new sylph-like format to a shelf in my office cupboard. At the time I began to feel self-righteous, another one of the endless boxes ticked for OFSTED. That was last Tuesday and the file hadn't seen the light of day since. Today was not the day for Health & Safety either, so the file went to my right hand side. The first file in the for another day category. This went on until it grew almost dark outside and I continued in the gloom, choosing not to put the lights on just yet. I didn't want to illuminate the crap. The black rubbish bag to my left was half-full with shredded notes, an old lip liner broken and abandoned, some leadership periodicals which I was always going to read but never did, and the minutes of two, virtually identical, diocesan meetings. The pile in front of me was optimistically called "to do this weekend" and consisted of anything and everything to do with our impending OFSTED inspection. As I determined to make it through the whole lot before Monday, I put the right hand pile back into my bag quickly as if in doing so it would diminish in size and lose its importance thus giving me a reprieve for another hour or two. I twisted the top of the black bag, knotted it and threw it into the bin just outside the front door with a little more enthusiasm than was necessary. The automatic light came on and lit the drive. I looked up and could just about make out Orion's Belt, visible at the moment prior to the street lights coming to life. It had been a strange day. I felt unsettled, my own impending departure appeared to be hurtling toward me at an alarming speed.

I stared at Orion and recalled the phone call from Matt which had determined my mood for the day. Brace yourself. He was announcing his exciting news. He was leaving the country, reinventing himself apparently. I had smiled encouragingly, and nodded over the phone knowing that it was pointless, rather like a Radio 4 wildlife journalist attempting to describe the flight of a thousand swifts across a west country sunset. I made all the right noises. I gushed congratulations and managed to squeeze out the all-important question, "When are you going?" sounding for all the world like a breathy Oliver Twist asking for more. And I *was* asking for more. More time, more fun, more book sharing, more walks, more laughter, more anything. I realised I'd flicked all my desk magnets onto the floor. Now realisation began to dawn on me. Matt's impact on my life had been substantial.

An Indian friend of mine once said, "Our personalities are the sum of all the relationships we have experienced." I understood what he was getting at.

As Joni Mitchell used to sing, "You don't know what you've got 'til it's gone..." Thanks, Joni, rub it in why don't you?

Who would've guessed slinging a bag of rubbish could motivate such Bohemian thoughts? Far too heavy for the weekend ahead. I put the kettle on then routed for a corkscrew in the drawer of useful things and took the top off a bottle of Merlot before I realised what I was doing! Taking a glass down from the cupboard, beverage decision made, I grabbed a chocolate biscuit...okay, two chocolate biscuits and stretched out in the darkened lounge.

Chapter 25

"Day forty-two in the Big Brother House…" I sometimes found myself saying this to no one in particular as I walked from the car park into school. Not that school was ever as dull or predictable, it just amused me sometimes. It doesn't take much!

As I walked through the foyer I smiled warmly at a couple of fidgeting parents. The dad glanced anxiously at his watch and I wondered if I had inadvertently forgotten an appointment. While checking my diary and running an apology through my mind, Belle followed me into my office. Belle was the school secretary. When you have a day or two to spare check out her job description and then ask yourself why she isn't head of MI5 and commanding a decent salary. Belle could tell at a glance what I was feeling and right now she read me well.

Belle assured me that there was no appointment with the parents, but that they had been waiting since 7.15am to see me. I asked Belle the purpose of the meeting. She glanced back at the door, furtively, before whispering that I had written to them on Friday following a racist incident in school during which their son had allegedly called a black child an offensive name. How she remembered everything I'll never know, but she could repeat conversations verbatim too. It all flooded back. I had phoned both the parents' work numbers, their mobiles, and eventually their home numbers after the incident, but their voicemails clicked into operation each time. I was only able to ask them to call me back as soon as they picked up the message. Naturally, Belle followed up with texts to parents as is normal practice these days.

Friday ended without a follow-up call. At the end of the day I emailed them with a brief description of the incident and asked them to call the office to arrange an appointment. I felt myself slip into sarcastic thought, much less hassle just to turn up. After all, what could be more important to a head teacher first thing on a Monday morning than their child's inappropriate behaviour on a Friday afternoon? Oh what a cynic I'm becoming!

Assembly was at 8.30am. My first scheduled meeting was at 10.00am. Should be enough time to have a quick word, I thought. They've probably come in to apologise and ask how to make reparation to the offended child. How naïve, after all these years, that I should assume the just and right response. As Belle showed in Mr and Mrs T. It was clear an apology and the pair of them were not going to be in the same room. Mr T pitched in with a diatribe accusing me of bullying his son who had done nothing wrong and was, as a result of my accusations, unable to sleep on Friday night and could hardly summon enough energy for his Saturday morning motocross competition. My heart sank as, yet again, I settled to listen to another parent giving me chapter and verse on the injustice meted out by us all in school as we failed to appreciate the angelic virtues of their children.

Mrs T was meek. Nodding, folding her arms, flicking her *Desperate Housewives* hair, and answering her phone which came to life with the dulcet tones of Robbie Williams' "Angels". Ahhhhh. I let Mr T finish. After all, he had put the record straight. His son was quoted as saying that he was, "nowhere near the victim on Friday and was inconsolable all the way home". Strange how accounts of the same event can be so far apart in content that it would seem to an outsider that there were two separate incidents. Two separate planets even! Belle walked past the door rolling her eyes. Not for the first time this year I envied her detachment.

Equally strange was the fact that their son – we'll call him Junior – demonstrated such imaginative prowess when explaining to his parents his version of events. Would that he showed such talent in his written work. Junior was averse to the written word or, should I say, Junior was dyslexic? At least that's the diagnosis of the parents who are experts in the world of education. After all, they too attended school once. Amazing that his spelling of *Fuck off you wankers*, in bold black spray paint on the outside wall of year six classroom was perfect, and that the handwriting would've been a strong contender for winner of the monthly handwriting competition. I guess there must be a new strain of dyslexia, selective dyslexia perhaps, or dyslexia by proxy.

Mrs T wasn't in the mood for listening. Robbie Williams went off again and I found myself wondering how many angels he loved each day, and how on earth could she stand it punctuating her life every ten minutes or so? No apology or acknowledgement regarding the ignored, dormant voicemails, texts or emails, naturally. Maybe carrier pigeons next time? I waited until she was figuratively back in the room before attempting to let them know what had happened. Before I was able to finish my first sentence they both launched. It was like facing a firing squad consisting of two trigger-happy snipers. They had me covered from all angles. With each of them attempting to be heard, their voices grew louder and louder as they poured forth in a sort of shout-fest. Very therapeutic I imagine. Clearly it was all my fault. I frightened Junior, caused his insomnia and subsequent energy-drained Saturday. I bullied him when no one else was around on Friday and, allegedly, verbally beat him to a pulp. I didn't recognise the person they described and wondered for a second whether I'd had an out of body experience on Friday, but I couldn't recall any compulsion to walk toward the light which, I believe, is a regular feature of the condition, and so drew the conclusion that Junior had been liberal with the truth. Liberal? The truth and Junior was an anathema.

I called Belle into the office. Belle had been there on Friday along with Pat, her partner in crime, the year six girls who witnessed the incident, the victim and Junior. It being the policy to keep my office door open at all times, any number of passing parent volunteer-helpers would also have seen, or possibly even heard the goings on. The alleged torturing of Junior, the out of control lambasting of said child, the coercion of hand-picked witnesses, all clearly observable. And yet, by some fluke, some simple twist of fate, none of this *had* been seen. Belle retold the whole episode from Junior's arrival in my office, exuding bravado, to his return to class thirty-five minutes later with his tail between his legs.

By now Mr T was maintaining that any adult present must've

seen and heard what Junior had reported to them between his bouts of hysteria and sleeplessness over the weekend because, "We know when he's lying!" I suggested calling Junior to the office. Innocent, dyslexic, bullied, ten-year-old Junior was collected from class.

Junior had sat in my office on Friday convincing himself of his innocence. I actually, momentarily felt a twinge of pity for him. The witnesses were girls from year six, squeaky clean, polite, reliable, no-nonsense girls, who couldn't be dishonest even if their lives depended on it. On Friday Junior had finally, begrudgingly, admitted his crime, but added a lame excuse in the vain attempt to divert his guilt. It was 9.35am, assembly missed. Almost forty minutes had passed. Surely this could be settled in time for me to grab my prep. for the meeting and arrive on time? Junior took a look at his parents. Mr T had been pacing my office. Not easy, as it's just about big enough to meet the requirements of the pre-second world war Factories and Shops Act, or more appropriately at times an Anderson shelter. His pacing involved navigating his way around a small coffee table, two chairs and the detritus from last Friday's senior leadership team meeting. Mrs T was on her third phone call rearranging her nail gel appointment. As it was an outgoing call we were at least spared Robbie. Both parents turned to face their son. He stood there, blonde haired, blue eyed, staring into the middle distance as if rooted to the spot by an unseen alien. He would've auditioned successfully for *Village of the Damned*. Dyslexic by proxy Junior, his eyes said it all as they took on a look I had not seen before. A look of *you still believe me don't you?* directed at his parents was met with an equally defiant *of course we do, darling* in silent unison.

What followed would've given *EastEnders* a run for its money. Ten minutes of cross-examination by Mr T trying desperately to convince me of his son's innocence proved too much for Junior, and I found myself understanding why he had lied. Mr T gesticulated, swore, accused Junior of wasting his precious time. No mention of *my* precious time you notice.

Finally, he checked his watch, a genuine, fake cheaper-than-Asda timepiece picked up on a recent holiday to Turkey taken in term time. He grabbed his jacket, previously slung over the coffee table so that he could roll his sleeves up and achieve maximum menacing effect, glanced at Mrs T, and strode out of my office almost flattening Pat, the school cook, as she bustled in to query dinner numbers for the day. His Mercedes purred out of the school car park as Mrs T and I were left with the fallout in my office. As if awoken from a bad dream Mrs T took Junior's hand, much to his embarrassment, and said she didn't care what everyone said. She knew Junior had been very upset by the whole incident and she was going to the shopping mall to buy him something special to make up for it. She stood up to leave hugging the by now mortified Junior who stood with his arms limp and his face nuzzled into her Per Una shirt. Robbie burst into song and she could be heard mouthing off at her boss as she struggled to reach the security switch to open the front door, while balancing her phone and her overstuffed leopard print handbag. I didn't know whether to reprimand Junior or commiserate with him for his unfortunate allocation of parents. I anticipated some kind of apology, some acknowledgement from Junior's parents that my time had been wasted, my honesty and integrity questioned, my staff called to account, but no, nothing from anyone. *Plus ça change*. Junior returned to class anticipating his treat from the mall, safe in the knowledge he would always win whether he was innocent or guilty. He had his parents where he wanted them, particularly his mother.

I was reminded of the book *We Need to Talk About Kevin* and wondered whether to recommend it to his parents. I flew out of the door to my scheduled meeting now already ten minutes late. What will become of the Juniors of this world I wondered as I drove into Weston-super-Mare. The thousands of children dropped at school by 8.00am to be picked up at 6.00pm by a stressed parent making no attempt to feign a welcome or proffer a smile. The thousands of children who think that love is getting their own way and the parents who think that love is giving their children everything in the Argos catalogue, driving them to school in the Mercedes four by four, and setting them up with a flat-screen TV, DS games console and computer in their bedrooms. Oh my. The countless children worldwide who are so busy communicating online that they are incapable of holding a conversation unless it's virtual. The overstimulated masses who have no comprehension of delayed gratification. God help them when they hit the world of work or, more realistically, the world of unemployment.

The meeting? The one I'd rushed to? The all-important-not-to-be-missed meeting? I surmised that I must've missed the all-important bit, or daydreamed my way through it yet again wondering whether Matt was making his mark in his new job, although I was sure that by now he would've wowed the entire community. Cue music as Sir Galahad's steed rears and heads off into the blazing glory of yet another perfect sunset.

Chapter 26

I woke up to the dying strains of the 10.00pm news. My laptop slid to the floor and the data I'd been analysing leapt to life again on the screen as if it too had been jolted awake unceremoniously from a deep slumber. I left it there and dragged myself off to bed trying hard to keep my mind from responding to the lure of percentages which I knew would keep me awake through the wee small hours if I allowed them a sneaky look in.

I don't remember getting undressed and getting into bed, but I do remember falling over my discarded dressing gown and flip-flops a few hours later as I beat a hasty exit from the bedroom to answer the phone before it woke Jeff. It was pointless. He always woke before me in a crisis and the phone ringing at 3.15am could only constitute a crisis. To my surprise it was a former teacher of mine, Kate, from St Mark's. We'd come across each other a couple of months previously. She was on maternity leave expecting her second child, and we'd exchanged news. She had been an inspirational teacher in my reception class, quirky, colourful, funny, strict and totally adored by every child she taught. We'd laughed as we recalled the good times and she made me realise how fortunate we had been in those four years when we had the dream team following the severe pruning of the previous years!

As we'd parted with hugs and best wishes, she turned to me and asked if I would help her if her husband was away when she went into labour. I agreed, of course, imagining babysitting her gorgeous son, Oliver, while her mother escorted her to the local maternity hospital. So it was with some surprise that I heard her say, "We've got to go,

Maggie, we've got to go *now*. Can you come over?" In my groggy state I tried to reassure her as I pulled on my jeans and struggled with my jumper which I later noticed was inside out. I mumbled something to Jeff and flew out of the front door. I was at Kate's home fifteen minutes later. She lived on the outskirts of Bristol, far enough away for there to be little light pollution. I drove slowly down the lane by her house and was unable to avoid the potholes and puddles in the pitch black. She was waiting in the porch with her Polish mother. I'd met her before at Kate's wedding. She was a lovely lady, but a worrier. I sensed her anxiety as I heard whispered Polish coming in fits and starts as if she was just remembering important last-minute advice which she obviously felt essential at this hour. Kate escaped from her enfolding arms weakly protesting, "Mama, mama, please let me go," and lurched toward my car. She looked back over her shoulder to tell her mama, "Oliver should sleep 'til at least 7.30am. He likes wheat flakes with warm milk for breakfast," pause to pant, "and…and he goes to nursery today. Sharon will collect him at 8.45am. He will need his all-in-one wetsuit and wellies, 'cos it's going to rain and they'll play outside. Bye, mama."

I registered the last two words, "Bye, mama". I stood staring at her mother's anxious face. In response she gently pushed me toward the car, nodding encouragement as she backed me along the path, and instructing me to, "Go, go…she is nearly ready…baby is coming soon."

Kate reached the car before me. "Ooh, we're going to have to get a move on, Maggie." Me? Get a move on? Oh, ME GET A MOVE ON! The facts registered like cherries in a row on a one-armed-bandit. Mama was babysitting, I was baby-delivering! Okay. First things first. How to get Kate into the car without the aid of a crane to lower her in through the roof. Luckily she had been a PE teacher and was still remarkably supple. She bent herself almost double, as double as is possible with a bump the size of an over-ripe pumpkin between her chest and the top of her thighs, and slid sideways onto the passenger seat where she froze. I thought she'd forgotten something and was about to call out for her mother when I noticed her face. Or rather I noticed her curtain of thick, blonde hair partially obscuring her transformed features. She was puffing, panting and trying hard not to whimper. I was trying hard not to worry that her waters might be breaking all over the cream leather upholstery, but she'd thought of everything with her usual efficiency and was attempting to push a large bath towel between her legs like an oversized nappy. I helped her into the seatbelt, pushed the seat back as far as it could go and set off in the lashing rain hoping against hope that my driving wouldn't initiate the airbag on the passenger side. I knew who would win that battle.

Driving through a deserted Bristol in the dead of night lent an air of mystery to the journey which took my mind off the air of near panic which, between us, was palpable. I swung into the car park of the maternity wing and levered myself out of the car, only to realise I was wearing one scruffy blue slipper and one black trainer sporting a luminous logo along the outside edge. How could I have done that? No time to dwell on that question. I opened the passenger door as Kate began another contraction. I crouched down on the gravel so that I was level with her face and panted with her. She stared at me as if I had lost possession of my faculties. "I thought it might help?" I whispered.

She scowled, looked at me and said, "How on earth am I going to get out of this bloody car?" I found myself apologising.

"Okay, grab the top of the door, no, undo your seatbelt, *now* grab the top of the door, no, forget that. Swing your legs round to the side, you know, like royalty. Now, edge yourself forward, put your arms round my neck and straighten your legs." All good so far.

Having got to semi-upright position, another contraction began. "Don't move, don't you dare move," Kate hissed through clenched teeth into my ear as we stood in a sort of bear hug / demi-plie position. More panting. I glanced around to see if there was a passing midwife in the car park. Where the hell were they when you needed one for God's sake? We prised ourselves to standing position. "Okay. Let's go." Kate relaxed and leant against the car. I groped for her bag in the boot and held her hand as we made our way, ever so cautiously, toward the fluorescent warmth of the maternity wing foyer. We were shown to her room and introduced to her midwife, who looked around in anticipation of an expectant father. "Don't even bother looking. He's in the Channel Islands," Kate glowered. James, Kate's husband, travelled a lot for work. He also commanded an enviable salary. "Here's his number," she said, thrusting an address book at me while beginning to pant again. "Call him, and," pant, pant, "tell him not to," wince,

wince, "come back without a massive," low growl, "DIAMOND!"

I did as I was told. I got through to James. He laughed when I relayed Kate's message. I thought it provident not to tell Kate that. I improvised along the lines that James was moving heaven and earth to board the next plane out of Jersey and fly to her side. One look at Kate was enough to know that he wasn't going to make it in time for the arrival of their second baby. The midwife, a rosy-cheeked young woman who looked about fifteen, asked, "Is your mother going to be your birth partner?" Kate guffawed,

"She's not my mother... She's my head teacher!"

"Oh," the midwife squeaked, "how...unusual." I think I detected a note of slight embarrassment as she held her notes tightly to her chest as if she thought I was about to check her spelling or reprimand her for appalling handwriting. Why do people do that I wondered, not for the first time.

I'd been mugged outside of school once by two lads on a motor-bike. When the police arrived to take my statement the young PC looked me in the eye and said, "Please don't look at my writing, Miss, it's embarrassing." Handwriting was the last thing on my mind then, as it was now.

Donning a pretty white cotton nightie, matching dressing gown, Chanel perfume and little else, Kate paced across her room pausing occasionally to grasp the end of the bed or the window sill, or the back of a chair. At one such stop we peered out of the window and watched the night shift leaving and the early morning shift arriving. It was still dark and the city lights gave the sky an eerie look, light which seemed to originate from another planet. Toward the south, Dundry Tower was visible and now and then the landing lights of an aircraft would punctuate the dark. With the best will in the world we both knew James wouldn't arrive until late morning.

At this stage Kate went into solitary mode. You know the kind of thing. "Don't touch me! Give me the Tens thingie! Get out of the way! Don't go! Just get out of the way!" I was reminded of Kate leading her class into the hall for a bout of Polish dancing. As if they weren't confused enough at the prospect, she led them, head held high, huge yellow flower clip clasping her hair up, as they marched along like a very long line of ducklings. They were in no doubt as to who was in charge and they thrived in her care.

The midwife and I were in no doubt about who was calling the shots here either. Kate barked out her orders and we jumped to it. After a rather fruitful visit to the bathroom it was as if any remaining barriers of propriety between Kate and I had simply been flushed away along with the contents of the meal she had devoured hours earlier. "Oh, good girl!" exclaimed the midwife. Easy for you to say, I thought. It wasn't her who'd supported Kate while the world fell out of her bottom! Now I found I was the Tens monitor. Such responsibility. I wished I could just change the flowers as I had as a carefree little flower monitor. When Kate gave the command, I'd push the button. When it didn't work fast enough it was my fault and she didn't take prisoners, so I tried to anticipate the next contraction and initiate the electrical current a little ahead of time.

"Did I say NOW? Well? DID I?" Kate had rumbled my ploy. I found myself thinking that if she spoke to her children in class in that manner she'd be up for a disciplinary from me! However, needs must as they say. At the time I would've forgiven her anything. In fact I was beginning to think I would give birth *for* her. Watching someone with whom you've had a strong working relationship, in addition to a few rough nights out with the staff, observing the pain of childbirth is terribly hard and demands a stoicism I began to believe I no longer possessed.

The midwife finally announced the last stage of labour. We already had an inkling of that. By now Kate had almost veered into "I can't do this anymore" phase which was swiftly followed by, "No! Don't touch my back! Where the hell is James?" phase.

"The head is crowning. Not long now," the midwife said. Kate was exhausted.

"Nearly there, Kate, good girl, you're doing really well." That was me saying all the things I hadn't wanted to hear at the final stage of labour with my own three babies many years ago. What else is there though? "It's going to be a lovely day... I got me meat in...what's your opinion on the Secretary of State's new plans for reception children?" I don't think so! Luckily Kate was in the zone with the only companion who really mattered, Mother Nature, and therefore was in no position to admonish me.

The midwife asked me to help by holding Kate's leg up and out of the way. She was lying on her side, this wasn't going to be the easy option. It also meant I'd be at the business end as I'd heard bashful husbands say on one of those dreadful reality programmes that are almost compulsive viewing. I wasn't sure whether that was in my job description but Kate helped things along by saying, "FOR GOD'S SAKE... JUST DO IT!" as an almighty contraction and a long, loud, "OH GOD... OH GOD... AAAAAAAAAAAHHHHHHHHHHH!" heralded the arrival of the most beautiful baby girl. I held her as the cord was cut, then she was whisked away and plonked unceremoniously on Kate's chest. By now we were both sobbing and laughing and hugging.

As if on cue James arrived once everything and everyone was clean and tidy, and looking immensely relieved. No diamond, but with a smile worth so much more...well at least I thought so. Not so sure about Kate at that moment. As the three of them had a family hug I realised it was 10.25am, and I had missed the beginning of the school day by two hours twenty-five minutes.

Having driven home, showered, changed and wearing enough slap to cover the lack of sleep and sheer trauma, I arrived at school in time for lunch. I walked through the front doors on an utter high. I truly had little idea of where I was or what I was going to do for the rest of the day other than bask in the bliss of the miracle I had witnessed.

A passing teacher greeted me and asked if all was well. I replied, "Yes, I've just delivered a baby. I think I need a cup of tea and an iced bun please."

This was followed by a shriek of disbelief and laughter as the teacher passed on what I'd said to the long-suffering admin staff in the office who were always up for a bit of fun. "Oh, Mrs C, you make me laugh you do."

It wasn't until I collapsed with a strong cuppa in the staffroom that I was able to tell the whole story in a blow-by-blow account, possibly slightly exaggerated, to everyone grabbing a quick salad before the afternoon began. More tears. The laughter and gasps of incredulity continued for days, and each time there was a pregnancy announced amongst the staff or parents during my remaining years someone was sure to say, "Don't worry, Mrs C is a qualified midwife, she keeps her enema kit and vinyl gloves in the office."

Chapter 27

On a capricious Tuesday afternoon I bought chocolates, Celebrations, for tomorrow's staff meeting. Sometimes this was to sweeten the pill of what was forthcoming in terms of the introduction of yet another initiative from the government, or some new project I dreamt up over the weekend. But today it was just because it was Tuesday and a pleasant lull amidst the normal day-to-day frenzy. I felt like making the most of it. Also, I was blessed with the most incredible team of teachers I had ever had. They never ceased to amaze me with their energy, ingenuity, commitment and, above all, thorough knowledge of their children. I took every opportunity to brag about them to parents. But, aside from those who took time to think things through, I felt that not many truly had any idea of the workload the teachers carried, and with little complaint. I was so blessed. Maybe I should quit while I'm ahead? I mused. Retire maybe.

This afternoon, as I emerged from the swamp of paperwork, I glimpsed a light at the end of the tunnel. I crossed my fingers, and prayed it wasn't the lights of an oncoming, inter-city train. As I was gathering up my notes and the Celebrations the phone rang. The gentle, long-suffering voice at the other end belonged to the secretary at the Catholic diocesan centre, Janie. My first thought was, What have I done? Talk about paranoid! I had no need to worry she assured me, as if reading my thoughts. The director simply wanted to come out to school on a visit. I quite relished this idea as we had lots to show off and I got on well with the director. However, there was a hidden agenda as I was to find out the next morning.

The diocesan director, a tall, dark-haired, intense man sat opposite me. He crossed his legs and I noticed the most garish pair of red socks I had ever seen. I immediately conjured up a recent TV scenario in which a local politician was being grilled by Jeremy Paxman, another man of my dreams. Just as the temperature rose above squeamish, the politician cleared his throat and crossed his legs revealing a flash of lurid scarlet socks. At the time it made me think of the warning signals in the reptile world, and how certain creatures can transform into florid, spiky little mini-monsters if feeling threatened. A bit like some children. Colours flashing like a brazen exotic dancer wearing a sequinned thong, and a whore-red lipstick smile. However, this was the real world. "So, we were wondering whether you'd be up for it and would like to meet the governors?" I realised I had only half listened to what appeared to be a proposal. "Obviously, time is of the essence..." he bumbled on, as I desperately tried to fill in the gaps of his previous soliloquy. I put enough together to work out that he was asking if I'd be interested in heading up another school. It was in trouble. The head teacher was leaving, the teachers were vulnerable, the parents were anxious, the pupils unsettled, and there was a suggestion that the governing body was in chaos. An offer you can't refuse, eh?

There it was. The challenge. Beguiling as it twitched behind the net curtains, surreptitiously kicking the passing "R" word into touch. PHEW! That was close. I agreed to meet the governors the following week.

At first sight they seemed the usual parade of humanity who took up the mantel of school governorship. Extremely well-meaning pillars of society with a childhood's experience of education. After two hours with them I had a better idea of who was who. I needed to concentrate on those, if any, who might have a clue about the workings of the school community, should I agree to the offer.

The most disturbing element was the lack of trust between them. I had already been taken aside by one of them and told that "Mrs T" was manipulative and renowned for saying one thing but doing another. The well-meaning governor imparting this information subsequently turned out to be as leaky as a dented school colander. The meeting was interesting and it was as plain as the diocesan director's socks that the schism existing between the governing body was as real and painful as those experienced by the Church over the centuries.

Still, there was something drawing me to St Christopher's. I sat in the church, which was next door to the school. It resembled the church of my childhood with its red-brick columns stretching toward the heavens. I could almost detect a faint whiff of incense. As I left I knew my decision, and it brought a sizeable lump to my throat.

I accepted the temporary position as head teacher pending the appointment of a substantive head teacher which was planned to take place in time for the following academic year. "What's the worst thing that can happen?" I asked myself. The stimulus of another school would take me off-piste for a while, and prolong the slalom which would inevitably deliver me at the finishing post and the banner emblazoned with the unavoidable retirement word. I also had a brilliant deputy head at St George's who would welcome the professional development of heading up our school for the year. She would, wouldn't she?

St. Christopher's was a stone's throw away from the sea front. Sitting in the head teacher's office, if I closed my eyes and listened to the seagulls, I could pretend I was a guest on *Desert Island Discs* about to be interviewed by Kirsty Young.

However, I was not alone on this particular desert island. A wander round the school during the summer holidays was as good as reading any report about the school. The building was large, empty, two storey. The decor, the gloomy corridors, ancient metal coat racks unashamedly hung with last term's moulding swimming togs in damp kit bags, all in desperate need of attention. Don't misunderstand me, the renovation had begun. The children's toilets were *beautiful*. "Pale grey-blue and white with a touch of peach, very seaside," I could imagine Laurence thinga-me-bob Bowen pronouncing. My gratitude knew no bounds. There's nothing more degrading than stinky toilets for children.

The staff toilets were laughable. Airless, windowless and with chain-flush mechanisms. Awful! How on earth had this morbid state of affairs been allowed to continue for so long? When I felt the call of nature I crossed my legs and decided to try the public toilets on the sea front on my way out. Yes, the staff toilets were *that* bad. Upstairs yielded even more abandoned PE kits and the left shoe of a pair of scuffed, black lace-ups. It never ceases to amaze me that in every school I have worked there is always a lonely shoe left behind somewhere, discarded, like an unwanted out-of-date meal for one during the summer holidays. Where do all the other shoes which make up the pair go? Maybe they all meet up at a predestined venue with the socks which disappear during the washing cycle. How is it that a child can reach home laden with art projects, filled exercise books, and grubby lunch boxes boasting sprouting yoghurt pots, while wearing one shoe, and neither they nor the parent notices or bothers? It's beyond me.

Displays were sad and jaded, as flat and predictable as the stretch of beach not half a mile away. Not a promising sign. Maybe I read too much into it, but dull or ageing displays convey a sense of apathy to me.

I hadn't met the staff at this stage, but I was beginning to put together a collective pen picture. To live and work in the conditions I had seen meant one of two things. One: Nobody cared any more, or two: Everybody cared, but was too embroiled in the current circumstances to make a fuss. Ever the optimist, I chose to believe two.

Next on my schedule was a meeting with the outgoing head teacher. The meeting lasted two hours and left me in no doubt as to why she was calling it a day. She was on the verge of a nervous breakdown and had been signed off for a couple of weeks unable to return to school due to relationship difficulties with a member of staff. We'll call the member of staff Mrs E. This particular teacher had allegedly bullied her way through countless years in school. She got the age group she wanted to teach, she got funding when others had been told categorically that the coffers were empty, and she made no secret of the fact that she held the majority of her colleagues in contempt. Lastly, she was in cahoots with a manipulative governor. I sat watching the tears line up and trickle, in single file, into the prematurely deep lines of the head teacher's cheeks. I wanted to hug her, pat her on the back and send her out to play in the sunshine. If only it were that simple. When I left the meeting I put the roof of my car down and roared up the motorway hoping to leave at least part of this tangled web heading out toward the Atlantic across the sand dunes in my wake.

At the start of the new term I looked forward to meeting the deputy head teacher. I speculated as to her response regarding my appointment. Something didn't ring true. The school's advisor had told me that the deputy had no desire to become acting head teacher for the year despite it being a fabulous professional opportunity. The governors had also told me she wouldn't be considered for the role. I had only ever seen her disappearing as she left through the back door. My curiosity had led me in ever decreasing circles throughout the holidays. I was at a loss to piece together how she must be feeling. After all, the first port of call when a head teacher is absent for any length of time is the deputy head. A child could work it out. It's in the title, DEPUTY HEAD. So, why didn't she want it and, more importantly, why had the governors not asked her? She had been a deputy in two schools to date, for a seven-year period. Her last school was in a challenging district in London therefore implying that she had some savvy. Oh, but one can be so wrong.

Ms Charles fell into my study ten minutes before the school bell for the start of the day. She was accompanied by a soft jingling sound which reminded me, against all odds, of Tinkerbell. She was forty minutes late for our scheduled meeting. She gasped, wheezed and stammered through an apology, at the same time retrieving her wayward hair as it sprang from her scalp like a manic shopping mall fountain shooting skyward from its source. "I suggest you join your children. You'll find them lining up on the playground," I said without looking up. Yes, you're right, you can detect a hint of a chill in my words. Another of my irrefutable rules is, never, ever, keep your children waiting.

Her response provided the answer to some of my unanswered questions to date. "Oh, it's okay, Mrs Kemp will see them in." I suspected a certain lack of commitment. She frowned as she dropped her bursting bags and sank, tinkling, onto the only other chair in the room. A timid line of sweat graced her upper lip, and I noticed a florid, creeping, blotchy wave progress from the deep V-neck of her Monsoon dress from which her breasts popped like two Galia melons. Swollen ankles bulged their way over the top of her sandals. Flat sandals... Oh God! Rows of bells graced her pastry-dough left ankle. Hence the Tinkerbell effect. From nowhere the song "Gypsies, Tramps and Thieves" by Cher started up in my mind. It was so loud that I feared she would hear it.

Ms Charles groped around the floor surrounding her seat exploring each gaping bag before sighing, pushing hair back from her by now glowing face, and moving on to the next bag. She finally found what she had been looking for. I hoped she was about to partially redeem herself, and that she was about to flourish the school's strategic development plan. Alas, with a smile worthy of an errant child trying to distract attention from the rapidly leaking milk carton headed for the carpet, she juggled eleven A4 folders in front of my eager face before dropping two behind her.

"I put these together over the weekend," she gushed. There was a pause and I knew I was expected to fill it with effusive congratulations. I didn't. Instead I enquired as to the purpose of the eleven files which she was still attempting to tame. "Planning files," she beamed. "I thought it would make things easier for you if everyone had a planning file." She was delighted with herself. I lifted one and opened it praying for a serendipitous surprise. My prayer fell on stony ground where it choked, smothered by thorny brambles. Somehow, I was expecting that. I glanced up at Ms Charles who was still *clearly* anticipating some expression of awe and gratitude. Oh God! I thought.

"Talk me through these," I managed to say, surprising myself with my calm.

Like an infant explaining a first tentative watercolour painting, Ms Charles gave me chapter and verse, and several repeated choruses, extolling the virtues of the heaped blue files threatening to helter-skelter off the edge of the desk. She had to be admired. Three minutes without hesitation, deviation or repetition was indeed admirable. Try as I might, I could find nothing in the files but the contents page. Not *any* contents page of course. Oh no, these were multi-coloured, illustrated, bold and *italic* contents pages. I cleared my throat, carefully replaced the threatening blue escapees, and looked into Ms Charles' inquisitive eyes. "Thank you, Ms Charles. I appreciate the time you must've taken to prepare the files." (It must've taken five minutes to compose the contents page, two minutes to hurtle from one font to another, likewise to create a rainbow of coloured text, and forty-five minutes in WH Smith choosing the colour of the A4 files.) "However, I prefer to access plans on the computer." As stealthily as the colour had crept from her cleavage to her eyebrows, it now began to descend with alarming speed, rendering her face ashen. Both hands flew to her hair not quite knowing which strands to capture first. She shoved every available clump behind her ears as if she were firmly placing an irritating child back in its seat.

My heart sank as I watched. I was awash with disappointment verging on the desperate.

She wrestled her bags behind her as she waltzed her voluminous Monsoon dress along the passage leaving the blue files on my desk. I scooped them up and found a place for them in the stock cupboard after removing the contents pages and dropping them into the recycling bin.

The room was squeezing every last breath from me so I took a learning walk around the classes. This never failed to restore my calm demeanour, and I hoped today would be no exception. The children were delightful in their inquiries. "Where's your *real* school?"

"Do you like it here?"

"Where's our own head teacher?"

"Why can't she come back?"

"We like her."

"Your hair's funny, do you like wearing glasses?"

"Is that sports car yours? Is it a Porsche?"

"My dad's got a fuel injection car with a GPS."

"I likes your shoes, Miss. Our ma's got some like it. She got 'em in H&M." I did everything in my power to smother my indignation at that. Not that I have an aversion to a good bargain. But shoes? Oh no. There's no bargaining there. I loved the children already. Whatever was to happen here at St Christopher's the children would have a fabulous year, and their school would become a place where they would enjoy participating in active learning with their enthused teachers (throw salt over left shoulder) in a learning environment worthy of them. The benefits would last for years to come, of that I was in no doubt.

Chapter 28

There were staffing issues. This had been hinted at prior to my accepting the role. Coming a close second to Ms Charles was Mrs E who had been absent for almost a year after a series of disagreements with the former head teacher and colleagues, all of which she denied vehemently, and very loudly to all and sundry.

Mrs E was introduced to me by the chair of governors, a well presented father of two stunning little girls who both attended St Christopher's. Although relatively young, his experience in the corporate world would stand him in good stead over the coming year. I'd invited them both in for a meeting to negotiate a return to work for Mrs E. I felt it would be a possible starting point for her in regaining confidence, and for me in assessing the extent of the existing troubles. I guess I hoped to extend the olive branch. I had no previous knowledge of her other than the briefing I'd had which was minimal. I was aware that we seemed to have reached an impasse, and I was eager to get it sorted and move on.

Having already survived an employment tribunal I had no desire to repeat the process, so leaving no stone unturned I had prepared, to the hilt, the content of the meeting. Initial pleasantries completed the meat of the meeting was laid before Mrs E. Unceremoniously, but with due respect, I welcomed her, explained the purpose of the meeting and told her where she was to be teaching for the year. I don't know if you've ever witnessed the science experiment to demonstrate how a volcano erupts – it involves bicarbonate of soda, water and brilliant timing. Mrs E was the human equivalent. She effervesced as the chair of governors and I watched. She sent out a couple of spurted phrases rather like a geyser in the wilds of New Zealand. She spewed, "This is discrimination…you're bullying me. I won't stand for it. You can't do this. I'm not coming back to teach unless I can have the class I want, and it's not in my best interest to teach in *that* year group. You can't dictate terms to me!" Remarkable. Oh dear, Mr Secretary of State, where are you now? I gave her a look which I hoped left her in no doubt that I could in fact dictate terms to her, particularly if my decision had been based on what was the best for the children. After her outburst came *déjà vu*. I could already see where this was heading, and I wasn't looking forward to it. In fact, I made a mental note to pull out every imaginable stop to avoid revisiting the rather unpleasant experience euphemistically called the employment tribunal.

We both attempted to placate Mrs E but it was futile. She had come for her pound of flesh and she was already into excess baggage on that front. She gathered her skirts, stood dabbing her eyes with a tartan handkerchief, and swept out of the room.

The school secretary poked her head round the door, "That's her for the next six months then. Tea anyone?"

If I haven't said it enough, "Thank you, God, for school secretaries." They invariably cut to the chase and follow up with a welcome cuppa.

The chair of governors looked up mouthing, "Sugar with mine, please" followed by "What d'you reckon then?" as he swivelled his chair in my direction.

With tongue firmly in cheek I took a deep breath, "I think we need a doughnut with that tea." So, that was Mrs E.

In the meantime I had received notification from several members of staff that, should Mrs E return to school, their resignations would follow. Fabulous. I found myself wondering what could possibly come next. Actually what came next lifted my spirits. Staff began to open up, to express their concerns, to offer their individual opinions on what had been happening at St Christopher's over the previous years. Initially I found it hard to digest, but one after the other teachers and teaching assistants told me of the fearful atmosphere which had led to their vulnerability and stress. Power struggles, bullying, threatening behaviour, dishonesty, all had taken their toll, and would have to be addressed individually before we could begin to rebuild a strong team.

It seemed to me that we needed our first INSET day to be firmly founded in trust. This had been a shock for some. Vulnerability and fear of rebuff had certainly caused a massive retreat in terms of proffering an opinion or making any contributions during meetings. They had no time to learn to trust me, or I them. We simply had to rally, take a leap of faith and move the school forward. No negotiation. I had one year to begin to turn the tanker, as it had been put by a governor, in the direction everyone knew it was tardy in taking. Time was a luxury we simply couldn't afford. I spent the next week or so preparing the in-service training day. Several Stephen Covey books were consulted, and I found some interesting anecdotes regarding trust, trust in a constrained timescale.

To my surprise the day went exceptionally well. There were smiles, questions, enthusiasm and generally a strong commitment to rally. We would make it through the year. Not only would we make it, we'd work hard, play hard and build up self-belief to kick the existing, rather deflated, egos into touch. St Christopher's was due a make-over on a massive scale.

Once the year's strategic plan was in place changes slowly began to happen. Structurally there were so many areas to be addressed, but first and foremost there were some fundamental shifts needed in terms of staff/children expectations and relationships. Each morning we met for a short period of reflection in the staffroom. I never forgot the difference this made way back when I was a supply teacher in the city. There's something strengthening about leaving the staffroom together at the start of the day and welcoming the children in from the playground. I emphasised the importance of being out there early, not dashing out on the bell simply because it was chilly. I went out and met parents, introducing myself and getting to know as many as possible. I wanted to portray a sense of energy and new beginnings, and I found the response from parents gradually became more upbeat and friendly.

One morning, after reflection, a young teacher met her children on the playground and skipped them into school. The giggling was contagious. The following day she imitated an American drill sergeant and marched them all in as they repeated her chants. Some parents stopped and watched. It was a time of major shift and it was contagious! Gradually a different relationship between teachers and children emerged. The biggest difference being that the teachers felt free to express what they had kept hidden for fear of ridicule or worse. It was remarkable and a privilege to watch unfolding.

Leaders also came to the fore. One erstwhile shy teacher in year three came forward with suggestions for after school activities and led the whole project by running a lively jazz dance class which was attended by aspiring boys and girls who clearly saw themselves as backing dancers for some cool boy band or Lady Gaga or Bollywood even!

One week several of us decided to join the class and treated the children to a great laugh as we rapped along with them and generally performed "daddy dances" to music which was insufferably monotonous and loud. They loved it. "Respect, Miss," was the verdict.

Each day brought more and more minor forays into the unknown as staff gained in confidence and felt motivated to experiment. The insecurities which formed one of the boundaries to their development were wilting and, as they were no longer treading on eggshells, creativity began to re-emerge. By giving teachers more responsibility they rose to the challenge and asked for more. Laughter was heard everywhere, and the atmosphere began to lighten up. You could almost hear the building groaning in relief. All was not perfect, however. Some members of staff clearly needed a helping hand into the twenty-first century. This could not be rushed. Also, Mrs E was making her presence felt by her prolonged absence. Staff tentatively asked where she was and I did my best to assure them that negotiations were taking place. What I didn't tell them was that negotiations were becoming hideous and bordered on harassment. Mrs E, her husband, and a friend wrote and phoned me to let me know that my behaviour was despicable, and that what was happening was nothing short of a vendetta or witch-hunt. Rumour was rife in the large parish too. I was the unknown against Mr and Mrs E who were pillars of the church. What was actually happening was now being directed largely by the diocesan legal team, and consisted of attempting to get Mrs E back into school for another return to work meeting as procedure demanded. I was clagged in procedures. They dragged me down into the mire, and there seemed to be no timely solution.

By this time Mrs E knew about the threat of resignation which had been handed to me by three members of staff. She maintained that I had dictated the letter in an attempt to influence the governors and persuade them that the only logical solution would be to pay Mrs E off. I have to admit I thought it was a damned good idea, so much more efficient. A clean cut. I wished I had thought of it. Even more, I wished I had the power to initiate it. But this is the airy-fairy world of human resources in education.

In another attempt to resolve the situation peaceably, Mrs E was invited back in to school. She arrived with her union representative. He was wearing a Fair Isle sleeveless pullover and I found myself thinking, Really?

The case he put forward on her behalf was as mesmerising as the pattern of his pullover and made just as much sense to me. Mrs E became fiery in her frustration, levelling inflammatory suggestions at all and sundry and denying any wrongdoing on her part. I began to fully comprehend how this lady had been a contributory factor leading to the early retirement of two previous head teachers, and the lengthy leave of absence of a third. She certainly had a hold over a number of the governors and, try as I might, I couldn't work out what it was, and haven't to this day. In the meantime she was garnering the support of others in the wider community. She was upping her campaign. She withdrew from church attendance in the parish where her husband was a leading light. He withdrew all support from church too and attended another parish refusing to speak to their parish priest of twenty-five years. She contacted the bishop on a number of occasions, pleading her case and citing the previous head teacher as another villain in the whole debacle with the chair of governors and myself supposedly conspiring against her. The *pièce de résistance* was writing to the Pope. I have no idea whether he replied to her or not. My guess is that there were more pressing situations assailing the Vatican at the time, but she may have been added to a prayer list of some sort. I found myself hoping it would bring her some comfort, if not rationale.

Later, staring out over the Bristol Channel, I recapped the situation at St Christopher's so far. A disturbed teacher emailing the Pope, and a jingling, tinkling, delusional deputy head, buildings on the brink of risking a health and safety shutdown, resources worthy of the city museum, a significant percentage of staff just coming out of the closet of indecision and vulnerability, a governing body well beyond its capability in most cases, a cluster of parents baying for blood and a history of less than amazing educational achievement. I shut the door and heard an irrepressible giggle as I wiped the tears from my cheeks. I couldn't help but notice I was the only person in the room.

Chapter 29

Approaching the first half term holiday the progress in school had begun to resemble a hovercraft rather than a mud dredger. There was a lighter feel to the school. Following a rather severe pruning at the start of the year, the inevitable blossoming was taking place. The parent community was a joy on the whole, and I felt privileged to be joining them in getting the best for their children. The number of parent volunteers was also increasing, and I remember feeling that the real school community was emerging from a seemingly endless hibernation.

Driving to work each morning I found myself invigorated and energised by the challenge of each day. I was also fond of listening to audiobooks on my drive to the coast. Travelling for longer than twenty minutes or so to school was new to me, and I found I quite enjoyed it. Teachers were planning with added confidence and a huge dollop of imagination. We had a temporary member of staff allocated to the school and she was heaven-sent. Imagine the most energetic, bright, humorous and creative young teacher and there you have it. Her name was Dee and she buzzed around the school like a warm whirlwind. Her remit was to lead by example, to demonstrate outstanding lessons and to work alongside the leadership team in driving up standards. She did this with boundless enthusiasm despite a few initial kick backs. Lesson content reached an all-time high, and the children began responding in ways which took their learning to previously unseen heights. Achievement rose too, and children started to arrive in school early, eager to experience the new ethos.

Teachers conversed professionally and learnt from each other.

They laughed, we had fun, we baked apple crumble, well, the one male member of staff did in response to a challenge! It was delicious and he was rightly proud, albeit slightly embarrassed. We went out socially and drank far too much. I think this must be a requisite quality when teaching in a Catholic school. Much of this was missed by the deputy head, Ms Charles. If there was a space in the *Guinness Book of Records* for excuses to duck out of social events she would be there. Ill health, childminding issues, too much work, lack of energy, mother visiting, mother-in-law visiting, budgie dying, impending emigration. I made the last two up, but you get the drift.

Her absence from school was also cause for concern. It was becoming obvious that she was simply out of her depth and treading water through all the changes hitting the school at the pace of a tsunami. Glancing through her employment record to date gave me an indication of where things had started unravelling in her career. It appeared she had been promoted out of the classroom into a leadership role at her previous school. She had spent five years or so in what was basically an administrative role mistitled, Deputy Head Teacher. No wonder she was struggling. How on earth she managed to get appointed at St Christopher's remains another mystery to this day. My intuition tells me it was something to do with religious fervour.

I began to fear the worst, that she had been promoted as a matter of damage limitation to get her out of the classroom and not because of her professional expertise. Regrettable though that is, there are so few options open to management in education. Trying to get shot of somebody clearly not suited to the job is almost impossible. I used to envy Jeff as he told me of corporate policies in human resources which enabled management to let an employee go if they didn't hit their targets. A person may be sacked if they are not producing the target number of Rich Tea biscuits, doctors are struck off if their performance isn't up to par, but the same rules don't apply if you have an incompetent teacher hindering the learning of thirty children per year. What a nonsense.

Here she was, out of touch with educational developments, teaching thirty year five children who had the measure of her. Granted, she was creative and came up with some wacky ideas which normally I would've welcomed and encouraged, the problem was that she had little idea of what she was trying to achieve in terms of the children's learning. Pretty essential that. Strangely, most of the parents really liked her. She had a winning way with her that had some of them eating out of her hands. This made my job even more difficult as it wasn't unknown for her to confide in them and be slightly liberal with the truth.

What was needed was accountability, some structure to which she would adhere and thus grow. However, with her rate of absence and the escalating number of disturbing gaffs witnessed almost on a daily basis, it was difficult to envisage scheduling such a programme. Surely, it was only a matter of time before she resigned? Ever the optimist.

Alongside the staff issues I was more than aware that the learning environment was less than satisfactory, using OFSTED terminology. Thank God money wasn't an issue at St Christopher's as I discovered a hidden backlog of unspent dosh. It was incredible that such an amount had not been investigated by the local authority auditors, but the reality was it had been missed. There was enough to transform the school and we launched into a renovation project which would've made us the envy of the programme *DIY SOS*.

First on the agenda was the relocation of the IT suite which was currently housed in what I named the Scout Hut in the playground. It not only resembled this from the outside, it *smelt* every inch a scout hut from the inside. The only dib-dib-dob that had ever taken place in there was that of the rain dripping along the mould-ridden window frames. Children were crammed in for each IT lesson, hence IT lessons were avoided if the slightest opportunity presented itself. Leaking roof, heating malfunction, dog on the playground were all stock reasons as to the lack of IT lessons actually happening. We had to act soon or be responsible for hordes of children leaving St Christopher's bemused by information technology and hanging on the jet stream of the twenty-first century by the skin of their teeth.

Within six weeks we had a state-of-the-art IT suite visible from the school foyer which by now resembled a display area worthy of Harvey Nicholls' shop front. It couldn't be overlooked by anyone whether parent, visitor or inquisitive child. It achieved everything we hoped for and more. It became a talking point. Children spilled out of lessons buzzing with delight and chatting about their learning, and it was a visible sign that things were moving in the right direction. Moving the furniture into the suite had been interesting. It had to happen quickly because stacks of chairs had been unloaded as close to the front door as possible, consequently blocking the fire escape. I was relying on the goodwill and muscle of the parent body, and planned to cajole or charm them into helping as they left their children on the playground at drop-off time. I figured parents were the only option. I strode out to the playground as the children were gathering and approached some dads who were lingering. Suddenly word got round that I was asking for some strong men with time on their hands, and suddenly the playground cleared with much jostling and good humoured remarks as the majority bid a hasty retreat. Luckily, a group of Asian families were animatedly discussing something as they strolled across the grass. As I approached one of the dads asked, "Is it help you are wanting, Headmistress? Come, let's go." And that was that. I had a large group of smiling, musclebound men moving all the furniture into the new IT suite. The good humour was contagious and we learnt more about each other in that hour than could possibly have been gleaned without the working group. As I sat with a much needed coffee and biscuit a couple of hours later, I began to realise what an exceptional multi-cultural community we had. Even more exciting, what future prospects could we conjure for their further involvement?

It was around this time of emerging hope and impending euphoria that I met Darren's mum. She was shown into the office on one of those bleak seaside days when the grey skies and buffeted seagulls herald the onset of the next ten hours weather. Ms A was mostly wearing the grey and buffeted look. She fused with the weather conditions seamlessly, so much so that I felt she could walk along the wide promenade unseen. The first thing I noticed as she slumped into the well-worn chair opposite me were her fingernails. Imagine coming in from an afternoon's gardening and examining your nails before reaching out for the nailbrush at a sink full of steaming water. Freeze. Move away from the sink, leaving welcoming water and primed nailbrush. You have the picture.

Nicotine stained her fingers and her front teeth. Blonde hair, naturally blonde, was swept into a fashionably untidy ponytail with one extremely irritating strand left to fall across her right eye until it curled under her tide-marked neck. I felt an overwhelming urge to push it back behind her multi-pierced ear. Within seconds the room smelt like the snug in a men-only bar in Newcastle upon Tyne I remembered being unceremoniously ushered out of many years ago.

I had asked to see Ms A because she frequently turned up late to collect Darren from after school club and I was looking for an explanation. She had skilfully avoided answering any questions posed by the play workers as she skulked off into the night with Darren following the glow of her cigarette across the deserted playground. Darren was partially sighted, possibly due to his mother's use of heroin during pregnancy. She made all the usual excuses which disappointed me. I had expected something a little more imaginative from a woman with copious piercings, including eyebrows, tongue and (so playground gossip had it) right nipple. OUCH! She also sported a tattoo proclaiming *The Grateful Dead* on her left shoulder. Apparently, she simply kept missing her bus from work. Careless, I thought.

Her eyes seemed to operate independently from each other and I found myself wondering if Darren's condition could actually be congenital. I didn't wonder for long though. I let her know that should the situation continue I would be notifying her social worker. She was unmoved. She coughed, sounding like an extra in *Oliver Twist*, and as she straightened and made her way to the door, she hesitated and grabbed the door handle for support. She regained her balance, lifted her head and left the room without a backward glance. I wasn't sure whether she was drunk or had been using, but I *was* concerned that Darren was to be taken home by her, and that she was his responsible adult.

I called the family social worker. I had already forwarded my concerns to her several times, and we had met briefly as is the custom with overworked social workers a couple of weeks beforehand. Social workers in the area were inundated with caseloads, and Darren was just one of a long list of children living in the chasm of uncertainty and chaos which constitutes life with a parent involved in substance abuse. The social worker said she was powerless because, despite living with an alcoholic and a drug addict, Darren had not been harmed. Why, oh why do we have to wait until it's too late? Something had to change, surely, but it had been years since I'd first found myself experiencing utter helplessness in the face of potential harm, and yet the system remained resistant to change.

The police were about to stake out Darren's home. They'd had plenty of tip-offs that the house was used to traffic and use drugs, and they were waiting for more concrete evidence serious enough to trigger the necessary action. They didn't have to wait long. Wednesday, 6.30pm the following week, and after school club (ASC) was due to close. All the children had been collected, some still eating the remains of the snack they enjoyed so much, jam sandwiches being the favourite, as they walked across the playground with mum or dad. The ASC manager rang through to my office to let me know that Darren hadn't been picked up. I closed down my computer and crossed the playground in the pitch black that seems reserved for school playgrounds early in the evening of mid-winter. I could feel the damp air cling to my face as a bitter onshore wind almost lifted me off the tarmac. After school club was warm and smelt of happy children. The play worker was washing up after snack time, and sitting at a table as close to her as he could get was Darren. He was colouring in his picture of the sea. His tongue was sticking out and moved backward and forward along his lower lip as he squinted before choosing his next colour. "You don't have to rush, Darren," I said, "you have plenty of time to carry on with your picture." And he did. Ms A finally arrived at 7.47pm, one hour and seventeen minutes late. Enough time for Darren and me to make some more jam sandwiches, have a picnic, wash up together and begin a game of Connect Four.

She stood in the doorway, the dim light of the passage at her back. She was stoned. Darren knew it, the ASC manager knew it, I knew it. She lurched toward us, her smile resembling a distorted reflection from the hall of mirrors on the newly refurbished pier. I stood between her and Darren while quietly telling the ASC manager to phone the social worker and the police. I asked if she'd like a jam sandwich. Well, you can hardly blame me for trying. We were clean out of smack! She didn't respond but leered at Darren. "Darren, my babber... I loves you, my little man."

Darren told me it was my go in the game. I turned to drop the counter into the slot. George yelled, "I won! I won didn't I, mum?"

"Yes, you fuckin' well did, my son!" she laughed, showing her stained teeth. She groped for a cigarette and I reminded her that she couldn't smoke at ASC.

I turned to Darren and said, "You deserve a prize for being such a skilful player. Not many children have beaten me at Connect Four you know. How about we go to the office and you can swing round in my chair 'til mummy has had her cigarette…outside?"

He jumped up, pulled his bag from under the desk where he'd left it four hours earlier and reached for my hand. "Come and get me soon, mum," he said. She was already lighting up and didn't hear her "little man".

By 8.15pm, Ms A had disappeared from the playground, Darren had been collected by the social worker and was on his way to a halfway house with foster parents he already knew from previous respite. Before he left he turned to me and said, "They've got a dog. I love dogs. They lets me walk her too, Miss. See you in the morning!" I remember the jam at the corner of his smiling mouth.

That night the police raided Ms A's house she was entertaining. Neighbours said fifteen people were escorted out of the house including Ms A who was found unconscious in the small back bedroom.

Darren spent the rest of the year with his foster parents and their loopy Labrador. His mother spent the same amount of time in rehab.

Chapter 30

After a series of failed attempts to negotiate with Mrs E we began preparing for the inevitable tribunal. This time I felt the stirrings of confidence which come with repetition of an uninvited experience. I also felt the nausea which accompanies it. As the full realisation sank in I began to have nightmares about the tribunal room, and I willed the days to pass so that we could get the whole thing over with expeditiously, and with the outcome we needed for the sake of the school. The extra spin-off being that Jeff and I could regain some uninterrupted sleep.

By now I had met Mrs E, her harassed husband, her solicitor and union representative. To clarify things, this was her *second* union representative, the first one having resigned after disastrous initial meetings with his client and her entourage.

The current rep. was a young man. His face was grey, as in the colour of pastry made by children, and his eyes darted about like balls in a pinball machine. Bless him, he was scared. What a baptism of fire. He couldn't help himself let alone state the case of a fiery client with all the fictional prowess of a Richard and Judy summer read. He tripped over fresh air as he mounted the steps of the town hall where we were meeting to ascertain a way forward and avoid a tribunal.

His file exploded as it hit the damp concrete steps, and A4 sheets flew from his grasp as the wind snatched them up and tossed them around like autumn foliage. We all grappled to help put him and his paperwork back into some kind of order. I found myself wanting to straighten his tie and had to restrain myself from patting his head and sending him back out to play. He nodded and sputtered out a mish-mash of an apology and thanks, all in the same breath. A silence ensued in which Mrs E, et al, gawped up at him. Finally, taking their cue from Mrs E, they processed through the heavily embossed doors and along the passage to the allocated room.

Details of the meeting are unnecessary. Suffice it to say we reached stalemate after the parish priest expressed his doubt as to the honesty of Mrs E's statement citing an incident at a parish dinner party where she had been less than discreet, or indeed truthful about the minutes of a recent governing body meeting, and had attempted to engage him in denigrating a fellow governor. OOPS. Mistake... BIG mistake. Eleventh Commandment: *Thou shalt not coerce the parish priest or diss thy neighbour at any parish social event.*

My heart went out to the parish priest, Father D. He was shaking as he spoke. I noticed a nervous tic in his left cheek. He was facing the lions in this suffocating arena, and it was clearly taking all of his conviction to speak out. He demonstrated such courage that day.

Mrs E had no response. She gathered up her notes, her rep, and her husband and swept out of the building. "See you in court, Mrs E," my solicitor murmured under his cool breath. I wondered whether Father D would see her first in the confessional.

Six weeks later we sat behind Mrs E, her legal team, her husband...and their burly, adult sons. Rumour had it that one of them had recently been released from a short-term sojourn at Her Majesty's pleasure. "But I'm not one to gossip," claimed the governor imparting this knowledge.

The tribunal played out over the next couple of days. Two of Mrs E's friends, one a governor, waxed lyrical about her teaching abilities. How come they were suddenly educational experts? Mrs E took the stand and I feared for her survival. I was right to be worried. After the shortest of cross-examinations she broke down becoming embroiled in a series of questions she found difficult to answer. She was confused, she said. She felt victimised, she said. She pointed the finger of blame toward head teachers past and present, to colleagues all and sundry, before making a tearful exit. After lunch, or rather after picking apart an under-filled sandwich in a local café with fly-ridden window panes, it was my turn to face the music.

Anticipating another marathon, as per my previous experience a few years back, I was prepared. Walking past the aforementioned hard-faced youths wasn't easy. Not that I felt intimidated in the least, I actually didn't want them to have to listen to the other side of the story, the one they hadn't heard, the one I was about to tell – the truth. The account which would eventually herald the end of their mother's career. I was sworn in and the questions began. Thirty minutes or so of flicking from one end of the bundle to the other, the barristers asked me to step down.

As we all filed out of the overheated room, Mrs E's group passed by fussing and preening over her as if she were some endangered fledgling. One of her sons swiped the end of his nose with his right hand which sported a faux-gold, oversized skull ring, and looked over to where I stood. As we made eye contact he looked down and shuffled, wiping his nose again. I wanted to tell him to be careful he didn't hurt himself with his ridiculous ring. I wanted to put my arm round him and offer him a tissue. He turned away following the crowd heading for the exit. The verdict was predictable and several years of heartache, bullying, manipulation and slanderous accusations came to an end with the dismissal of Mrs E. I didn't feel the euphoria I'd anticipated. I felt pity for Mrs E. I had no doubt that in her youth she had been as idealistic as the rest of us on leaving college in the late 60s. I found myself wondering what had blighted her career so badly that she had become so disillusioned and bitter.

The fastest year of my career came to an end with alarming speed, and not before I had suffered a minor stroke. Nothing too alarming and I quite enjoyed the imposed train travel for a few weeks as driving was off limits for a while. At the end of the summer term I walked out of an almost state-of-the-art school equipped to face the twenty-first century with its head held aloft. The teachers were confident and embraced new technology and the many challenges of the new curriculum. They were confident and happy, and the children were excited about learning as they began to flex their increasingly independent learning muscles, and achieve standards of which to be proud. The school community was taking on a more pro-active role too, and what had been a wilting PTA was now accustomed to planning fund-raisers and family events which were very well attended. New staff members were appointed to replace Ms Charles and Mrs E. A brand new head teacher had been appointed and was already showing encouraging signs. She was young and incredibly well equipped to take up the mantel at St Christopher's. I had grown to love the children, their parents and staff, and leaving felt like missing the final act of a three-act play. Part of me wanted to stay and lead the ascent of the school and parish family. Part of me knew that what was needed was a continuation of the newly acquired energy to take the school into overdrive. They needed a head teacher who would grow with them as leaders, and journey with them into the foreseeable future. Now they had one. "My work here is done..." as my son was known to say at the successful completion of a job. As I drove up the motorway for the last time I felt good, if tired and tearful. I had learnt so much. We had made a difference if the staff and parents are to be believed, and I left them smiling. I had achieved the remit I had been handed at the start of the academic year and, in addition, had managed the budget well enough to revamp the internal structure of the school building. The very last project, which I kept for the summer holidays, was the complete gutting and redesign of the school kitchen and, pause for fanfare please, new staff toilets! During the holidays when I went into school to sign off the projects I added the last-minute fripperies to the loos. Flowers, beautiful hand-wash, the like of which is normally only found in the upmarket corporate world, and a handwritten sign for the door which I knew the staff would find amusing. At the start of the next academic year the loos, now pimped to perfection, would mean all staff could at last pee in pleasant surroundings.

St Christopher's was fit for purpose in all aspects.

Chapter 31

My return to St George's was strange, wonderful, affirming and a wake-up call shot across the boughs of my career. Events led me on a road less travelled, to coin a phrase – the road to retirement.

In retrospect, the R word never lodged in my thought processes much before my year at St Christopher's. Although Matt was no longer in the country, I was beginning to reap the benefits of our friendship. When you've experienced a relationship of that emotional magnitude, which helps to shape you and expand your outlook, then you will know exactly what I mean. At the risk of sounding like a latter day Bridget Jones, imagine excitement, hilarity, meteoric rise in self-image, an inexplicable connection and, yes, you're there. Wonderful isn't it? Now, just for the hell of it, and believe me I do mean the *hell* of it, reverse those emotional meanderings at speed and, as any good aerobics teacher would say, "Don't forget to breathe!" You find yourself vulnerable, seeking anonymity, deflated like a Christmas balloon found behind the sofa at the end of January, wrinkly with a film of dust. At the outset of the year at St Christopher's I had felt like that, alone and unsure, without my *confidante*. Returning to St George's was akin to entering a room full of friends and sensing a lull in the conversation. More significantly, I was different. I was stronger for standing on my own two feet, for making my way in unknown territory, a solitary explorer without expedition leader, and enjoying some success. St Christopher's had changed me and given me the impetus I needed to face my future.

There's no rewind button of course. Wrinkled balloons do not a party make, but we are all capable of finding our way through the flotsam the waves entangle around our sinking feet. Tuck those transitions in your life into the end of term box and you can ditch them during the hols along with all those unnecessarily printed emails accumulated in the office.

Meanwhile there was the ever-present threat of the Secretary of State for Education who was snorting and pawing the ground with restless hooves before bursting forth into the arena brandishing the NEW CURRICULUM. Except it wasn't, and I found myself yawning at the prospect of heading up yet another wave of change for the sake of change, change for which I discovered I couldn't summon up any enthusiasm. My poor staff. How could I honestly lead them with the passion and commitment it would demand? How could I enthuse my leaders with the verve it needed to motivate others when my verve had up and left with the school bus? How would I be able to look the children and their parents in the eyes and tell them that these developments were in their own best interest, when clearly they were not?

My heart was pounding and I was curiously moved to tears. Suddenly, everything was too much and I wanted to magic the whole school community off and over the hills to a fantasy school where we could all learn the REAL things, real as in *The Velveteen Rabbit*. I found I loved them too much to stay and lead them into this mind-numbing exercise of creeping up the league tables to make the politicians look good in their unending game of political football.

My thoughts tumbled out unheeded. Children are not tea bags. They are not clones trundling off the conveyor belt of primary education. No matter what the game plan, no matter who the Secretary of State, there will always be high achievers, average achievers and lower achievers because that's how nature intended it. Or, as a dyed in the wool teacher once said in the staffroom of a local primary school, "You can't make a silk purse out of a sow's ear." I thought that was a tad extreme, but we all knew where he was coming from didn't we? The world needs all types of learners, academic, practical, creative, radical thinkers, lateral thinkers, autistic thinkers, you name it, the world needs them.

Our role is to help them fully explore the gifts they have and introduce them to the amazing process of learning to learn for themselves, for life. I thought of the excitement of opening up the realms of possibility in thirsty little minds. The privilege of encouraging children not just to think outside the box, but coaxing them to ask "What box?" Improve the world we share, *that's* the target. Whether children can "jump through the hoops" that we know as SATs after a year of spoon-feeding English and maths within the confines of a constrained, bland curriculum is irrelevant and, in my opinion, morally wrong.

I was beginning to feel re-energised. It was then that I realised that "refirement" was what I needed, not retirement. I heard myself saying, "The day we are charged with pushing *all* children to leave primary school with level five and six in English and maths is the day I…oh my goodness…the day I RETIRE!"

I had seen colleagues hedging their way toward retirement, testing the water or rather testing the ice like a novice skater, and wondered what it would be like to be that old and that cautious. I could spot the forced optimism in conversations about farmhouse renovation in France and cruises with the wife or the reluctant husband. It all seemed so tired, hanging there like sad curtains in a charity shop.

Those of us not yet on the slippery slope discussed colleagues who were careering down it, smiles fixed in place like some failed Botox experience, eyebrows permanently reaching toward ever-receding hairlines. The luge hurtling toward extinction. It was as if they were out of focus, still present, but not with any clarity, comparable to the last line of an optician's sight chart. We all know it's there, but is it really worth the time and effort to read it? They were no longer important. Their views mattered once. In fact last week their views mattered, not now though, no, not now the R word had been uttered. They had nothing to say, or rather they had nothing to say that meant anything to us. After all, we were *staying*. We were in it for the long haul. We were committed. We had value, purpose, and status. People listened to us and we were revered by eager young head teachers as elders with wisdom. Why on earth would anyone even so much as consider jacking it in? Unless, of course, they could no longer cope, or choice slipped under the door unnoticed.

Retirees? Sympathy was the most any of us could offer. We felt sorry for them, pitied them, even offered them support, while covertly agreeing that they were beyond help, washed up on the shoreline of disillusionment as they were. We survivors could surely afford them that, our condescending offers falling, as the last leaking lifeboat into an unforgiving sea. It was as if we were all protecting a family secret, a terminal illness, a teenage sibling coming out of the closet...best not discussed. I guess support was an improvement on derision, although there was still plenty of that to be had should those dishing the dirt need a boost to their own tottering self-image. The class bullies could be relied upon to come up with the goods with the regularity of the speaking clock. Innuendo doled out at each meeting with sidelong looks at the apprentice retiree. It was part of the agenda, expected, like the dish of discoloured imperial mints dipped into with the nimble fingers of nonchalance. At least *we* weren't retiring – yet. We weren't throwing in the towel, or taking an early bath. No, we were warriors of the light, kings of the high plains! Nothing could touch us unless we allowed it. Surely we were blessed with hidden strength? How else could we function year after year on the Disney-ride that is the UK's education system? By way of sustenance we thrilled at the notion of some off-piste action such as I'd experienced during my year at the seaside. Something to distinguish us from the banal. So we conjured up projects and inter-school initiatives with which to taunt the less adventurous, the tired, the weary, the *retiring*, who smiled and shook their heads as if passing up the offer of a Belgian chocolate. We humoured the retiring, we even told them we envied them and wished we could afford to go too, and then joked about possible leaving gifts behind their backs. Incontinence pads featured high on any list closely followed by Viagra, large print versions of *Nigel Slater's Suppers*, and Zimmer frames. Such fun, savoured from behind the latest file of initiatives from the government. Yes, the head teachers' conference wasn't just a bad dream to be rinsed off with lavender body scrub the following morning. It was here to stay, clinging with the scale on the shower head. However, here was I allowing the R word an increasingly prominent space in my head. I kept it quiet and attempted, at times, to play it at its own game by filing it in the black hole of pending. But it was as insistent as a four-year-old calling "finished" from reception class toilets. A response was called for...from me. This time there would be no delegation.

I spoke with a friend, Marcie, who had been a deputy head in a comprehensive school in Bristol. She'd been retired for a number of years. I managed to catch her between her two-month visit to friends in Florida, and an impending ten-week sojourn in Catholic missions in India. You couldn't fault the balance could you?

We arranged to meet on Wednesday afternoon after school. This would mean that my current deputy head would lead the staff meeting for me, not much of a change there, I was fast becoming an advocate of ever more delegation. I filled my briefcase with everything I thought I might need for the evening's work, and when it was stuffed to oblivion realised that I only *really* needed my memory stick, the fount of all knowledge, and ever-increasing angst. Where was it? I looked in the usual places, the USB dock, my favourite black leather pencil case, the floor, the surface of my desk, lifting each paper, scanning it before replacing it exactly as it was, and the pile next to it, and the heap next to it. Fearing the domino effect if not settled in precisely the same order, I wondered if I was developing obsessive compulsive disorder. I slumped in my oversize executive chair, the one we always joked about. It was a perfect replica of the *Mastermind* chair. It was sleek, black faux leather. It could spin and move from one side of the room to another with the merest hint of a foot touching the carpet. Very Fred Astaire. I glanced at the school car park from my misted up window. It was dark, wet and took on the appearance of a car showroom forecourt, with neatly parked rows of teachers' cars lining up obediently, waiting to be collected at the end of the day. The after-hours school day that is, the norm being around 6.30pm. Usually the last cars leaving were that of Ian the caretaker, or me. Often Ian would pop his head round my door and ask whether to set the alarm zones to exclude mine, in which case I would stay for the duration.

Other times I thought, Enough! and left at the same time as Ian, especially when, on those dark, rain-slashed, winter nights, I struggled to find the right key for each door and gate while juggling a bursting briefcase.

I shook myself back to the present moment. "Think!" I told myself, with more consternation than necessary. "Where the hell did you leave your memory stick?" Then the superficial question popped up: When did you last see it? My anxiety cranked up another notch. What a ridiculous question and yet one I'd asked children for the previous forty years. I took a moment to wonder how many of them I had truly hacked off with that question, amongst others.

I rammed my diary into my briefcase with the force of a Waitrose packer attempting to save the world by shoving every item of my shopping into one hessian carrier bag, and out popped the memory stick, no bigger than a child's eraser. It had become wedged inside my A4 diary. I realised, not for the first time, why the teachers wore their memory sticks around their necks like a recently acquired piece of bling. "Why are they so bloody *small*?" I asked no one, as I thrust it into the pocket of my jacket.

I left school early, 5.45pm, and made my way to a local pub. I say local but in fact it was far enough from school not to be greeted by wide-eyed children gazing with incredulity as their head teacher scanned the lounge bar as though checking to see if her online date had arrived yet, while embarrassed parents wished they had gone to McDonald's instead. I also had a thing about being seen this soon after the end of the school day. It was as if I was adding credence to the, "Teachers? They only work half a day...and the holidays!" If you've seen the film *Madagascar,* there's a lovely moment when the monkeys have been caught like rabbits in the headlights by their enemies. The leader of the pack, in desperation, says, "If you have any poo, fling it now." That's the best comparison I can come up with for how I felt being seen out of school, and not burning the usual midnight oil. "Accountability, justification and guilt" my constant companions, as loyal as *The Three Musketeers*, keeping me in the black, worn, leather saddle.

Marcie, was already there and had the foresight to order a boatload of chips and two G and Ts. She looked ten years younger. It's a *cliché* I know, but she really did look ten years younger! Her hair had lost its fractious perm and was gently falling into a very subtle highlighted bob. Never one to worry, or even concern herself about her clothes here she was looking...okay. Actually, looking almost colour co-ordinated in varying shades of lilac and pink. I complimented her and she replied, "Charity, all of it... Not *ordinary* charity shops, obviously, I go to Bath...so many more upmarket cast-offs there." She had a point, but even as she was talking I thought, Charity shops are for impoverished teenagers and a haven for young mums looking for designer toddler outfits. They are NOT for me, not now, not ever. I held onto my pride while carelessly handing over my debit card in Karen Millen, Ghost or All Saints. I even suffered when dropping things off at St Peter's Hospice Shop. I literally threw bulging bags of last year's shirts and skirts at the assistant while backing out of the shop like a potential criminal risking recognition, while here was Marcie looking like a Gok Wan client swathed in last season's colours. Well girlfriend, the butterfly leaves the cocoon!

We spent almost two hours together by which time I had mindlessly demolished too many chips and was bloated on Marcie's monologue "So, Madeira was amazing, incredibly relaxing and the weather was glorious. Australia next, yes, flying out next week. Can't wait to see the children again, and the grandkids of course. Did I tell you about Canada? I'm thinking of Canada in September. Always wanted to go there, and then of course New Zealand, and the most exciting news of all, I'm moving house!" It was early evening by now, and the time was approaching when I'd have to make my exit. I needed to be home by 8.00pm if I was ever going to put in a couple of hours work before calling it a day. I looked at Marcie, her mouth was still moving. She was even more animated now as she launched into a monologue about a house she'd seen in Cambridge where her daughter and young family lived. They meant the world to her and her face lit up as she described how she had plans to redesign the garden to make it more child-friendly. She got to the part where she was about to ask my opinion on decking when the automatic timer device in my brain kicked in and I just *had* to make my move.

She looked disappointed, but didn't make me feel churlish about leaving. She slowed her speech down and simply said, "No worries. I remember what it was like. I bet you've already calculated how much time you have left this evening to get home, log on to your laptop, check your emails, and begin something which can't possibly wait 'til another day." All the while she was smiling, a carefree smile bearing no resemblance to my own apologetic "you know how it is" grin. As I got to my car in the already full car park, Marcie hugged me, stepped back and said, "Don't leave it too long."

"Yes, chips on me next time," I replied with Girl Guide joviality as I suggested that we arrange another get together after her globetrotting adventure.

"Oh, I didn't mean that," she said, "I mean...you know, don't leave it too long, you know...to retire." WHAM! There it was again.

As I manoeuvred my car onto the drive half an hour later,

Orion was beginning to fade behind a cover of cloud, flimsy as a strip of white muslin, and I remembered a friend showing me the constellation for the first time many years ago as hundreds of us piled out of a conference centre after a one-day retreat. I found his stories romantic and determined to revisit the Greek classics I'd loved at school. It was as if he had reopened a familiar yet tucked away world.

I remember the train journey home from a residential retreat last spring mulling over the lack of time we afforded ourselves simply to stop and stare. I was all too soon forced out of that reverie. That was the stuff of retreats, not the real world, not the fast lane we inhabited. Little did we know that pretty soon the government would insist that head teachers take time out to concentrate on their well-being. This came too late for a colleague who took early retirement when diagnosed with cancer and died seven months later.

So Orion, are you another sign on this strange day? I fiddled with the key in the front door and fumbled for the light switch in the hall. No one was home. I stumbled over a pair of boots abandoned on the doormat, and stubbed my toe, the one with the in-growing nail. I yelped like a wounded puppy, a wounded puppy mouthing "SHITE!" I sank onto the weary hall carpet and cried. The final sign.

Chapter 32

Feeling more like a prisoner on death row than someone about to embark on a journey entitled "Freedom", I laboured for two days on my letter of resignation. It shouldn't be difficult should it? *Dear whoever, it's been fun, goodbye.* But there's something profound about a letter of resignation, pending retirement. After all, I wouldn't be going on to another job would I? This was *it*. The final act of a theatrical performance lasting forty years was playing to a finale, a production even outrunning *Les Miserables*. Each time I approached the computer I became distracted. Once the theatrical references took hold I launched into a reverie of reminiscence, recalling a programme of musical plays which could be applied to my forty years in education. A new and intriguing delaying tactic. It was fun and, more importantly, kept me from having to frame those oh so final words for a while longer.

"Hair" could be applied to the 60s decade in schools. Of course, we didn't get naked, often, but such a candy-shop of options presented itself in rows of unabashed shiny glass jars for new teachers to reach up and grasp. Revolution was in the air we breathed. No prescribed curriculum, no targets, no timetables, no data crunching, just experiment, use your creative skills and nurture spirituality. After all, that's why you became a teacher isn't it? And all the while, children flourished and grew in confidence just as surely as they grew in knowledge and understanding. Freedom of expression was the order of the day and we relished the opportunities. They don't pen classics the like of "I met a boy named Frank Mills on September twelfth right here in front of the Waverly" in the twenty-first century. Maybe we're losing our ability to dream.

"Anything Goes" would describe the 70s. Head teachers pushed the boundaries in an attempt to outdo neighbouring schools. Walls between classrooms were demolished and more teachers became avid football spectators in order to pick up any tactics they could on crowd control. We all drifted about in an aura of "Lucy in the Sky With Diamonds". No one knew what was happening in the classroom on either side of their own most of the time, despite the lack of dividing walls. Continuity and Progression wasn't even a twinkle in anyone's eye at that stage, yet somehow children progressed and achieved well. I recall a dance lesson I had with my seven-year-olds at the time. We were floating around the hall as soap bubbles, with puffed up cheeks, arms wide, light steps, when I glanced up to the balcony where the young male head teacher stood grinning down at us. I pretended not to notice. I had little respect for him and, at best, considered him just another warm body in the room, at worst, a complete bastard. I was content to be blobbing along with my forty-two little bubbles "in an octopus's garden in the sea".

It was like that. "Pinball Wizard" must be the musical equivalent of education in the 80s. Tommy, of course, being the Secretary of State for Education, firing off shots at random in an attempt to score the jackpot which would reap rewards for children all over the country, leaving teachers as dizzy as those crazed coloured balls plopping into the abyss to be fired up again with the next initiative. *Les Miserables* must be my choice for the 90s. Aside from the only positive fact that French was now being taught in some enlightened primary schools, teachers all over the country were manning the barricades as boroughs and local education authorities hurled more and more work at them. Bureaucracy arrived in spades. Little did we know we were simply in the warm-up stages of the exercise. Teachers attended endless meetings where policies and schemes of work were discussed, dissected and constantly failed to satisfy officialdom. Revolution was in the air once more and I loved it! One meeting in particular stands out in my memory. Fifty subject co-ordinators gathered to compare schemes of work at a countywide conference. Any untrained eye observing the action would have been forgiven for thinking it was a nursery for grown-ups housing a predominance of two-year-olds on the verge of tantrum status.

We all stood around tables upon which we had all possessively placed our schemes of work. What followed was a large scale cut and paste using actual scissors and glue! Yes, that expensive stuff! Our painstaking offerings fell under the knife as infant teachers took their place at the table and commandeered the operation. They were the undisputed experts with scissors and PVA glue. It was more than a nip and tuck. This was a full-on surgical make-over. The room felt like a sauna as waterproofs, damp woollen scarves and over-zealous armpits joined forces. Surfacing from this stifling cacophony, a teacher of some standing in the borough appealed for order. As silence gradually rolled out across the room, hesitating, like fog on the Tyne, he stood on a chair and said, "This is madness. This is timewasting bloody madness. Hundreds of hours of work have just been condensed into a one-size fits all document we can all adapt to meet the needs of our children. What could be more simple? My question is this. Why the hell didn't the government do this in the first place?" We cheered like the rowdy 60s students we once were and, amidst futile attempts from local authority officials to convince us that we needed ownership to make this work, we headed for the photocopier and proceeded to churn out fifty copies of the jigsaw-ed schemes of work. Own *that*, Mr Secretary of State!

The dash for our cars was comparable to the flight from London trading floors at the beginning of the recession, as we ducked and dived through the worst thunderstorm that summer, clutching our newly acquired schemes of work safely inside a rush of waterproofs.

I resumed my reverie with the new millennium. It had brought with it expectations which could best be described using the immortal words "to infinity and beyond", from *Toy Story*. Standards demanded by the end of Key Stage 2 meant that the notion of above average, average and below average were to be rendered redundant because every child was to leave primary school with a level four/five or even six! It seemed as if the government would only be satisfied if they had their cake, ate it and regurgitated it on an unsuspecting nationwide nest of open-mouthed chicks. On the one hand child-centred education had teachers burning the midnight oil to ensure that every type of learner in the class would have his/her needs met with a bespoke delivery of maths, English and science, and on the other hand we were charged with ensuring that every child reached levels previously taught at secondary school by the end of their last year at primary school. And all this with just the customary twenty-four hours in the day.

Head teachers sat through sessions with their education advisors poring over targets set with challenge and reality in mind. After an hour or so I realised that the challenge element was vastly over-proportionate to the reality. Apparently, it didn't matter whether or not a child had special needs, the pressure was on for *every* child to meet the government's targets. What an utter waste of time those meetings turned out to be. Yet here I was, right now, in one such lengthy session with a particularly obdurate advisor who listened with one eye on her laptop and one eye on my target sheet. Occasionally they crossed, skewing her vision even further. I was at pains to explain that reaching the local authority's targets for my year six was not possible this particular year. The targets had been determined by information submitted at the end of year two and, since then, three and a half years had passed. Three families had emigrated, one child had suffered bereavement when a close family member committed suicide, and two children had transferred from different schools bringing with them moderate behaviour problems and English as an additional language respectively. I began to wonder if the advisor also had English as an additional language as she didn't appear to understand a word I said. She wasn't that interested in listening. I wondered if she had ever been a head teacher, or whether she had been nudged into the advisory role from mediocre attempts at teaching. She looked at me with the vacant stare of a child skipping around the playground completely oblivious of the fact that her skirt is hitched up in the leg of her knickers. She simply didn't want to know. It was patently clear that she had no intention of leaving my study until I'd agreed the targets, *her* flaming targets!

I glanced at the clock. It was 11.45am and I was due to join the children on the top table in the hall for lunch, top table being where six children identified for their good manners were invited to dine with a class teacher and me. There was only one way out. I stopped mid-sentence and agreed the targets. She wasn't surprised. She was practised at the art of wearing down the weary. We'd nicknamed her The Rottweiler. Rumour had it she'd been trained at a madrassa on the outskirts of Pakistan. As soon as she left I looked back over the local authority targets. I Tipp-Exed them, photocopied the proforma and entered our original percentages. The percentages which included both challenge and realism and which had taken hours, nay days, of analysis at which to arrive, and painted a true picture of the current year six cohort. The whole thing was faxed to the local authority office before she turned her Skoda onto the main road.

Then, turning away from the window, I had an epiphany moment. There was a little girl called Olivia standing at my door with her hand extended to grasp mine. I smiled at her, how could I not? In a glance lasting no more than a second or two I saw my professional life summed up in her glorious upturned face. "Come on, Mrs C, it's sausages and apple crumble." She spoke with all the assurance of an adult offering a welcome diversion to a friend. Interesting combination, I thought, as I took her outstretched hand. Olivia stopped and bent to retrieve a sheet of paper from under my chair. "Is this important, Mrs C?" she asked as she handed over my draft letter of resignation.

"Not terribly important," I replied, "more of an obstacle/opportunity thing." She smiled and skipped me into the dining hall.

I was surprised at how cathartic it felt.

Acknowledgements

I wish to thank my dad, for knowing me far better than I ever knew myself; my mum, for the sacrifices she made in order to be sure we always had good shoes; my husband, for his enduring encouragement and delicious cooking; my children, for suffering all the pitfalls of having a parent as a teacher, without complaining, and for becoming the best friends I could ever hope for. And finally to every child I have encountered and every selfless member of staff I have had the privilege to work alongside. I have been blessed to have you all in my life.

Lightning Source UK Ltd.
Milton Keynes UK
UKOW04f2309030215

245621UK00001BA/9/P